Across the Great Divide

CW00739506

The sent-down youth movement, a Maoist project that relocated urban youth to remote rural areas for "re-education," is often viewed as a defining feature of China's Cultural Revolution and emblematic of the intense suffering and hardship of the period. Drawing on rich archival research focused on Shanghai's youth in village settlements in remote regions, this history of the movement pays particular attention to how it was informed by and affected the critical issue of urban–rural relations in the PRC. It highlights divisions, as well as connections, created by the movement, particularly the conflicts and collaborations between urban and rural officials. Instead of chronicling a story of victims of a monolithic state, Honig and Zhao show how participants in the movement—the sent-down youth, their parents, and local government officials—disregarded, circumvented, and manipulated state policy, ultimately undermining a decade-long Maoist project.

Emily Honig is Professor of History at University of California, Santa Cruz. She has written extensively on issues of gender and sexuality during the Cultural Revolution. Her books include *Sisters and Strangers: Women in the Shanghai Cotton Mills, 1919–1949* and *Creating Chinese Ethnicity: Subei People in Shanghai, 1850–1980*.

Xiaojian Zhao is Professor of Asian American Studies at University of California, Santa Barbara. She is the author of *Remaking Chinese America: Immigration, Family and Community, 1940–1965*, which was awarded the History Book Award by the Association for Asian American Studies. More recently, she authored *The New Chinese America: Class, Economy, and Social Hierarchy*.

Cambridge Studies in the History of the People's Republic of China

Series Editors

Jeremy Brown, Jacob Eyferth, Daniel Leese, Michael Schoenhals

Cambridge Studies in the History of the People's Republic of China is a major series of ambitious works in the social, political, and cultural history of socialist China. Aided by a wealth of new sources, recent research pays close attention to regional differences, to perspectives from the social and geographical margins, and to the unintended consequences of Communist Party rule. Books in the series contribute to this historical re-evaluation by presenting the most stimulating and rigorously researched works in the field to a broad audience. The series invites submissions from a variety of disciplines and approaches, based on written, material, or oral sources. Particularly welcome are those works that bridge the 1949 and 1978 divides, and those that seek to understand China in an international or global context.

Across the Great Divide

The Sent-Down Youth Movement in Mao's China, 1968–1980

Emily Honig

University of California, Santa Cruz

Xiaojian Zhao

University of California, Santa Barbara

CAMBRIDGE
UNIVERSITY PRESS

CAMBRIDGE
UNIVERSITY PRESS

University Printing House, Cambridge CB2 8BS, United Kingdom

One Liberty Plaza, 20th Floor, New York, NY 10006, USA

477 Williamstown Road, Port Melbourne, VIC 3207, Australia

314–321, 3rd Floor, Plot 3, Splendor Forum, Jasola District Centre, New Delhi – 110025, India

79 Anson Road, #06–04/06, Singapore 079906

Cambridge University Press is part of the University of Cambridge.

It furthers the University's mission by disseminating knowledge in the pursuit of education, learning, and research at the highest international levels of excellence.

www.cambridge.org
Information on this title: www.cambridge.org/9781108498739
DOI: 10.1017/9781108595728

First published 2019

Printed in the United Kingdom by TJ International Ltd, Padstow Cornwall

A catalogue record for this publication is available from the British Library.

ISBN 978-1-108-49873-9 Hardback
ISBN 978-1-108-71249-1 Paperback

Cambridge University Press has no responsibility for the persistence or accuracy of URLs for external or third-party internet websites referred to in this publication and does not guarantee that any content on such websites is, or will remain, accurate or appropriate.

Contents

Illustrations

Acknowledgments

This book is the product of multiple collaborations, not only because it is coauthored, but also due to the numerous colleagues in both China and the US who contributed to the research and thinking. Jin Dalu, Zhou Gongzheng, Liu Qi, and Hu Xiaolan traveled with us from Shanghai to some of the remote counties in Heilongjiang and Yunnan to conduct research. We are grateful for their guidance in navigating access to local archives, their insights, and the conversations we had while traveling. This book would not be possible without the assistance of many other individuals. We want to thank all those who shared with us their personal experiences as well as letters, diaries, and artifacts from their private collections, especially Cao Jianhua, Xue Weimin, Chen Jiang, Wang Pei, He Xinhua, Hu Xiaolan, Zhu Kejia, Yang Xiaohu, Qinshu Qian, Peisheng Hu, Zhiqing Shi, Hengyuan Wang, Weilong Xu, Jianhua Wang, Jian Ye, Xiaoxia Wang, Jianmin Zhao, Sam Shixiong Yang, and Zhou Gongzheng, as well as villagers and locals at Le'an (Jiangxi), Xunke, Aihui, Heihe (Helongjiang), and Jinghong (Yunnan). Special thanks to He Xinhua, Feng Xiaocai, Chen Baoping, Sun Jianzhong, Zhao Jianchang, Yan Jing, Xie Chunhe, Zhang Gang, Ruan Xianzhong, Fang He, and Yanjun Liu for their assistance in archival research. We are very grateful to many county and regional archivists in Yunnan, Jiangxi, and Heilongjiang, and in district and municipal archives in Beijing and Shanghai. Their enthusiasm about sent-down youth research encouraged and inspired us.

Over the years of conducting research, we were fortunate to be included in conferences hosted by Fudan University and East Normal University in Shanghai, and the Sent-Down Youth Research Institute in Heihe, Heilongjiang. We also had many opportunities to participate in gatherings of former sent-down youth associations and groups. A number of participants provided us with ongoing engagement, particularly Jin Guangyao, Xie Chunhe, Zhang Gang, and Ruan Xianzhong. In addition, a number of scholars in China contributed to our project, and we are grateful to Feng Xiaocai, Jiang Jin, Ruan Qingquan, Gao Xiaoxian, Tan Shen, Ding Yizhuang, and Wang Yan.

Graduate students at both UCSB and UCSC assisted our research. At UCSB, we would like to thank Yanjun Liu for conducting research through Chinese-language newspaper databases and translating archival documents from Chinese to English and conference papers from English to Chinese. He also assisted with the bibliography, editing, indexing, and technical issues. Fang He conducted archival research in China and assisted with conference paper translation. Tian Wu was the first to join the research team, and we appreciate Angela He's assistance in the final phase of the project. At UCSC, we would like to thank Xiaofei Gao for identifying materials available on Chinese sent-down youth websites, and also for translation work. Xiaoping Sun, Sarah Chang, Jinghong Zhang, Wilson Miu, and Jeremy Tai also provided valuable research assistance.

We would like to thank several funding agencies for their support of this project. A system-wide University of California Pacific Rim Research Program Faculty collaborative grant provided funding for our trips to Yunnan and Heilongjiang; a UC–Fudan faculty collaborative grant enabled us to organize an international conference at UCSC in 2014. The UCSC Committee on Research of the Academic Senate Special Research Grant and Faculty Research grants provided funding for Emily Honig to conduct research in China and also for research assistance throughout the project. Xiaojian's early research trips to Jiangxi were supported by a Fulbright Senior Scholar Fellowship. Grants from UCSB's Academic Senate and Institute for Social Behavioral and Economic Research from 2013 to 2017 provided additional funding for research trips, graduate student research assistance, indexing, and other publishing expenses.

From the time we submitted the manuscript, the senior China editor at Cambridge University Press, Lucy Rhymer, has been its guardian angel, deftly guiding us through revision of the manuscript. We are indebted to Lisa Carter and Natasha Whelan for overseeing the production process. We are also the grateful beneficiaries of John Gaunt's long experience as an editor. We also want to thank the two readers who offered insightful comments and suggestions. The order of the authors' names was determined by a coin toss.

In addition, Emily Honig would like to thank the crew of colleagues and friends who contributed in myriad ways to this book. Members of the UCSC History Faculty East Asia reading group commented on several chapters of the book, and thanks are due to Noriko Aso, Alan Christy, Jennifer Derr, Gail Hershatter, Minghui Hu, and Juned Shaikh. Over the years of working on this project, conversations with Elizabeth Perry have called attention to the broader context of PRC politics that informed the sent-down youth movement. China scholars Marilyn Young and Susan Mann also provided insights and encouragement. More ongoing and casual conversations with many friends provided sustenance throughout the years working on this book: Susan Basow, Wendy Brown, Laurie Coyle, Cheryl Jacques, B. Ruby Rich, and Susan Salisbury. No words are adequate to express gratitude to Gail Hershatter for the hundreds of runs spent discussing this project, for seriously long-term friendship, and for being the best intellectual interlocutor one could have. Finally, Emily wants to express the deepest gratitude to her mother, who unfortunately died before she could see the book in print, but who expressed continual curiosity about almost every point and did not hesitate to convey her disagreements and opinions. Emily's son, Jesse, provided wise counsel and great humor throughout the years spent growing up alongside the evolution of this project.

Xiaojian Zhao would like to thank colleagues and friends who have read parts, or the entirety, of the manuscript and who offered critical suggestions and encouragement at various stages of book: Gail Hershatter, Bryna Goodman, Paul Harvey, John Park, Yanjun Liu, Weijing Lu, Angela He, and Jian Zhao. She wants to express her gratitude to family members, colleagues, and friends who encouraged and advised her through the process. She appreciates the generous assistance and support from Arlene Phillips.

The word "across" in the book's title emphasizes the boundary between urban and rural China. The process of writing the book enabled us to see far more clearly the layers of multiple social boundaries that are not always easy to cross. Recognizing these boundaries will most surely inform our future research and writing on issues of race, gender, class, and power relations.

A version of Chapter 3 appeared in "Sent-down Youth and Rural Economic Development in Maoist China," *The China Quarterly*, 222 (June 2015), 499–521.

Stylistic Note

Most sources cited in the footnotes are listed in the bibliography with the Chinese characters for the authors and titles. However, all the references to archival documents include the Chinese characters in the footnotes the first time the item is cited; the archival documents are not listed in the bibliography. Chinese terms in the text are in Pinyin. The glossary lists the terms with the Chinese characters as well as the definition (except for names of individuals or places).

Introduction

Of all the political campaigns that reconfigured daily life in the first three decades of the People's Republic of China, the sent-down youth movement that sent 17 million urban youth to live in rural China in 1968–1980 is one of the most vividly remembered and hotly debated. Mao's 1968 call for re-education catapulted urban youth into a world of rural poverty they would otherwise never have known. Memorialized in fiction, films, art exhibits, and even an orchestral performance,[1] the movement is commonly branded a misguided revolution, a forced relocation, and a sacrifice of youth. The victimization of sent-down youth has been invoked to symbolize the suffering of all Chinese people during the Cultural Revolution (1966–1976). Whether former sent-down youth look back on that era as one of deprivation that handicapped them or as one that honed their ability to navigate adversity, their years living in the countryside constituted the pivotal experience for a generation that came of age during the Cultural Revolution.

This book differs from other accounts and studies of the sent-down youth movement. It is the first to draw primarily on archives in remote rural areas that hosted sent-down youth, offering a local perspective on the movement. Aiming to understand more than the ups and downs of this political campaign, the hardships experienced by urban youth, and the difficulties implementing Mao's directive for urban youth to be "re-educated" by the "peasants," this study centers on how the movement was informed by and affected relations between state and society, between the city and countryside, in the PRC. It highlights divisions as well as connections and interdependencies created by the movement, calling particular attention to the conflicts and collaborations between

---

[1] The orchestral performance is *Ask the Earth and Sky: An Oratorio for the Sent-Down Youth*, performed in San Francisco as well as several cities in China in 2016. For a description of some of the exhibitions about sent-down youth, see Xiaowei Zheng, "Images, Memories, and Lives of Sent-Down Youth in Yunnan," in James Cook, Joshua Goldstein, Matthew D. Johnson, and Sigrid Schmalzer, eds., *Visualizing Modern China: Image, History, and Memory, 1750–Present* (London: Lexington Books, 2014), 241–258.

urban and rural officials. Instead of chronicling a story of victims of a monolithic state and its powerful cadres, we show how participants in the movement—sent-down youth, their parents, and even local government officials—disregarded, circumvented, and manipulated state policy, ultimately undermining what was ostensibly a decade-long Maoist project.

Our study of the sent-down youth movement has its origins some thirty years ago when we first met at Fudan University in Shanghai. Emily Honig was an American graduate student researching the history of Shanghai factory workers; Xiaojian Zhao was a Chinese undergraduate in the Department of History who had recently returned to Shanghai after spending seven years as a sent-down youth. Living in the same dormitory in 1980, we hoped to visit the Jiangxi village where Zhao had lived, a plan thwarted by then restrictions on foreigners' travel to the countryside. In subsequent decades, we were otherwise occupied with establishing academic careers in the United States, Honig as a historian of modern China, Zhao as a historian of Asian America. It was not until 2010, when our paths intersected in Shanghai again, that we resurrected the idea of visiting the village in Jiangxi.

The village landscape had changed dramatically in the three decades since sent-down youth returned to the city. Large tracts of terraced land on the surrounding hillsides were left unattended. As most young adults had left to work in towns and cities, only elderly residents and their young grandchildren remained. Interspersed with the old mud houses were new two-story family dwellings featuring gated courtyards with fruit trees. Earnings from those working in cities had eased worries of the past about adequate food, and older villagers could now afford leisure time during this winter slack season, sitting outside in the sun or gathered indoors to play cards. The house where Zhao had lived with eleven other sent-down youth was now empty, only a faded picture of Mao remaining on the wall of the dusty interior. The bedrooms were completely dark on a sunny afternoon, their tiny windows boarded shut to keep out the cold winter air.

Though the trip was long overdue and meeting old friends was emotionally powerful for both the villagers and Zhao, it was our almost serendipitous visit to the county archives that catalyzed this project and prompted us, over the next several years, to seek access to a number of other county archives in areas that had hosted large numbers of sent-down youth from Shanghai. In addition to counties in Jiangxi, we collected records of sent-down youth offices in the far northern counties of Heilongjiang just across the Black Dragon (Heilong) river from Siberia, and in semi-tropical areas of Xishuangbanna, Yunnan, close to the

Laotian and Burmese borders. We also visited municipal and district archives (including Putuo, Jing'an, and Zhabei) in Shanghai. The documents in these archives—reports, meeting minutes, work plans and proposals, statistical tables, texts of conference speeches, correspondence, records of telephone calls, grievances, accusations, confessions, and investigative reports—made us realize just how much more complex a history of the sent-down youth movement remained to be written.

From its outset in the late 1960s, Western observers were captivated by this seemingly bold experiment launched by a socialist state to contend with the dual problems of urban unemployment and rural poverty, advocating the idealistic goal of closing the gap between the city and countryside.[2] For this reason, accounts of the sent-down youth movement, including scholarly studies, began to appear even before the movement ended in 1980.[3] Whether produced in the late 1970s or the 1990s and early 2000s, these accounts almost all relied on newspaper reports, memoirs, and interviews (first with refugees in Hong Kong and later with former sent-down youth who remained in the PRC). These earlier scholars of the sent-down youth movement lamented the impossibility of accessing local archives and wondered how such materials might change their analyses.

This study is the first to do just that. The documents that comprise records of the sent-down youth offices held in those archives, many handwritten, were produced for internal use among cadres tasked with the implementation of Mao's directive for urban youth to receive "peasant re-education." They were not for public consumption, but rather for government agencies to evaluate progress and report to their administrative superiors. The authors of these reports were individuals enmeshed in the implementation of the movement, whose futures depended in part on how well or poorly they performed. Yet many reports, even if infused with a determination to chronicle local success, invariably also convey problems, sometimes in a relatively short section at the end. In contrast, reports by teams of urban cadres (referred to as the *weiwentuan*) tended to focus more on problems, as their members were tasked with investigating conditions for urban youth on rural production teams.

---

[2] See, for example, Thomas P. Bernstein, *Up to the Mountains and Down to the Villages: The Transfer of Youth from Urban to Rural China* (New Haven: Yale University Press, 1977), 2–4. Also see Martin M. Singer, *Educated Youth and the Cultural Revolution in China* (Ann Arbor: University of Michigan Press, 1971).

[3] See Bernstein; and also D. Gordon White, "The Politics of Hsia-hsiang Youth," *China Quarterly*, 59 (July–September 1974), 491–517; and John Gardner, "Educated Youth and Rural–Urban Inequalities, 1958–1966," in John W. Lewis, ed., *The City in Communist China* (Stanford: Stanford University Press, 1971), 268–276.

Although, like any and all historical documents, these records cannot be interpreted as representing a truth of what transpired, they are the first set of materials that provide insight into how a broad range of participants in the movement—cadres in county governments and sent-down youth offices, provincial officials, municipal government leaders, and the *weiwentuan* sent by cities to provide comfort for, investigate, and manage problems of sent-down youth—navigated the daily work of the movement, expressed frustrations, and sometimes articulated ideas on how policies should be modified. Reports from the county offices of sent-down youth include accounts of visits by urban and rural officials to sent-down youth settlements, often recording conversations with the youth and villagers that suggest the everyday interactions between the two. They reveal the conflicts that erupted at the local level, not only the most obvious between youth and their rural hosts, but between officials located at different administrative levels and in urban versus rural institutions.

Most importantly, the archival collections make audible the voices of rural villagers and cadres, previously overshadowed by the testimonies of sent-down youth themselves. While adjusting to harsh conditions in the countryside was difficult for urban youth, it was local officials, shouldering the blame for almost everything that went wrong, who expressed deep frustration about their job of managing hundreds of urban teenagers sent to their villages. Many archival reports voiced the worries of local officials about sent-down youth who did not tend their vegetable plots or collect firewood, and who overstayed their winter home visits and therefore could not earn enough work points to support themselves. Officials grappled with issues concerning dating, cohabitation, and pregnancies among sent-down youth. Groups of youth whom urban officials regarded as hoodlums, and were anxious to send to the countryside, sometimes refused to work and engaged in gang fights, causing local authorities particular consternation. They also complained about the intervention, if not the subversion of their authority, by the *weiwentuan*.

The integration of rural voices with those of urban participants changes the ways in which we understand the history of the sent-down youth movement. It becomes not simply a story of China's "lost generation," but instead one that reveals the burdens imposed by this campaign on an already beleaguered and impoverished rural population, which served to intensify an urban–rural divide that permeated all sectors of the Chinese population. Although the stages of the movement that we describe (mobilization, settlement in the countryside, recruitment to factories and universities, and returning to the city) echo those that frame other studies, the archival records make visible the processes, conversations, and negotiations that underlay each of these phases. They reveal how relocating young urban residents to remote rural villages re-enforced the belief that rural and urban people were fundamentally different. Although attention to the voices of rural cadres articulated in the archival records attest to the rural–urban divide that both informed and was intensified by the movement, they also expose surprising linkages that were established.

Authors of the documents in local archives were by no means empowered to make decisions about policy. But the reports and communications unwittingly show the more local and everyday decisions made by low-level cadres. Maoist slogans and state directives may have been promulgated and implemented through mass campaigns, but urban and rural government officials infused them with their own meanings, sometimes reconfiguring the original intent, other times conforming to the letter of the directive while altering its spirit, and in some instances ignoring them altogether. The decision to end the sent-down youth movement, ten years after its launching, was not the result of popular resistance, nor can it be reduced to the death of Mao. Rather, it may be understood as death by documents, the extraordinary proliferation of local reports that increasingly conveyed the unwelcome message that "the problems cannot be solved."

Although archival materials are at the center of this analysis of the sent-down youth movement, our study also benefits from sources of several other types that have become increasingly available in recent decades. Document collections, local gazetteers, and institutional histories published since the late 1980s make it possible to understand the archival records in a broader historical context. Personal accounts of participants in the movement also help contextualize the archival records. There are also memoirs published in the first two decades after the movement ended, some crafted to satisfy the sensibilities of an English-speaking readership, chronicling a story of suffering and victimhood.

Beginning in the 1990s, many former sent-down youth began to claim their experience in the countryside as a source of pride and became prolific in chronicling this period of their lives. They established associations; organized reunions and conferences; published magazines and newsletters; collected historical records of their experiences; and raised funds to provide financial relief, social services and support to former sent-down youth. The websites established by their associations began to provide a forum for extended informal recollections and conversations among sent-down youth, and between the youth and those who once hosted them. Many provinces and rural counties that had accommodated sent-down youth have in turn compiled collections of oral histories of both the youth and locals, published selections of local government documents, and incorporated accounts of the sent-down youth into their local gazetteers. At the same time, personal recollections of *weiwen-tuan* members and officials who worked in sent-down youth offices have appeared. All of these accounts, in addition to our own interviews with former sent-down youth and villagers who hosted them, enable us to put a personal perspective in dialogue with the documentary record.

In addition to these newly available sources, we also consulted newspapers, particularly the Shanghai local paper *Jiefang ribao*. On the surface, newspapers issued government propaganda to the public, with articles praising the success of the movement: stories of idealistic urban youth who selflessly committed to life in the countryside as well as portraits of villagers who welcomed the youth with excitement and enthusiasm. Yet newspapers can also be read against the grain, as reflecting problems with the movement, reporting, for instance, on city parents who were not sufficiently enthusiastic about sending their sons and daughters away or on Shanghai cadres who were reluctant to be dispatched to the countryside to monitor the movement.

All these materials complemented the archival records of the sent-down youth offices. Based on this research, our study both builds on and departs from prior analyses of the sent-down youth movement. One of the first major studies, Thomas Bernstein's *Up to the Mountains and Down to the Villages: The Transfer of Youth from Urban to Rural China*, explores whether the movement, revolutionary in its premise that "educated urbanites can become peasants," could ever have achieved its goal of closing the gap between urban and rural China.[4] Drawing on media accounts as well as interviews with refugees in Hong Kong, his careful analysis of the ideological and practical rationales for the movement details the challenges of mobilizing urban youth and accommodating them in remote rural areas. Bernstein highlights the ways in which sent-down youth, even if resentful of the requirement to live in impoverished villages, contributed to rural economic development, a theme amplified in more recent studies, such as those by Sigrid Schmalzer and Miriam Gross, of scientific and technological development under Maoist policies.[5] Our study adds a new dimension to these observations by considering the extensive and complicated negotiations between urban and rural officials that made such development possible in the context of the sent-down youth movement, and the particular ways in which a large industrial city such as Shanghai, in order to improve the welfare of its

---

[4] Bernstein, 3–4.
[5] See Sigrid Schmalzer, *Red Revolution, Green Revolution: Scientific Farming in Socialist China* (Chicago: University of Chicago Press, 2016); and Miriam Gross, *Farewell to the God of Plague: Chairman Mao's Campaign to Deworm China* (Berkeley: University of California Press), 2016.

youth in the countryside, mobilized urban resources to support these developments.

The most recent comprehensive study of the sent-down youth movement, authored by French historian Michel Bonnin, reviews the goals and rationale for the movement as well as the implementation of its policies. *The Lost Generation*, partly aiming to consider the "limits of totalitarian power," analyzes the extent to which sent-down youth, victims of what he describes as harsh Chinese Communist Party policies, engaged in what he terms both passive and active resistance.[6] Our study shares his interest in noncompliance with state policies, but rather than categorizing types of resistance, our attention turns more to the explicit and implicit, blatant and muted ways in which all participants in the movement, including urban officials, rural cadres, parents, members of the *weiwentuan*, and sent-down youth themselves, interpreted and manipulated state policies. In this sense, our study is informed by and engages theories of state–society relations in socialist China, such as Vivienne Shue's early challenge to Cold War assertions of state control over all aspects of individual lives. The archival documents that inform our study repeatedly affirm her insistence that China's bureaucratic apparatus routinely "delayed, distorted, deflected and destroyed central intentions," and that state policy itself was often "a series of forced compromises and squalid bargains."[7] Our study speaks as well to more recent scholarship that, focusing on the "grass roots," emphasizes the disjuncture between the goals of mass campaigns and their results, as well as the subversion of state policies by local officials.[8] And in its consideration of individuals who were sent to the countryside, it reinforces the early observations of Shaoguang Wang

---

[6] Michel Bonnin, *The Lost Generation: The Rustication of China's Educated Youth (1968–1980)* (Hong Kong: The Chinese University Press, 2013). The book was first published in French in 2004. One other recent study of the sent-down youth movement is based on interviews: Helena K. Rene. *China's Sent-Down Generation: Public Administration and the Legacies of Mao's Rustication Program* (Washington, DC: Georgetown University Press, 2013). There are also a number of Chinese studies of the sent-down youth movement, most importantly Huo Mu, *Guangrong yu mengxiang: Zhongguo zhiqing ershiwu nian shi* (Glory and Dream: The Twenty-Five-Year History of China's Sent-Down Youth) (Chengdu: Chengdu chubanshe, 1990); Liu Xiaomeng, *Zhongguo zhiqingshi: Dachao (1968–1980)* (History of China's Sent-Down Youth, 1968–1980) (Beijing: Dangdai Zhongguo chubanshe, 2008). Some of the extensive Chinese research on sent-down youth is compiled in a three-volume collection, Jin Dalu and Jin Guangyao, eds., *Zhongguo zhishi qingnian shangshan xiaxiang yanjiu wenji* (Collected Research Essays on Sent-Down Youth in China) (Shanghai: Shanghai shehui kexueyuan chubanshe, 2009).

[7] Vivienne Shue, *The Reach of the State: Sketches of the Chinese Body Politic* (Stanford: Stanford University Press, 1988), 17.

[8] Jeremy Brown and Matthew D. Johnson, *Maoism at the Grassroots: Everyday Life in China's Era of High Socialism* (Cambridge, MA: Harvard University Press, 2015), 1.

that while Cultural Revolution activists identified themselves as loyal followers of Mao, they invoked and interpreted his messages to pursue their own self-interests.[9]

Focusing on the urban–rural relations that informed and were created by the sent-down youth movement, this book also builds on scholarship that has highlighted the chasm between city and country-side in China. Although this issue is often treated as particular to Maoist China, recent scholarship reveals that its origins go back to the early twentieth century. Prior to that time, as Martin King Whyte observes, the "status barrier between rural and urban residents was not large."[10] The divide emerged first in the context of nation-building projects that followed the 1911 revolution, and then became central to discourses of modernity. Throughout the Republican era, urban cosmopolitanism represented the modern, in contrast to pea-sants, who epitomized backwardness, if not the antithesis to moder-nity, most vividly exemplified in popular films featuring "country bumpkins" as stock figures.[11] Throughout the Republican era, the Nationalist government sponsored numerous projects to modernize the countryside: programs for agricultural improvement, rural educa-tion, and health care, alongside campaigns to combat superstition and religious practices. None of these projects proved very effective, in part because of the war with Japan and subsequent civil war between the Communist Party and the Guomindang, leaving most reformers to deplore what they believed to be the collapsing rural economy.[12] Meanwhile, left-wing social scientists conducted myriad investigations of peasant poverty, which also became a prominent theme in left-wing literature by writers such as Lu Xun and Mao Dun.[13] No matter their political persuasion, Susan Mann observes, Republican-era intellectuals became increasingly concerned by the urban–rural gap: "social change and cultural crisis," she concludes,

---

[9] Shaoguang Wang, *The Failure of Charisma: The Cultural Revolution in Wuhan* (Oxford: Oxford University Press, 1995), 278–279.

[10] Martin King Whyte, "Introduction," in Martin King Whyte, ed., *One Country, Two Societies: Rural–Urban Inequality in Contemporary China* (Cambridge, MA: Harvard University Press, 2010), 1. Also see Jacob Eyferth, *Eating Rice from Bamboo Roots: The Social History of a Community of Handicraft Papermakers in Rural Sichuan, 1920–2000* (Cambridge, MA: Harvard University Press, 2009).

[11] See Yingjin Zhang, *The City in Modern Chinese Literature and Film: Configurations of Space, Time, and Gender* (Stanford: Stanford University Press, 1996).

[12] Kate Merkel-Hess, *The Rural Modern: Reconstructing the Self and State in Republican China* (Chicago: University of Chicago Press, 2016), 17.

[13] Xiaorong Han, *Chinese Discourses on the Peasant, 1900–1949* (Albany: State University of New York Press, 2005), 19–25.

"were intimately bound up with the differences between the city and the countryside."[14]

If the urban–rural divide was prominent in the first half of the twentieth century, it stubbornly endured after the establishment of the PRC in 1949. Maoist policies did not create this divide, but, as Jacob Eyferth puts it, they did intensify it.[15] Scholars including Edward Friedman, Paul G. Pickowicz, Mark Selden, and Martin King Whyte have emphasized how socialist economic policies privileged the cities while turning the countryside into an impoverished periphery and rendering its villagers powerless.[16] This was primarily the result of two sets of policies. First, in order to finance the development of urban industry, rural residents were required to sell grain to the state at artificially low prices.[17] Excessive demands for grain to feed the cities reduced the production of commercial crops, as David Zweig points out, "impoverishing many parts of rural China."[18] And, as Jacob Eyferth more cynically notes, "The Maoist ideal for the countryside was the self-reliant, insular collective that produced surplus grain and other inputs for cities but required nothing from the urban sector."[19] Second, in 1955 the government institutionalized a household registration system, known as *hukou*, which both forbade migration of rural residents to cities, and also identified all citizens as members of either "agricultural" or "nonagricultural" (or rural/urban) households.[20] Both policies not only solidified the rural–urban divide but also contributed to the popular belief that villagers and urban dwellers belonged to entirely different social categories. Most recently, in a study of Tianjin and its surrounding countryside, Jeremy Brown shows that even when urban and rural districts were in extremely close proximity, the household registration and state planning systems made the boundary almost impermeable for rural residents, although their efforts to challenge the boundary never ceased.[21]

---

[14] Susan Mann, "Urbanization and Historical Change in China," *Modern China*, 10, 1 (1984), 87–88.

[15] Eyferth, 8–10. Also see Jeremy Brown, "Spatial Profiling: Seeing Rural and Urban in Mao's China," in Cook et al., *Visualizing Modern China*, 212.

[16] Edward Friedman, Paul G. Pickowicz, and Mark Selden, *Chinese Village, Socialist State* (New Haven: Yale University Press, 1991); Martin King Whyte, "The Paradoxes of Rural–Urban Inequality in Contemporary China," in Whyte, *One Country, Two Societies*, 9–10.

[17] Brown, "Spatial Profiling," 203.

[18] David Zweig, "From Village to City: Reforming Urban–Rural Relations in China," *International Regional Science Review*, 11 (1987), 44.

[19] Eyferth, 10.

[20] Xiaogang Wu and Donald J. Treiman, "The Household Registration System and Social Stratification in China: 1955–1996," *Demography*, 41, 2 (May 2004), 363–384.

[21] Jeremy Brown, *City versus Countryside in Mao's China: Negotiating the Divide* (Cambridge: Cambridge University Press, 2012).

The sent-down youth movement, a rare encounter between privileged urban youth and disadvantaged villagers, provides an ideal context in which to revisit scholarship on urban–rural relations in China. In surrendering their urban residency and relocating to the countryside, the sent-down youth might seem to have traversed this great divide. Yet the divide was so ingrained that even when rural villagers and urban residents were physically together in the countryside, social boundaries between the two remained intact. The presence of urban youth in rural China, if anything, intensified the social categories of "urbanite" and "peasant." Though stripped of their official urban status, sent-down youth never compromised their identity as urbanites, nor did rural residents ever perceive them as peasants.

At the same time, however, the sent-down youth movement connected cities and remote rural areas in ways that were unprecedented in Maoist China. For the first time since the introduction of the *hukou* system in the mid-1950s, impoverished counties geographically distant from cities suddenly had both personal and institutional connections to urban resources. These connections often produced unanticipated results, such as the transfer of industrial equipment from cities to rural areas. Recognizing these relationships suggests a reconsideration of conventional beliefs that the post-Mao economic reforms represented a complete disjuncture with the Cultural Revolution: the ways in which connections forged during the sent-down youth movement effectively undergirded subsequent economic reforms become more apparent.

Shanghai and Its Sent-Down Youth

Unlike other studies that treat the sent-down youth movement in a national context,[22] this study centers on Shanghai and the youth it sent to the countryside. Focusing on a single sending city offers an opportunity to examine how municipal government officials and residents deployed human, material, and institutional resources to ensure the welfare of their youth. It also enables us to see how the sent-down youth, after surrendering their urban residence permits and relocating to the countryside, remained a primary concern not only of their families but of the city government as well. Shanghai also manifests the ways that a major nationwide campaign launched by the central government was implemented, interpreted, and sometimes modified by municipal

---

[22] The single exception is Stanley Rosen's early book, *The Role of Sent-Down Youth in the Chinese Cultural Revolution: The Case of Guangzhou* (Berkeley: University of California, Berkeley Center for Chinese Studies, 1981).

officials, and how their efforts to support the movement could unwittingly undermine it.

Shanghai dispatched more youth than any other city in China, sending a total of 1.1 million to the countryside over the decade of the movement (1968–1980). The next-largest city, Beijing, had some 700,000 sent-down youth, and Tianjin approximately 400,000.[23] Shanghai in the 1960s and 1970s was not only China's largest city, but also its most prominent commercial hub and advanced industrial center. Its residents were among the most privileged citizens in China, many enjoying access to subsidized housing, education, health care, food, and basic consumer goods, as well as running water, electricity, and public transportation, amenities that were beyond the reach of rural residents. For Shanghai residents, the gap between city and countryside was particularly acute.

Rather than considering all sent-down youth from Shanghai, this book focuses more specifically on Shanghai youth sent to production teams (*chadui*) in remote regions far from the city. As other scholars have pointed out, the term "sent-down youth" has often been loosely used to describe all middle and high school graduates who were sent to the countryside during the Cultural Revolution. This could include rural youth who left their villages to attend secondary school at the commune or county seats and then returned to their home villages after graduation. These "returning-to-the-village youth" (*huixiang qingnian*) have often been included in sent-down youth statistics.[24]

Although the term "sent-down youth" is most commonly used to refer to those sent from the city to the countryside during the Cultural Revolution, the idea of sending urban youth to rural areas actually originated in the mid-1950s. At that time, youth from Shanghai (as well as from other cities) began to go rural areas, in large part because of urban unemployment, although some went voluntarily, such as the first Shanghai Voluntary Reclamation Team of close to 100 members who went to Jiangxi in October 1955.[25] Over the decade from 1955 to 1966,

---

[23] Shanghai qingnianzhi bianzhuan weiyuanhui, ed., *Shanghai qingnianzhi* (Shanghai Youth Gazetteer) (Shanghai: Shanghai shehui kexueyuan chubanshe, 2002), 553; Beijing shi difangzhi bianzhuan weiyuanhui, ed., *Beijingzhi zonghejuan: Renmin shenghuozhi* (The Beijing Comprehensive Volume: People's Livelihood Gazetteer) (Beijing: Beijing chubanshe, 2007), 12; Tianjin listed 415,000 sent-down youth from 1962 to 1978. See Tianjin shi difangzhi bianzhuan weiyuanhui, ed., *Tianjin tongzhi: Renshi zhi* (Tianjin Gazetteer: People and Events) (Tianjin: Shehui kexue chubanshe 1999), 145.

[24] Bernstein, 21.

[25] In 1954, officials noted that some 60,000 youth in Shanghai could not find employment. Jin Dalu and Jin Guangyao, *Zhongguo xin difangzhi: Zhishi qingnian shangshan xiaxiang shiliao jilu* (China's New Gazetteers: Historical Materials on the Sent-Down Youth Movement) (Shanghai: Shanghai renmin chubanshe and Shanghai shudian chubanshe, 2014) vol. 4, 2223.

some 164,000 Shanghai youth went to Jiangxi, Anhui, Hubei, and Xinjiang; the majority mobilized between 1961 and 1965. Roughly half of those sent went to Xinjiang, where they worked on farms as members of the Production and Construction Corps under the military.[26]

This earlier iteration of sending urban youth to the countryside is important to recognize for several reasons. First, many of the problems that Cultural Revolution-era officials confronted as they worked to relocate urban youth to the countryside had emerged in the initial project: the reluctance of rural officials to accommodate urban adolescents; the resentment of villagers that their income, in the form of work points, was reduced; and attempts by rural families to lure young urban women into marriage.[27] Second, the voices of Shanghai youth sent to the countryside prior to the Cultural Revolution had a major impact on mobilization efforts following Mao's 1968 directive. Nevertheless, the number of Shanghai sent-down youth in the 1950s and early 1960s represented only a small fraction of those sent in the context of the Cultural Revolution, and it is therefore appropriate to consider those sent after 1968 as part of a distinctive movement.

If the term "sent-down youth" referred to those sent before as well as after the beginning of the Cultural Revolution, it also encompassed those who, following Mao's 1968 directive, were sent to state and army farms alongside those sent to production teams. This study focuses on those sent in the context of Mao's 1968 directive, and, more specifically, those sent to production teams. We focus on production teams for several reasons. The state and military farms were large-scale state-managed units where thousands of sent-down youth worked on projects such as clearing forests and planting rubber trees in Yunnan and cultivating vast tracts of barren land in Heilongjiang. Although they also engaged in agricultural labor, youth on these farms received a fixed salary and had set work hours. Managed by cadres and under the auspices of the

---

[26] Jin Dalu and Jin Guangyao, *Zhongguo xin difangzhi: Zhishi qingnian shangshan xiaxiang shiliao jilu*, vol. 4, 2199, 2205. At the beginning of the Cultural Revolution in 1966, this program of sending youth to rural areas was curtailed, and, according to Yiching Wu, "many rusticates abandoned their rural posts and returned to Shanghai, often with the acquiescence or even encouragement of local officials who were eager to rid themselves of the troublemakers." Yiching Wu, *The Cultural Revolution at the Margins: Chinese Socialism in Crisis* (Cambridge, MA: Harvard University Press, 2014), 101–102, 109. For a detailed account of the earlier sent-down youth movement, see Ding Yizhuang, *Zhongguo zhiqingshi: Chulan 1953–1968* (History of the Early Sent-Down Youth in China, 1953–1968) (Beijing: Zhongguo shehui kexue chubanshe, 1998); as well as Bonnin. Jeremy Brown also provides an analysis of the Tianjin youth sent to rural areas during the early 1960s, prior to the outset of the Cultural Revolution. Brown, *City versus Countryside.*

[27] See Ding Yizhuang for an account of problems of the earlier phase of the movement.

government, these farms were not home to ordinary local workers. In contrast, youth sent to village production teams lived and worked in rural communities and earned work points, the value of which depended on local harvests.

Youth sent to production teams were the ones who most deeply experienced rural life and had daily interactions with villagers, thereby providing the most clear index of how the sent-down youth movement reflected and changed urban–rural relations. Of the 1.1 million youth sent from Shanghai to the countryside over the decade-long duration of the movement, more than 400,000 went to villages in other provinces, most sent in the early years of the movement.[28] Precisely because *chadui* required urban youth to live in rural villages and required villagers to accommodate urban youth, it was plagued by problems from the outset. Within two years following Mao's directive, Shanghai no longer mandated that school graduates join production teams in remote regions, but they could instead go to state farms administered by the Shanghai municipal government. Problems of youth already on production teams received by far the most attention from the municipal government throughout the movement. The intervention of the municipal government in the management of the *chadui* youth reveals conflicts and collaborations between a major urban center and administrations in remote rural regions.

Focusing on Shanghai makes particularly visible issues of privilege and inequality. This was a period when Maoist rhetoric of class struggle was ubiquitous: the Cultural Revolution glorified the proletariat, while those classified as members of the bourgeoisie became the targets of mass criticism.[29] For residents of Shanghai, beliefs about class status did not necessarily conform to this binary. When Shanghai youth went to villages, those from families of intellectuals, government officials, and relatively well-off individuals could find themselves assigned to live and work with youth from working-class families in Shanghai's factory districts or even from the city's shack settlements. Although sent-down youth recognized class differences manifested in dialect, dress, behavior, and the food and material goods they were able to bring with them to the countryside, once in the villages these differences were often overshadowed by the articulation of an identity as "Shanghai people" versus those sent from other places: the latter had access neither to the wealth of urban material goods nor to the support of a powerful city government that was accessible to those from Shanghai. Yet by far the vastest distinction was between urban

[28] Shanghai qingnianzhi bianzhuan weiyuanhui, 552–558.
[29] For a critical analysis of Maoist class categories, see Yiching Wu, 39–40.

youth and their rural hosts. Rural hosts may not have been able to distinguish youth from the wealthier or poorer quarters of Shanghai, but they had no doubt that these youth came from China's most wealthy and glamorous city.

Organization of the Book

This book begins with the inauguration of the sent-down youth movement. Chapter 1 examines the mobilization following the promulgation of Mao's 1968 directive mandating that urban youth be sent to the countryside. The movement initially seemed to provide solutions for some of Shanghai's most pressing problems: unemployment, chaos associated with the Red Guard movement, and gang violence. In a widespread campaign to enlist participation, the municipal government organized mass rallies and parades celebrating idealistic youth who volunteered to sacrifice their privileged urban life for this new revolutionary cause. It also mobilized thousands of urban officials, school administrators, teachers, and neighborhood representatives to work relentlessly to persuade middle and high school graduates to register for assignment to remote rural areas. With no hope of securing jobs, as well as the prospect of jeopardizing future personal and political advancement by not complying with this state policy, most urban youth agreed to leave the city, some enthusiastically and some begrudgingly. An examination of the mobilization efforts in Shanghai reveals the class dimensions of popular responses. Ironically, it was the most marginalized residents of Shanghai—those outside the state employment system who earned a living by working in private trades as peddlers, barbers, carpenters, or tailors—who knew how to help their children support themselves without relying on government employment and thereby circumvent relocation to the countryside.

It would have been simple if the role of the Shanghai government was merely to send its youth out of the city, but as Chapter 2 illustrates, settling urban youth in remote villages proved to be extremely difficult. From the beginning, the sent-down youth movement was beset with problems related to the gap between urban and rural conditions. The municipal government received a multitude of reports that urban youth experienced inadequate housing, food, and medical facilities, and that physical labor was backbreaking and potentially injurious for individuals raised in the city. This chapter calls attention to the perspective of rural officials who, completely unprepared for the arrival of urban teenagers, faced the overwhelming job of accommodating and managing them. Given the paucity of rural resources, sent-down youth often required provisions from the city. While youth were geographically distant from their homes, and may have bemoaned the loss of their legal residence in Shanghai when their *hukou* was transferred to a rural production team, they maintained close connections with their families in the city, on whom they depended for both financial and material goods. Most importantly, their welfare was continually monitored and managed by the Shanghai government through the sent-down youth office and its teams of Shanghai cadres stationed in areas where the city's youth were sent— the *weiwentuan*.

An inadvertent result of the sent-down youth movement was the creation of not only individual, but also administrative and institutional, connections between remote rural regions and Shanghai. Although intended to facilitate the discussion of problems encountered by sent-down youth, these new connections turned out to have some unexpected functions. Chapter 3 focuses on how the network of connections established by the sent-down youth movement provided rural leaders a way of bypassing state planning policies to obtain directly from Shanghai materials and equipment they desperately needed to establish small local industries. At a time when state planning policies favored large industrial centers such as Shanghai, most remote rural counties had almost no way to acquire resources, in spite of Mao's advocacy of rural industry. Were it not for the sent-down youth movement, these county leaders would have had no connection to Shanghai, nor would agencies in Shanghai have had reasons to donate materials to places unfamiliar and irrelevant to them. Now, when rural local leaders issued requests for equipment, officials in Shanghai hustled to identify bureaus that could satisfy them, as the otherwise far more powerful Shanghai municipal government found itself dependent on small and peripheral local governments to take care of the city's youth.

If the sent-down youth movement connected Shanghai and remote villages and in this sense may have slightly narrowed the urban–rural gap, investigations of abuse of urban youth by local villagers illuminated the breadth and unbridgeability of this gap. Popular and scholarly literature has long decried the plight of young urban women who were victims of sexual assault during the sent-down youth movement.[30] While there were surely far more such incidents than were ever reported, Chapter 4 revisits this highly controversial issue from the perspective of the state: the reasons for and impact of its intervention. Texts of accusations,

---

[30] Ba Shan, "Bei pohai de qingchun: Dalu shangshan xiaxiang nü zhiqing canzao roulin lu" (A Record of the Tragic Oppression of Female Sent-Down Youth), *Zhongguo zhichun*, 108 (May 1992), 58–64; Deng Xian, *Zhongguo zhiqing meng* (The Dream of China's Sent-Down Youth) (Beijing: Wenhua shehui chubanshe, 1996). Also see Bonnin, 296–300.

confessions, investigative reports, and sentencing records make it clear that the compilation of statistics and conduct of investigations were part of a campaign triggered by a state directive in 1973 concerning "harm to sent-down youth," a campaign that pressured local officials to identify, expose, and investigate locals who had romantic relations with female sent-down youth, and punish individuals found guilty of sexual assault. This was not limited to rape, but included a range of behaviors and relationships previously deemed inappropriate but now classified as criminal: seduction, adultery, and molestation, as well as flirting, dating, and affairs. Regardless of what type of intimacy was the basis of accusation and investigation, in almost every case individuals found to be guilty perpetrators of abuse were local men, and those they abused were urban women. Male sent-down youth who engaged in similar intimacies with fellow sent-down youth or local women were exempted from the investigations, as were local men who engaged in such intimacies with rural women. The stated aim of the campaign was to punish individuals for undermining the sent-down youth movement, but it was the zealousness of the investigation campaign that ultimately subverted it by creating a stereotypical image of villagers as abusers who were unfit to host, let alone educate, urban youth.

The directives of 1973 and the campaign to criminalize abusers of sent-down youth raised serious questions about the principles of the sent-down youth movement: the wisdom of having Shanghai youth live in close proximity with peasants and the role of peasants as educators for urban youth. As Chapter 5 shows, in the wake of the 1973 campaign, the Shanghai government intensified efforts to help urban youth leave the fields, launching projects such as technical workshops in Shanghai in which youth could participate during their home visits as well as distance-learning courses offered for sent-down youth in rural areas. This promotion of education and technical training enhanced the opportunities for sent-down youth to escape fieldwork and take on less physically taxing jobs in rural areas as office clerks, accountants, electrical engineers, machine technicians, and barefoot teachers and doctors. In some areas, the Shanghai government provided material and financial resources for the establishment of small factories and sent-down youth stations, urban outposts scattered across the rural landscape that were entirely independent of the village economy. Although these programs were ostensibly initiated to support the sent-down youth movement, they inadvertently intensified a new boundary in the countryside that divided sent-down youth and villagers. They also turned urban youth into educated and skilled rural residents who became some of the most privileged residents in the countryside.

In spite of all these efforts by the Shanghai government, by the mid-1970s the sent-down youth movement was beset with insurmountable problems. As Chapter 6 demonstrates, an increasing number of urban youth did not want to stay in the countryside, while urban cadres became equally unwilling to join the *weiwentuan* teams dispatched to provide relief. Relations between rural governments and the *weiwentuan* from Shanghai became conflictual, paralleled by mutual antagonism between urban youth and rural leaders. At the same time, *weiwentuan* reports on conditions of sent-down youth became desperately pessimistic about the prospects of long-term settlement of urban youth in the countryside. The flow of youth back to Shanghai increased, primarily without official sanction. What stand out in archival reports are the ways in which the Shanghai government, *weiwentuan*, and rural officials, all charged to support the sent-down youth movement, began to collaborate to enable youth to return to the city and re-establish their official urban residency. By the time dramatic protests by youth on the Yunnan state farms took place in 1978–1979—commonly cited as bringing the movement to a halt —almost all the Shanghai youth assigned to production teams had already left or were in the process of leaving.

The termination of the sent-down youth movement, then, was not simply a product of the work stoppages, hunger strikes, and demonstrations that took place during its final year. The movement's end must be understood in the context of the myriad acts of circumvention and manipulation of state policy engaged in by sent-down youth, their families, urban and rural officials, and ordinary villagers throughout the decade of the movement. Many of these actions were disconnected individual initiatives that did not represent a history of protest against an all-powerful state. Yet their cumulative effect fundamentally shaped the course of this movement and eventually played a major role in bringing it to an end. In the case of the sent-down youth movement, the reach of the Maoist state, to invoke Vivienne Shue's words, had to confront its limits.

1   Farewell to the Huangpu River

On October 9, 1967, just before their departure from Beijing to Inner Mongolia, a group of ten students from the Beijing Number 25 High School congregated in front of a picture of Chairman Mao at Tian'anmen Square. Witnessed by a crowd of a thousand local residents, they swore allegiance to Mao, declaring,

For the great goal of spreading red Mao Zedong thought throughout the world, we would, if it were necessary, be willing to go up to the mountain of knives or down to the sea of fire. Following [Mao's] great directive to integrate intellectuals with workers and peasants, we are taking the first step. We will go all the way on this revolutionary road and never look back.[1]

This event, publicized through national radio stations and newspapers, generated enthusiasm throughout the country. By the end of 1967, official media reported that 4,000 high school graduates had left Beijing for the countryside, many more following the next spring.[2]

In Shanghai, it was more than half a year later that idealistic students began to volunteer to go to the countryside. After several exploratory trips to Anhui and Heilongjiang in July 1968, the first delegation set off in August. "Farewell to the Huangpu River," declared the Shanghai *Jiefang ribao* on August 12, 1968, announcing the departure of forty-five of "our city's little soldiers" for remote mountain districts of China, where they would join village production teams. This contingent had secured the "glorious approval" of the Shanghai municipal government, which held a reception for them on the morning of their departure, praising them for their decision to go, and instructing them to closely study Chairman Mao's works, learn from the poor and lower-middle peasants, and participate in both production and class struggle. As they prepared to board the train that evening, the station was brightly lit and adorned with red

---

[1] Liu Xiaomeng, *Zhongguo zhiqingshi*, 71.   [2] Ibid., 69–71.

flags; drums beat as the "little soldiers" said goodbye to the 10 million citizens of Shanghai.[3]

These voluntary departures of urban youth to the countryside took place in the context of the first years of the Cultural Revolution when, since its inception in summer 1966, student Red Guards in cities throughout China attacked educational, cultural, and administrative institutions, as well as individuals, including their own family members and teachers, whom they deemed to be counterrevolutionaries, or class enemies, or guilty of bourgeois thinking and habits. As with students from the Beijing Number 25 High School, Shanghai newspapers explained that the decision for urban youth to go to the countryside was a way of expressing their loyalty to Chairman Mao and the Chinese Communist Party as well as their commitment to revolutionary change.[4] The emergence of these volunteers culminated in the directive issued by Mao and publicized in the *Renmin ribao* on December 22, 1968, announcing, "It is necessary for educated youth to go to the countryside to receive re-education from the poor and lower-middle peasants," and that "rural comrades throughout the country should welcome them." This directive signified a turning point of the sent-down youth movement, shifting voluntary initiatives by a relatively few idealistic students to a state-led nationwide campaign.

Immediately after the announcement of Mao's directive, the Shanghai municipal government announced its policy of "uniform redness" (*yipianhong*): all the 507,000 middle and high school graduates of 1968 and 1969, along with graduates of the previous two years who were still waiting for job assignments, would be sent to the countryside.[5] The practice of sending city youth to the countryside continued until 1978, some 1.1 million youth from Shanghai having been sent.[6] Over the course of the decade, these youth were assigned to village production brigades, state farms, or military farms. Persuading youth to go, transporting them, and settling them required an extensive mobilization campaign, as well as the creation of new administrative structures to manage the program.

This chapter focuses on the process of mobilizing Shanghai's urban youth to go to the countryside, as well as responses to mobilization by youth themselves, their parents, and municipal government officials during the peak years of the movement in 1969 and 1970. During this time, the mobilization campaign aimed to achieve the goal of "uniform redness": all the graduates were required to go to the countryside. Moreover,

---

[3] *Jiefang ribao*, August 12, 1968.   [4] Ibid.
[5] Shanghai laodongzhi bianzhuan weiyuanhui, *Shanghai laodongzhi* (Shanghai Labor Gazetteer) (Shanghai: Shanghai shehui kexueyuan chubanshe, 1998), 111.
[6] Ibid.

almost all were sent to production teams and state farms in places distant from Shanghai.

Mobilization

The mobilization of urban youth to go to the countryside had its origins in the mid-1950s, when a small number of idealistic and progressive youth volunteered to go to the countryside, and newspapers publicized model volunteers such as Dong Jiageng, Hou Jun, and Xing Yanzi.[7] Before the Cultural Revolution, the Shanghai government strongly encouraged "social youth" (*shehui qingnian*)—students who had not been admitted to high school or colleges and had not found employment—to go to the countryside.[8] By 1962, the central government formulated policies and established administrative offices for the resettlements. From 1955 to the beginning of the Cultural Revolution in 1966, the Shanghai government claimed that some 164,015 youth from the city were sent to the countryside.[9] In relation to the total Shanghai population, which was over six million in 1955 and nearly eleven million in 1966, this number, fewer than 15,000 per year, was small.[10] The effort to send youth to the countryside before the Cultural Revolution, therefore, affected a limited segment of Shanghai residents.

At the same time, however, this earlier phase of sending youth to the countryside is a significant backdrop to what took place during the movement's reconfiguration and expansion during the Cultural Revolution. During the early months of the Cultural Revolution in 1966, a large contingent of youth sent to the countryside in the early 1960s returned to Shanghai and protested their assignment, demanding that the municipal government reinstate their urban residence permits. And in the unprecedented political opening afforded by the Cultural Revolution, many of the youth returning to the city formed their own rebel groups.[11] This meant that many sectors of the Shanghai population became well aware of the hardships endured by the earlier contingent of sent-down youth.

The sent-down youth movement of the Cultural Revolution, therefore, was not an entirely new phenomenon, even if it was instituted in

---

[7] See Liu Xiaomeng, *Zhongguo zhiqing shidian* (Major Events and Documents of China's Sent-Down Youth) (Chengdu: Sichuan renmin chubanshe, 1995), 719–722, 731–739.

[8] Ding Yizhuang, 47–48. For a discussion of "social youth" in Hunan sent to the countryside before the Cultural Revolution, see Yiching Wu, 162–170.

[9] Shanghai laodong zhi bianzhuan weiyuanhui, 114; Liu Xiaomeng, *Zhongguo zhiqingshi*, 43.

[10] Jin Dalu and Jin Guangyao, *Zhongguo xin difangzhi*, vol. 4, 2205.

[11] See Yiching Wu, 108–110. Also see Bonnin, 63.

a completely different context than the earlier movement. The dislocation of the first years of the Cultural Revolution, particularly the disruption to schools and factories, caused the problem of unemployment in Shanghai to reach an unprecedented level.[12] Red Guard attacks on schools resulted in the closure of all academic institutions above middle school. Students graduating from middle school, starting in 1966, could not be admitted to high schools; those graduating from high school could not go on to colleges or universities. There was also a scarcity of jobs for these school graduates, as most factories curtailed production during these early years of the Cultural Revolution when Shanghai worker rebels, endorsed by Mao, seized control of the municipal government and later occupied schools and government institutions.[13] This reduction in potential jobs became particularly acute in 1968 when, in order to restore classroom instruction, students in the middle and high school classes of 1966, 1967, and 1968, referred to as *lao san jie* ("three old classes"), would have to be graduated to make classroom space needed for new entering students.[14] The first policy to deal with these *lao san jie*, announced in April 1968, was to assign them jobs according to the "four directions": to the countryside, frontier, factories, and mines.

Although most students hoped for urban factory jobs, a large number of them were sent to the countryside.[15] At this point the countryside to which most youth were sent consisted primarily of state farms near Shanghai (such as those in Chongming, Nanhui, and Fengxian) or more distant ones administered by Shanghai (such as Huangshan in Anhui and Dafeng in Jiangsu).[16] In early June 1968, the Shanghai Party Committee sponsored a mass rally in Hongkou Stadium to mobilize the 1966 high school and middle school graduates to go to the countryside.[17] A week later, the city established an office to oversee the mobilization.[18] Still, many students did not want to go to the state farms and instead

---

[12] See Bonnin, 32–46.

[13] Elizabeth Perry and Li Xun, *Proletarian Power: Shanghai in the Cultural Revolution* (Boulder, CO: Westview Press, 1997).

[14] During the Mao era, it was the responsibility of city governments to either provide jobs for graduates from colleges, middle and high schools, and vocational and technical schools, or to send them to the countryside. Bernstein, 33.

[15] Jin Dalu and Lin Shengbao, *Shanghai zhishi qingnian shangshan xiaxiang yundong jishilu* (Chronicle of Shanghai Sent-Down Youth) (Shanghai: Shanghai shudian, 2014), 2.

[16] Shanghai laodongzhi bianzhuan weiyuanhui, 185. Also see Jin Dalu and Lin Shengbao, 21.

[17] Shanghai qingnianzhi bianzhuan weiyuanhui, 552. In 1966, there were almost 150,000 middle school graduates in Shanghai and nearly 31,000 high school graduates.

[18] This "Shangshan xiaxiang bangongshi" preceded the establishment of the Shanghai office of sent-down youth—Shanghai shi zhishi qingnian shangshan xiaxiang bangong-shi—under the State Council.

chose to wait for the possibility of a preferable assignment.[19] Meanwhile, a small number of youth from Shanghai—following the example of their counterparts in Beijing—volunteered to go to distant production teams. In June, the Shanghai government dispatched two small teams to explore the possibilities for assigning youth to production teams in Anhui and Heilongjiang.[20]

This is the context in which Mao issued his directive in December 1968. His directive added two new elements to the project of sending youth to the countryside. First, by the directive stating that it is "necessary" for educated youth to be re-educated by peasants, going to the countryside became a requirement, not one of several options. Second, it mandated that rural communities welcome the urban youth. The directive transformed what had been a relatively modest set of policies to deal with unemployed school graduates into a full-blown movement that required the participation of a far larger number of urban families.[21]

Leaders of the Shanghai government announced that all students waiting for job assignments, along with the entire class of 1968 graduates, would be required to go to the countryside. Demonstrating loyalty to Mao and formulating policies that supported him was crucial for the personal and political survival of high-ranking government officials. Although the 1968 directive was not at all specific about how youth should be mobilized and where they should be settled, the Shanghai government, like that of Beijing and several other large cities, defined the countryside as remote rural regions. During these early years of the sent-down youth movement, the Shanghai government defined the countryside as remote production teams and state farms, excluding state farms administered by the municipal government that were in closer proximity to Shanghai.

Within several weeks, the Shanghai government arranged to send youth to state farms and villages in Heilongjiang, Jilin, Inner Mongolia, Anhui, Jiangxi, Yunnan, and Guizhou. This policy was strictly implemented for two years, and impacted 507,000 middle and high school graduates, including the entire 1968 and 1969 classes as well as the remaining

---

[19] By the end of December, about 47,000 graduates from the 1966 and 1967 classes were still waiting, making it difficult for the government to start job assignments for the class of 1968. Shanghai laodongzhi bianzhuan weiyuanhui, 112.

[20] Jin Dalu and Lin Shengbao, 3; also see "Lishi de tiankong: Zhiqing shangshan xiaxiang dashiji" (The Sky of History: A Chronology of Sent-Down Youth), May 18, 2007, at www.chsi.com.cn/jyzd/jygz/200705/20070518/908609.html, accessed April 18, 2017.

[21] *Renmin ribao*, December 28, 1968, CCRD. For a more extensive analysis of the ideological underpinning of the sent-down youth movement, see Bonnin, 19–24; Bernstein, 33–83; and Liu Xiaomeng, *Zhongguo zhiqingshi*, 36–41.

1966 and 1967 graduates who were still waiting for assignments by December 1968.[22]

For the Shanghai government, the prospect of sending youth to the countryside offered a practical solution to some of its most vexing problems. As noted above, the curtailment of high school and college admissions since the beginning of the Cultural Revolution had prevented middle and high school students from graduating for two years. Until these students received job assignments and graduated, enrolling new students would be increasingly difficult. Mao's sent-down youth directive might well have seemed a much-needed, even if temporary, solution to this problem.

Mao's directive also offered a means of terminating the two years of urban violence and disorder that had erupted since the beginning of the Cultural Revolution, when Red Guards trashed neighborhoods and occupied schools and some private residences. In Shanghai disorder was not only a product of Red Guard activities, but also involved gangs of neighborhood youth labeled in government documents as hoodlums (*liumang afei*). The Cultural Revolution increased the ranks and activities of *liumang*, whom local newspapers accused of engaging in gang fights, theft, assaults on women, and killing people with knives.[23] By early 1969, some districts in Shanghai were arresting *liumang* (many identified as elementary and middle school students) and also organizing them into study groups; throughout that summer, city newspapers included numerous reports on efforts by the municipal government to crack down on them.[24] Exporting them to the countryside became one of the most effective ways in which the Shanghai government could deal with the problem. Commenting on the negotiation conducted by Shanghai authorities with Anhui Province to accept 10,000 *liumang*, one provincial official stated that the arrangement was "to relieve the pressure of these youth on the city."[25] Whether such a sizeable number actually went and whether rural officials had any say about accepting these *liumang* remains unclear.

---

[22] Shanghai laodongzhi bianzhuan weiyuanhui, 112.

[23] PTDOSY, Putuoqu Jiaozhou diqu Mao Zedong sixiang jiaoyu xuexiban 普陀区胶州地区毛泽东思想教育学习班, "Jiaozhou diqu Mao Zedong sixiang jiaoyu xuexiban zongjie" 胶州地区毛泽东思想教育学习班总结 (Summary of the Jiaozhou District Study Group on Mao Zedong Thought), March 13, 1969, PTDA.

[24] On the problem of *liumang afei*, see *Jiefang ribao*, July 20, 1969; July 24, 1969; July 25, 1969; July 26, 1969.

[25] Jiang Danping, "Nongnong de qingsi: Huiyi Anhui sheng shangshan xiaxiang gongzuo" (Thick Affections: Recalling "Up to the Mountains and Down to the Countryside" Work in Anhui Province), in Zhonggong Anhui shengwei dangshi yanjiushi, ed., *Anhui zhiqing koushu shilu* (Oral History of Anhui Sent-Down Youth) (Anhui: Zhonggong dangshi chubanshe, 2014), vol. 1, 47.

The Shanghai government launched a massive mobilization campaign to achieve "uniform redness." Echoing the *Renmin ribao*, Shanghai newspapers did not refer to any of the practical rationales for launching the movement, but instead focused on its espoused revolutionary ideology and benefits: the virtues of hard labor in the countryside for urban youth, the opportunity the movement would provide them to learn about China's social and economic problems, and the potential contributions to rural development they could make. It also glorified going to the countryside, depicting those who went as loyal followers of Mao willing to sacrifice the comfort of their urban homes for the cause of the revolution and presenting them as models of worthy revolutionary successors.[26]

Mobilization consumed the city of Shanghai. Its streets were plastered with bright red posters proclaiming Mao's directive about sent-down youth, depicting young students excitedly boarding trains bound for distant provinces. Newspapers published detailed accounts of mass rallies and parades celebrating those who agreed to go. The *Jiefang ribao*, for example, claimed that in early 1969 some 400,000 youth and their parents joined a parade to publicize their excitement about the movement.[27] Large assemblies took place every time groups of youth departed from the Shanghai train station, such as the 10,000 people who gathered to support the 4,000 urban youth leaving for Heilongjiang.[28] On a single occasion of 1,800 youth boarding a train for Anhui, the Zhabei district staged a sending-off parade with 200,000 participants, including both the "old and young" of the neighborhood.[29] The same district government also organized a "propaganda week" in May 1969, during which it commanded all work units to hang up banners and posters and stores to exhibit photos of and letters from sent-down youth in their windows. It also sent performing teams to schools, bus stations, major streets, and alleys to reach "every single family."[30]

In propagating the virtues of "going up to the mountains and down to the villages," the media, particularly in the very early phases of the movement, made clear that the ideal version of going to the countryside was

---

[26] *Jiefang ribao*, January 8, 1969; January 27, 1969; February 26, 1969.

[27] *Jiefang ribao*, February 12, 1969.

[28] *Wenhui bao*, July 9, 1969, cited in Jin Dalu and Lin Shengbao, 62–63.

[29] Zhabeiqu geming weiyuanhui 闸北区革命委员会, "Guanyu zhishi qingnian xiaxiang shangshan da dongyuan de qingkuang baogao" 关于知识青年下乡上山大动员的情况报告 (Report on the Mobilization of Sent-Down Youth), January 21, 1969, ZBDA.

[30] Zhabei qu geming weiyuan hui 闸北区革命委员会, "Guanyu Zhabei qu kaizhan dongyuan zhishi qingnian fu Heilongjiang, Neimeng, Jilin, Anhui chadui luohu xuanchuan zhou huodong de jidian yijian" 关于闸北区开展动员知识青年赴黑龙江，内蒙，吉林，安徽插队落户宣传周活动的几点意见 (Ideas Concerning Propaganda Week Activities in Zhabei District to Mobilize Educated Youth to go to Villages in Heilongjiang, Inner Mongolia, Jilin, and Anhui), May 1969, ZBDA.

Photo 1.1 Holding a portrait of Chairman Mao, students from Shanghai's
Putuo district bid farewell to the Huangpu river.
Photo courtesy of He Xinhua.

chadui luohu, joining village production teams and living like villagers in
poor and remote areas.[31] The government had to confront large numbers
of students who imagined they could comply with Mao's directive by going
to less impoverished areas or to state farms. One district report highlighted
the problematic residents who asserted that "the worst thing is to be sent to
chadui luohu," and preferred to go to state farms instead.[32] Newspapers
also boasted headlines such as "You Must Be Determined to Endure the
Greatest Hardships!" "Take the Path to the Production Brigades!"[33]
"Joining Production Brigades Is Forever Revolutionary!"[34] They praised
youth accepting assignments to production teams, with headlines such as

---

[31] See, for example, PTDOSY, "Xiaxiang shangshan bangongshi gongzuo dasuan" 下乡上
山办公室工作打算 (Plan for the Work of the Sent-Down Youth Office), July 1969,
PTDA.
[32] Zhabeiqu geming weiyuanhui, "Guanyu zhishi qingnian xiaxiang shangshan da dongyuan de qingkuang baogao."
[33] *Jiefang ribao,* January 17, 1969.   [34] *Jiefang ribao,* December 19, 1968.

Photo 1.2 A photo released by the media featuring a happy departure of sent-down youth at the Shanghai train station. Xn-irro5qn0bv6c.com

"Spring Thunder on the Banks of the Huangpu River: Waves of Youth Are Going Up to the Mountains and Down to the Villages."[35]

To complement these calls to join production brigades, Shanghai newspapers published accounts, often culled and reprinted from provincial newspapers, of the enthusiastic welcome urban youth received from rural hosts. The *Yunnan ribao* (*Yunnan Daily*) declared, "We welcome you sent-down youth from Beijing and Shanghai!"[36] The *Jilin ribao*'s (*Jilin Daily*) bold-lettered welcoming of sent-down youth was followed by an account of the careful preparations being undertaken by villagers for the arrival of urban youth: making arrangements for food, housing, fuel, and furniture; preparing to provide political education; ordering Mao's books as a welcome gift. According to one report, "Everything is in place" in the countryside: many villages had organized residents to repair old houses, build new stoves, and paint the walls; some villagers were saving vegetables for the sent-down youth, and some others happily vacated their

[35] *Jiefang ribao*, February 12, 1969.   [36] *Jiefang ribao*, February 27, 1969.

rooms, decorating them as if for newlyweds.[37] *Jiefang ribao* also reported that Inner Mongolia had organized leadership committees and transportation teams to greet sent-down youth and would provide food for the youth during their journey to villages. Even local stores were reportedly prepared: they set up special counters to provide sent-down youth the commodities necessary for daily life in the region; some herdsmen made Mongolian gowns and leather boots for the arriving urban youth.[38] In Heilongjiang, local residents were said to have declared that their "great leader Chairman Mao" had bestowed upon them "this heavy responsibility to re-educate the educated youth ... the greatest trust given to us peasants." These villagers, the report said, wanted to assure urban parents that they would treat the students as if they were their "own sons and daughters."[39]

As soon as some Shanghai youth settled down in the countryside, newspapers began to publish accounts of their heroic accomplishments. A Shanghai youth sent to Jiayin, Heilongjiang, received lavish praise for having donated blood to save the life of a village woman who had lost consciousness during childbirth.[40] Other accounts described sent-down youth who provided medicines for villagers and who, as barefoot doctors, treated those who were seriously ill.[41]

Negotiations

In spite of the relentless enthusiasm propagated by the national and local media, many urban residents were ambivalent about the call to go to the countryside. A cadre from Heilongjiang sent to Shanghai to receive potential sent-down youth described the "sea of noisy people" occupying the street in front of the prestigious Jinjiang Hotel where she and delegates from other provinces stayed. Hoping to obtain information about conditions in the countryside and potentially to negotiate the best possible assignments for their own children, people crowded the entrance to the hotel. At a high school gathering, this cadre found herself encircled by students desperately asking questions such as, "The winter must be cold. Will my ears freeze off?" "If I go out to pee, do I have to break the ice to make a hole with a stick?" "Are we getting guns? Is there going to be a war?" "Is there rice to eat?"[42]

[37] *Jiefang ribao*, February 24, 1969.   [38] *Jiefang ribao*, March 16, 1969.
[39] *Jiefang ribao*, February 3, 1969.   [40] *Jiefang ribao*, July 20, 1969.
[41] For example, see *Jiefang ribao*, July 20, 1969. Other issues of the newspaper published many similar stories.
[42] Liu Lianying, "Wo qu Shanghai jie zhiqing" (I Went to Shanghai to Pick Up Sent-Down Youth), *Zhiqing* (Sent-Down Youth), 2 (2013), 42–43.

Despite their worries about rural conditions, the majority of urban students did join the movement. It is difficult to determine to what extent they did so voluntarily. Although newspapers relentlessly reported stories of young volunteers guided by revolutionary ideology, what might appear as voluntary participation sometimes turned out to be more complex. One early volunteer, a student from the high school affiliated with Shanghai Normal University, offered to go to Jiangxi before the movement became mandatory, hoping that this would enable his younger brother to have a factory job in Shanghai. This strategy to spare his brother from being assigned to the countryside failed. "Unfortunately," he recalled, "the policy changed with Mao's directive a month later, and my brother was sent to Jilin."[43] Had he known in advance, he most likely would not have volunteered.

Once the government mandated that all graduates must go, many Shanghai residents tried to negotiate the best possible situation. One former sent-down youth explained her father's efforts:

My younger sister and I were one year apart and in the same class of 1969. We were told there were four provinces where we could be sent: Heilongjiang, Jiangxi, Anhui, and Yunnan. My younger sister, who had some health issues, was assigned to Jiangxi, while I was assigned to the most distant location in Heilongjiang. I was upset and was informed that the Jiangxi slots were filled. Then my father, hearing that a work team from Jiangxi was staying at the Jinjiang Hotel, rode his bicycle there and met with the team leader. Fortunately, that person understood that if siblings were together they would be more secure and settled, and he promised to add me to the Jiangxi list. Did we resist? No! Everyone had to go and there was no alternative. And we were happy to have gotten the best possible assignment.[44]

Although some Shanghai students expressed passion about going to the countryside, their passion was not always an expression of revolutionary zeal. One young woman explained her excitement as desire for independence from her family: "I was a little excited because I could finally escape the control of my parents and become my own boss. The sky is high so that birds can fly; the ocean is wide so that fish can jump."[45] One student, a former Red Guard, explained the naivety of his enthusiasm:

---

[43] Yang Shixiong, "Shouyinji li de gushi" (Story from the Radio), February 12, 2012, at http://zhiqingwang.shzq.org/jiangxArtD.aspx?ID=4773, accessed April 10, 2014.

[44] Interview with Wang Pei.

[45] Pan Ying, "Li kai muqin de na tian" (The Day I Left My Mother), in Zhu Mingyuan, *Nanwang Makuli: Heilongjiang sheng jiangchuan nonchang zhiqing huiyilu* (Unforgettable Makuli: Memoirs of Sent-Down Youth in Jiangchuan Farm, Heilongjiang) (self-published, 2011), 166.

At that time I was at an age when I didn't really understand reality. I had no idea what kind of impact giving up my *hukou* would have on my future. I had no idea how precious a Shanghai *hukou* was. It took me only a few minutes to sign up.[46]

Another attributed his enthusiasm to an effort to perform ideological correctness and compensate for the political problems of his deceased father that limited his future prospects. His family's economic situation was also a factor: after his mother's death, he lived with his aunt, who, regardless of her poor health, had to support a family of four on a monthly salary of sixty *yuan*. The aunt had tried to commit suicide because of poverty and her illness. His enlistment to go to the countryside represented a desire to relieve her burden.[47]

To be sure, most youth did not readily volunteer or accept their assignment, and the mobilization campaign to persuade more than half a million students to go to the countryside required the involvement of the entire organizational infrastructure of the municipal government as well as extensive "ideological work" (*sixiang gongzuo*) on the youth and their family members. Schoolteachers and administrative officials, responsible for determining assignments for graduates, would try to persuade them by addressing their real or imagined objections: "'You are afraid of going far away from home?' they might ask," as one sent-down youth recalled. "Then Anhui would be ideal: it is only a few hundred *li* from Shanghai and it would only take you one day to get home."

You're not used to eating wheat products? Then you can go to Jiangxi where they cultivate rice. If you are afraid of cold weather, then you can go to Yunnan where all four seasons are like spring and you can always wear a T-shirt and go barefoot. If you are worried about economic security, then you can go to a state farm where they pay you a salary every month.

Teachers and leaders insisted that these were one-time offers and that such choices would not be available for long.[48]

Many students were still not persuaded. Some stayed away from school meetings, and others refused to accept their assignment. In these cases, neighbors organized to cajole them. Street committees, composed mostly of housewives, could be relentless: members took turns visiting homes and talking exhaustively, posting on people's doors sheets of red paper on which Mao's directives were printed. According to the cadre from Heilongjiang,

---

[46] Zhang Liang, *Cong hei tudi zoulai* (Coming from the Black Soil) (Shanghai: Xuelin chubanshe, 2011), 9–10.

[47] Zhu Xiaohong, "Xiaxiang" (Going to the Countryside), in Zhu Mingyuan, *Nanwang Makuli*, 185–186.

[48] Zhang Liang, 10. One *li* is approximately 0.5 kilometer.

the street committee was more active than school officials. They would go to the homes of graduating students to engage their family members in ideological work. If the student disagreed or showed even slight resistance, those cadres would stay at their home every day from morning until night, until the student was actually persuaded to leave for the countryside.[49]

Residents did not always appreciate these tactics, and in some instances vandalized the homes of street committee members.[50] If the strategies of schools and street committees were inadequate, parents of those who refused to leave were likely to be subjected to additional pressure from their work units, where they could be stigmatized and barred from privileges such as joining the CCP.[51]

A number of parents, to avoid sending their children to remote regions, tried to arrange for their sons and daughters to go to villages in the relatively affluent areas of Zhejiang and Jiangsu near Shanghai. Although during the early years of the movement the government did not send students to these areas, many Shanghai residents had relatives in these two provinces who could accommodate their youth, a practice referred to as "finding one's own road" (*zixun chulu*). From the perspective of parents, sending their youth to live in nearby areas under the care of relatives was far preferable to having them assigned to impoverished and faraway places, where they would be overseen by complete strangers. Although this could be understood as a way of nominally participating in the movement, the Shanghai government did not encourage this, and pressured residents to accept assignments to remote counties. The *Jiefang ribao*, for example, chastised such individuals, declaring, "if you do not go where you are assigned but instead go to where you have relatives, this is shameful!"[52]

The stubborn resistance of some parents to having their children sent to the countryside proved to be a major problem, as reflected in the number of articles in major Shanghai newspapers addressing this subject. "There are some parents," one reported,

who say, "The countryside is bitter and our children will not be able to adjust." Actually, it is precisely the fact that they cannot adjust that proves how imperative it is for them to receive re-education by peasants ... If billions of peasants can adjust to life in the countryside, then why in the world can't educated youth adjust?[53]

---

[49] Liu Lianying, 42–43.   [50] Liu Xiaomeng, *Zhongguo zhiqingshi*, 107.

[51] Bernstein is more skeptical about the effectiveness of the mobilization campaign, particularly the role of the neighborhood committees. His study deals with both large and small cities, and also deals with mobilization over a longer time period. Bernstein, 93–96.

[52] *Jiefang ribao*, January 24, 1969.   [53] *Jiefang ribao*, January 8, 1969.

Another news report focused on parents at the Tobacco and Sugar Company in the Nanshi district of Shanghai. To persuade them to encourage their children to enlist for the sent-down youth movement, the company held more than 100 study sessions in summer 1969, with some 4,800 participants. Unfortunately, leaders found that although those attending expressed enthusiasm at the meetings, many still refused to send their children.[54]

In spite of rallies, study sessions, and pressures on parents, a significant number of youth did not volunteer. In Putuo district, for example, 25,000 graduates were determined eligible to go to the countryside in 1969. After four months of intensive efforts to mobilize them, some 7,500 refused to comply. The district sent-down youth office developed a plan to improve its effectiveness: to provide training for the cadres from the schools, district, and neighborhood committee; to hold a large-scale rally with inspirational speeches; to organize an exhibition of photos featuring participants in the movement. The plan also called for special attention to Red Guards and their parents, and an analysis of the reasons for their lack of enthusiasm for the movement. In an effort to instill excitement among the district residents, the plan instructed cadres to "use every possible means" to publicize the movement. To this end, it proposed that broadcast speakers be installed in front of the district government office and at the intersections of the busiest commercial streets.[55]

In addition to broadcasting the virtues of going to the countryside, the city government also began to publicize the consequences that would be faced by those who tried to undermine the movement. By fall 1969, public sentencing meetings began to take place. At one held in Putuo district, a woman found guilty of introducing prospective marriage partners to female youth so they could avoid being sent to remote regions was sentenced to twenty years in jail for having "tried to destroy the sent-down youth movement."[56] In 1970, in response to a central government directive to crack down on those who subverted the movement, some thirty-seven individuals in Shanghai were identified as criminals guilty of undermining the movement. Beginning that year, 145 rallies were held to publicize these crimes, attended by 310,000 people (the largest had an audience of 5,000).[57]

---

[54] *Jiefang ribao*, August 19, 1969.
[55] PTDOSY, "Putuo qu shangshan xiaxiang bangongshi dang qian gongzuo dasuan" 普陀区革命委员会上山下乡办公室打算 (Plan for Work of the Putuo District Office of Sent-Down Youth), July 1969, PTDA.
[56] Ibid.
[57] Shanghai shenpanzhi bianzhuan weiyuanhui, *Shanghai shenpanzhi* (Shanghai Trial and Sentencing Gazetteer) (Shanghai: Shanghai shehui kexueyuan chubanshe, 2003), 247.

Looking more closely at the mobilization efforts in Shanghai, it becomes clear that their effectiveness was often shaped by the political, social, and economic status of individuals. Those labeled as members the "five black categories" (*heiwulei*)—landlords, rich farmers, antirevolutionary individuals, bad individuals, and rightists, as well as capitalists or anyone under scrutiny for historical or ideological problems—could not afford to resist having their sons or daughters participate in the movement, as it would likely intensify their already vulnerable position. For youth belonging to families with problematic backgrounds, complying with the policy could both protect their parents and express their determination to distinguish themselves from their inherited class identity. The majority of youth went to the countryside either because they believed it was the right thing to do or because they had no other choices. Ironically, it was most often residents of working-class neighborhoods, particularly those living in the city's shack settlements, who defied the mobilization campaign.

Contradictions of Class

Class struggle dominated the media in Maoist China, particularly during the Cultural Revolution when the proletariat was valorized and the bourgeoisie condemned. This official discourse of class, however, obscured more popular notions of social status, which may not have used the vocabulary of class but manifested deep sensibilities about economic and social relationships. Most broadly, the residential registration system, which made urban residency a privilege inaccessible to rural people, marked the distinction between the agricultural and nonagricultural population, or between rural and urban status, particularly prominent. Residents of Shanghai were even more conscious of their city's privileged status: they considered almost everyone else "outsiders" (*waidi ren*), a term commonly used interchangeably with *xiangxia ren* ("country bumpkins"). There were also popular perceptions of class identity within the city of Shanghai, based on employment, school, neighborhood, and place of origin. For example, Shanghai people identified some areas, such as neighborhoods in the former foreign concessions, as "upper quarters," and the shantytowns and shack settlement districts where many of the so-called *Jiangbei* people lived as "lower quarters."[58]

---

[58] Jiangbei people were immigrants from areas in Jiangsu province north of the Yangzi river, an area considered poor and backwards by the Shangai elite, most of whom hailed from southern Jiangsu and Zhejiang. For an analysis of Jiangbei or Subei people in Shanghai, see Emily Honig, *Creating Chinese Ethnicity: Subei People in Shanghai, 1850–1980* (New Haven: Yale University Press, 1992).

Investigations of the mobilization campaign suggest that residents of the working class and shack settlement districts proved to be the most problematic, some openly challenging the government's policy, and some ignoring it altogether. A report concerning the Shanghai Number 11 Textile Mill in Putuo district observed that in summer 1969, close to 20 percent of the youth in workers' families who should have already gone to the countryside as members of the *lao san jie* remained at home in the city. One worker claimed that the family needed its child to perform household chores; another argued that his/her child had a high school education and was therefore "overqualified" to live in the countryside; another, having declared, "I do not believe there will be unemployment in a communist society," was confident his child would obtain an urban job if they waited. The investigative team found a worker who cursed the unfairness of the policy every day, and expressed frustration that sometimes factory cadres sympathized with the needs and desires of individual workers to keep their children at home. Even some Party members set a bad example for others. According to the report, one Party member claimed that he had prepared all the materials his son would need in the countryside, but could do nothing more to force the unwilling child to go. Another used his old age as an excuse, saying that he needed his child to be home to take care of him. Citing the fact that a Party member appointed workshop head had not sent her own child to the countryside, some workers said they would send their children only if she sent hers.[59] Reports of other factories in Shanghai described similar problems. A certain Wang Zhengling, a CCP member who also served on the revolutionary committee of the Shanghai light bulb factory, was described in a special investigative report as a "typical case" of a leader who had not sent his children to the countryside.[60]

The difficulties mobilizing factory workers to participate in the movement are also manifested in newspaper reports. Invariably providing a happy ending, these reports revealed problems that needed to be resolved. Leadership at the Number 9 Textile Factory, for example, called on all workers to make mobilization of the graduates in workers' families a top priority. Visiting families and holding study groups to encourage enlistment for the countryside, factory cadres encountered

---

[59] PTDOSY, "Jiu guomian shiyi chang qingkuang diaocha tichu dui gongchang shangshan xiaxiang gongzuo de jidian kanfa" 就国棉十一厂情况调查提出对工厂上山下乡工作的几点看法 (Several Suggestions Regarding the Work of Sent-Down Youth in Factories Based on the Investigation of the No. 11 Textile Mill), July 1969, PTDA.

[60] PTDOSY, "Ge jiedao jieji douzheng dongxiang chubu huibao" 各街道阶级斗争动向初步汇报 (Preliminary Report on the Signs of Class Struggle on Neighborhood Streets), July 1969, PTDA.

an older worker, Tian Gendi, who adamantly protested sending her second son to the countryside. Master Wu, who belonged to her workshop, used his break time to talk to her. "We workers," he reportedly instructed her, "need to listen to Chairman Mao. Have you thought about that? We came to the factory as teenagers. Do you remember conditions at that time and how much has improved? It is Chairman Mao who has brought us happiness and we cannot forget that." Not only did Tian change her mind, but she also began to educate her coworkers. Half a year into the mobilization campaign, 1,500 of this factory's 8,000 workers had agreed to send their children to the countryside. Although this report surely intended to convey success, it did indicate that many workers had expressed reluctance to send their children to the countryside.[61]

There are several reasons why workers at these factories could brazenly complain about sending their youth to the countryside. As members of the politically privileged working class, they had far less at stake than intellectuals or people with problematic class backgrounds. Working for state enterprises, their work units could pressure or stigmatize them, or deny them Party membership, but most often their jobs were secure.

If government officials found it challenging to mobilize factory workers, they confronted even more frustrations in contending with residents who constituted a "sub-proletariat," who had far less attachment or loyalty to the state. The critical role played by class in shaping responses to Mao's directive on sent-down youth is particularly conspicuous in a detailed report on one of Shanghai's best-known slum districts, Yaoshuilong. One of three major shantytown settlements in Shanghai, Yaoshuilong had its origins in the early twentieth century, when migrants from northern Jiangsu, Shandong, and Anhui came to the city to beg or engage in menial labor. The migrants made homes along the southern bank of Suzhou Creek in huts built of straw, bamboo poles, and broken wooden boards.[62] In the early 1950s, some one-fifth of Shanghai's population lived in shantytowns, some of which, only in the latter part of the decade, were gradually replaced by brick housing compounds.[63] Running water and electricity (but not indoor plumbing) were also installed in these settlements. Although the Shanghai Institute of City Planning claimed that on the eve of the Cultural Revolution,

---

[61] *Jiefang ribao*, April 1, 1969.

[62] For those who lived there, factory work was, as historian Hanchao Lu puts it, "a highly coveted form of employment." See Hanchao Lu, "Creating Urban Outcasts: Shantytowns in Shanghai, 1920–1950," *Journal of Urban History* 21, 5 (1995), 564; Hanchao Lu, *Beyond the Neon Lights: Everyday Shanghai in the Early Twentieth Century* (Berkeley: University of California Press, 1999), 118–137.

[63] Janet Y. Chen, *Guilty of Indigence: The Urban Poor in China, 1900–1953* (Princeton: Princeton University Press, 2012), 223.

many of the residences of Yaoshuilong had transformed from straw huts to simple dwellings with clay roofs, it nonetheless remained a slum with some of the worst housing conditions in Shanghai.[64]

The authors of this 1969 report about mobilization in Yaoshuilong described it as Jiaozhou district's most difficult neighborhood to organize. Reporting to the district government, the report described the slum neighborhood as a residential area of "the working class," but this did not refer to members of the industrial proletariat. Instead, what emerges from the report is an account of a segment of the Shanghai population that to all intents and purposes was self-employed and engaged in private enterprises, albeit ones that were not particularly lucrative and offered no security and government benefits. As the report suggested, these residents earned a living doing jobs such as driving rickshaws; pulling carts; or working as carpenters, barbers, tailors, and street vendors.[65]

The report about Yaoshuilong reveals that residents there were openly negative about the sent-down youth movement. Of the 239 youth graduating, only ninety-six had gone to the countryside and 140 had refused to go. According to the investigation, some cited physical disabilities or illness as their reason to remain in the city, while some 70 percent of the youth simply refused to go. One female student threatened to hang herself if forced to go to the countryside. Another, a male student about to marry a woman factory worker, was quoted as saying, "Even if you use a stick to break my leg, I will not go!" Parents shared their reluctance to leave the city. One parent said, "My child is young and let's wait a few years." Another reasoned that she had four daughters and only one son, upon whom she would be dependent in future and therefore she would not let him leave. One, who already had a daughter in the countryside, declared that she "would rather die" than let her son go. Described as suffering "ideological problems," the report concluded that people from the slum "love the city and are scared of hardship and the countryside."[66]

The investigation also revealed residents of Yaoshuilong who avoided going to the distant countryside by negotiating marriages with people in

---

[64] Shanghai shi difangzhi bangongshi, "Shanghai chengshi guihua zhi" (Gazetteer of Shanghai City Planning), at www.shtong.gov.cn/node2/node2245/node64620/index .html, accessed March 2, 2014. The observation about the transformation to clay roofs is based on an investigation conducted in 1965 by the Shanghai City Planning and Construction Institute.

[65] Jiaozhou jiedao xuexiao xiaxiang shangshan lianhe bangongshi diaocha zu 胶州街道学校下乡上山联合办公室调查组, "Guanyu Jiaozhou jiedao yaobei liweihui zhishi qingnian xiaxiang shangshan qingkuang diaocha" 关于胶州街道药北里委会知识青年下乡上山情况调查 (Investigation of the Sent-Down Youth in Yaobei Alley, Jiaozhou Street Neighborhood), August 26, 1969, PTDA.

[66] Ibid.

nearby Jiangsu and Zhejiang provinces. A certain Wang Xiuying reputedly had connections with people in Huzhou, Zhejiang, and introduced young girls in the neighborhood to potential mates there. Eventually the investigative team of Yaoshuilong suggested that she be criticized and that her marriage arrangements be labeled a crime. She retorted that there was nothing wrong with her activities as she was actually helping "send people to the countryside." Another Yaoshuilong resident reportedly had arranged a marriage for her son in Kunshan, just beyond the limits of Shanghai proper, in order to avoid him being sent to a remote and difficult place. One youth who married in a nearby county had a sixteen-table banquet at the wedding celebration.[67]

In the context of these early years of the Cultural Revolution, when adherence to state policies was mandated of all citizens, the attitudes and activities of the Yaoshuilong residents may have concerned the investigators. They attributed the resistance to the fact that Yaoshuilong, although a "working-class" neighborhood, was populated by "enemies and bad influences." The report went on to assert that "before Liberation it was a notorious place for bankrupted farmers, landlords, and gangsters."[68] While some residents of Yaoshuilong may have been former landlords from Subei who fled to Shanghai during land reform, the majority could not obtain jobs in the system of state enterprises for which Shanghai was famed. Because they did not enjoy its benefits (such as secure employment in a state-owned enterprise, health insurance, and housing), they had less to lose by ignoring government efforts to mobilize them.

Another factor in Yaoshuilong residents' resistance to the sent-down youth movement is that relocating youth to the countryside was not an entirely new phenomenon for them. Many of the "social youth" sent by the Shanghai government to the countryside from the mid-1950s to the mid-1960s came from districts like Yaoshuilong, where many residents had only temporary urban household registration permits and many youth had long ago dropped out of school and were not officially employed by the government. This meant that their families and neighbors were deeply familiar with the harsh conditions that sent-down youth would encounter. Families who had youth that had been sent to Xinjiang before the Cultural Revolution, for example, were most likely very reluctant to see their other children sent and resentful of those who came to mobilize them.[69] In one case, a youth named Wang Yugen, who had been sent to Jiangxi in 1963, adamantly opposed the prospect of his younger

[67] Ibid.   [68] Ibid.
[69] Chen Yingfang, *Penghu qu: Jiyi zhong de shenghuoshi* (Shantytown: Life History through Memory) (Shanghai: Shanghai guji chubanshe, 2006).

brother being sent to the countryside. He was back in Shanghai without a residence permit during the early years of the Cultural Revolution. When, in 1969, his brother received the notice assigning him to Heilongjiang, Wang tore it to shreds, and declared, "So long as I have porridge, he will have porridge! So long as there is food for me, he will not go hungry!"[70] Another youth who had returned from Jilin reportedly "told everyone how hard it was there, that they had to go out in the middle of the night to work, there was not enough food, and that wind and sand would get in your eyes." A girl who had been in Heilongjiang informed neighbors and friends in Shanghai that "they were at war" and "life there is very hard." "Lots of people were influenced by this and do not want to go," the authors of the report lamented.[71]

Residents of Yaoshuilong could refuse to go to the countryside for practical reasons as well. They knew how to survive without state-assigned jobs or government assistance, and were accustomed to finding ways of earning a living by providing services to local residents. Of the youth who refused to go to the countryside, one married a man who worked at the Xikang vegetable market and offered to buy a sewing machine so she could earn money as a tailor; several young women paid five *yuan* for sewing lessons, while several young men apprenticed a "master" carpenter, earning one *yuan* a day, a free lunch, and a packet of cigarettes. Others made a living by cutting hair or pulling bicycle carts.[72] One sold crickets for five cents each.[73] Authors of the report identified this as a "bad influence," suggesting to neighborhood residents that one could ignore government directives and still make a living in the city. They described these self-employed people as "making a pretty good living."[74]

Among other things, the above account sheds light on the ways in which attitudes toward going to the countryside were sometimes shaped by the social and economic situation of individual families. The most disenfranchised, such as residents of Yaoshuilong, learned to survive outside the state employment system in ways unfamiliar to most Shanghai residents. More than the ability to make a living was at stake: anyone with occupational or political ambitions could not refuse government mobilization, as failure to comply would have closed doors for their

[70] PTDOSY, "Ge jiedao jieji douzheng dongxiang chubu huibao."

[71] PTDOSY, Jiaozhou jiedao xuexiao xiaxiang shangshan lianhe bangong shi diaocha zu, "Guanyu Jiaozhou jiedao yaobei liwei hui zhishi qingniang xiaxiang shangshan qingkuang diaocha."

[72] PTDOSY, Jiaozhou jiedao xuexiao xiaxiang shangshan lianhe bangong shi diaocha zu, "Guanyu Jiaozhou jiedao yaobei liwei hui zhishi qingniang xiaxiang shangshan qingkuang diaocha."

[73] Ibid.   [74] Ibid.

future. People with such ambitions may have looked down on these Yaoshuilong types, but the petty laborers of neighborhoods such as Yaoshuilong saw themselves as far better off than their relatives in the countryside.[75]

Conclusion

Mobilizing its city's youth to go to the countryside was anything but straightforward for the Shanghai government. The widespread propagation of Mao's directive that aimed to create widespread enthusiasm for the movement did not produce instant support and enlistment. Instead, municipal government officials had to mobilize all of their organizational resources to stage rallies and parades, as well as organize school administrators and teachers, neighborhood committees, and cadres in work units, to overcome the reluctance of students and often their parents to participate in the sent-down youth movement. With few choices available, the vast majority of middle and high school graduates from the 1968 and 1969 classes, and some of those from the previous two classes, participated in the movement and relocated to distant places. Some 615,517 Shanghai youth were sent to other provinces, of whom 401,147 went to production brigades and the rest to state or military farms.[76]

Reports from Shanghai's district offices of sent-down youth highlight two aspects of the mobilization effort that have not been previously observed. First, the most significant resistance to the government's campaign was not staged by "class enemies," but instead by factory workers and residents of the city's shack settlements. Second, the reports suggest a dual role played by the city's low-level cadres: on the one hand, they assumed responsibility for implementing Mao's policy, but at the same time, their reports, even if not intended to do so, conveyed to their superiors some of what Elizabeth Perry refers to as the "fault lines" and "sites of potential rupture" in the political order.[77]

One manifestation of the seriousness of these ruptures is that the idea of "uniform redness" in sending youth to remote provinces to live and work with peasants was relatively short-lived. Newspapers continued to glorify

---

[75] For a description of the contemptuous attitudes toward petty laborers, see Zhang Liang, 11.

[76] Shanghai laodongzhi bianzhuan weiyuanhui, 113.

[77] Elizabeth J. Perry, "Trends in the Study of Chinese Politics: State–Society Relations," *China Quarterly* 139 (September 1994), 710. This point also appends one made by Bernstein, that changes in policy are often "influenced by implicit assumptions about what is or is not acceptable to the masses, and what the masses can be brought to accept." Bernstein, 71.

the project of sending youth to learn from peasants, suggesting that the policy was fully alive and that nothing had changed. Yet, by 1971, when the class of 1970 was to receive assignment, the meaning of being sent to the countryside had been transformed.

No matter whether youth in the late 1960s and early 1970s embarked for the countryside with enthusiasm or dread, idealism or cynicism, few who had grown up in Shanghai knew much about the rural areas where they were sent to settle. Nor did they know what this relocation would mean for their future: how long they would be required to stay in the countryside, whether they would ever have the chance for further school-ing, whether they could someday return to Shanghai, and what impact time in the countryside would have on their lives.

Rural officials awaiting the arrival of sent-down youth harbored at least as many questions and concerns. If mobilizing youth to leave required the involvement of the entire administrative infrastructure in the city, then settling them in the countryside would require an even more extensive complex of rural management involving local residents and government officials at the village, commune, county, and provincial levels. As the next chapter shows, the difficulties for Shanghai youth to settle in remote villages of the countryside exceeded the imagination of both rural and urban government officials, compelling the Shanghai government to become involved in the supervision of its youth already in the countryside for years to come.

2   Not All Quiet on the Rural Front

The campaign to mobilize urban youth for relocation to the countryside did little to prepare them for rural life. Media reports depicting beautiful planting seasons and happy harvest times; editorials praising the ideological superiority of peasants, eager to provide re-education; photographs and posters depicting joyful urban youth marching with farming tools to the fields, along with stories of urban youth who had been transformed by their rural experience—all romanticized conditions in the countryside, so most Shanghai youth were shocked by the level of poverty they encountered. Rural residents and officials were equally unprepared, overwhelmed by the sudden, heavy responsibilities for transporting, housing, feeding, and organizing agricultural work for large teams of urban adolescents. Although many production brigades made great efforts to welcome the newcomers, the accommodations they provided were often far below the expectations of their urban guests. For both urban youth and villagers, the sent-down youth movement made it starkly clear that the world of the city and that of the countryside were entirely different.

The difficulties urban youth encountered in remote rural areas compelled the Shanghai government to find ways to support them. Created initially to mobilize the city's students and send them away to the countryside, the Shanghai Office of Sent-Down Youth soon became engaged in coordinating efforts to solve problems for the youth who had already left. Through teams of Shanghai cadres stationed in the countryside, the *weiwentuan*, the Shanghai government maintained an ongoing connection with its sent-down youth. Although youth may have been geographically distant from their homes and were no longer registered as urban residents of Shanghai, individuals and institutions in Shanghai continuously monitored their welfare. Institutional and economic support provided by the Shanghai government for its sent-down youth created new channels of communication and collaboration between Shanghai and rural communities, but this support also created distrust and tension between them. Most importantly, the administrative and material support to youth in the countryside could

Photo 2.1 Although his older brother had already left for Jiangxi, Yang Shiguang (third from right) was sent to Jilin after Mao issued his directive in December 1968.
This photo, taken by a news reporter, features Shanghai youth marching to the fields with villagers in a Korean-Chinese community.
Photo courtesy of Xiang Shixiong.

make barely a dent in the improvement of the conditions under which rural residents lived. From the very beginning, settlement of youth in the countryside proved to be complex and deeply problematic, raising questions about the viability of the program.

Crossing the Great Divide

When they boarded trains to settle in rural destinations, sent-down youth crossed one of the most profound divides in China: not only between city and countryside but between privilege and poverty. Having grown up reading newspaper accounts describing the ever-increasing prosperity of the countryside, Shanghai youth were surprised to discover the gap between urban and rural conditions. A young woman from Shanghai, Xu Yiming, described her journey to Heilongjiang in June 1969.

When the train stopped in Anhui, a swarm of young kids suddenly rushed toward the train window. They were dressed in rags and a few were completely naked.

Photo 2.2 Sent-down youth joyfully going to work in the fields.
Remin huabao image.

They stared at us with hungry eyes, begging with their small dirty hands reaching toward us. We youth immediately all grabbed our snacks and tossed them to the kids. This was my first step into real life, and I already saw many Chinese peasants were barely surviving or were even starving.[1]

Many youth experienced travel to their destinations in the countryside as an unanticipated ordeal. One described waiting three hours with twenty-four other Shanghai youth for a truck to arrive at the train station. Huddled on the floor of the covered truck bed, they headed for the commune, and then had to walk, dragging their luggage on a cart, four miles to the village.[2] Another described his travel from Shanghai to Yunnan that began with a three-day train ride, sleeping under the seat every night, followed by several days on a truck to Mengla. "I thought this

[1] Xu Yimin, "Fu Beidahuang sishiwu zhounian ji" (45th Anniversary of Going to the Great Northern Wilderness), in Shen Guoming, ed., *Zhiqing hui mou Yinlonghe* (Sent-Down Youth Looking Back at Yinlonghe) (Shanghai: Shanghai renmin chubanshe, 2014), 520.
[2] Ibid.

was our destination," he recalled, "but actually there was still a long way to go." They transferred to tractors that transported them along an extremely bumpy road to the border of Laos. From there, they had to walk a long way into the mountain forests before arriving at their village.[3]

Conditions in their new rural homes were equally shocking. One Shanghai youth was unprepared for the absence of electricity, the only light provided by a small oil lamp.[4] Another compared the straw houses in which they lived to a "rough bird's nest," in which they used tree branches and bamboo sticks to make beds.[5] Although often greeted with the best food villagers could provide, some urban youth were appalled, one complaining that he and his classmates could barely swallow the dark-colored steamed buns, pickled vegetables, and preserved soybean curd offered to them.[6]

Unprepared for the bleakness of rural China, some youth refused to get off the trucks, would not open their luggage, stayed indoors, and were unwilling to work.[7] Three female students sent to the Yuxi district of Yunnan in 1969 saw the house provided for them and asked, "How could humans live in this kind of pitch-dark mud house?" According to one villager, they moved in and refused to come out for three days.[8] And some youth expressed cynicism about the notion that they would be "re-educated" by the poor peasants, who, as one put it, were not educated themselves, not able to "say complete sentences," and "selfish at heart." Another complained that the "older brother" he was assigned to work with "talks a lot and doesn't even read a newspaper. How could he educate us youth?"[9]

While the disillusionment experienced by sent-down youth when they first arrived in rural villages is well chronicled in retrospective accounts,

[3] Hua Zefei, "Zhiqing shenghuo shi wo de rensheng jishi" (Being a Sent-Down Youth Is the Cornerstone of My Life), in Zhonggong Yunnan shengwei dangshi yanjiushi, ed., *Yunnan zhishi qingnian shangshan xiaxiang yundong* (The Sent-Down Youth Movement in Yunnan) (Kunming: Yunnan daxue chubanshe, 2011), 200.

[4] Fan Kangming, "Wo de zhiqing rensheng" (My Life as a Sent-Down Youth), in Fan Kangming, Yang Jidong, and Wu Hao, *Guntang de nitu: Sange Shanghai zhiqing de wangshi* (Boiling Hot Soil: Stories of Three Shanghai Sent-Down Youth) (Hangzhou: Zhejiang daxue chubanshe, 2008), 21.

[5] Hua Zefei, 200.   [6] Fan Kangming, "Wo de zhiqing rensheng," 21.

[7] Cao Wensheng, "Shanghai ganbu zai Huma" (Shanghai Cadres in Huma), in Liu Shijie, ed., *Huma zhiqing fengyunlu xuji* (The Story of Huma Sent-Down Youth), vol. 2 (Shanghai: Shangwu lianxi chubanshe, 2004), 611.

[8] Chen Ping, "Yuxishi zhishi qingnian shangshan xiaxiang yundong zongshu" (Overview of the Sent-Down Youth Movement in the city of Yuxi), in Zhonggong Yunnan shengwei dangshi yanjiu shi, *Yunnan zhishi qingnian shangshan xiaxiang yundong* (The Sent-Down Youth Movement in Yunnan) (Kunming: Yunnan daxue chubanshe, 2011), 65.

[9] XKCOSY, "Xunke zhishi qingnian daibiaohui wenjian huibian" 逊克知识青年代表会文件汇编 (Collected Documents of the Conference of Sent-Down Youth Representatives in Xunke), December 1970, XKCA.

the challenges local residents had to confront receiving them are far less well known. Rural hosts, it turns out, were equally unprepared for, and sometimes not altogether enthusiastic about, the arrival of sent-down youth. Although many of the problems faced by rural officials and villagers in accommodating urban youth had surfaced during the sent-down youth program of the 1950s and early 1960s, the number of rural localities involved as well as the number of urban youth they had to manage was now far greater.

For many officials, news of the movement triggered by Mao's 1968 directive came quite suddenly through radio and loudspeaker broadcasts. Jiang Danping, a senior provincial cadre assigned to head the Anhui Office of Sent-Down Youth, recalled that on December 21, 1969,

> the loudspeaker made a lot of noise about urban youth going to the countryside. News of the movement was broadcast repeatedly, and thousands of people paraded in front of the provincial government office ... This reminded me of when I was very young and experienced the zealous movement to oppose the Japanese invasion, and when the call for patriotism was so passionate and overwhelming that I joined the revolution.

The actual arrival of the youth was "like a storm," Jiang recalled. "We were completely unprepared mentally, organizationally, and materially. Nothing we had was sufficient."[10] Jiang recalled that three weeks after hearing news of Mao's directive, the head of the Anhui provincial revolutionary committee, Li Desheng, informed him of his responsibilities:

> I was supposed to create a plan for all the cities, districts, and counties in Anhui to present to the revolutionary committee the next day. I was told this plan must be careful and thorough, because it would involve tens of thousands of families. "We trust that you can handle this job well," Li told me. I did not sleep that entire night. I had no documents or information about how to formulate policies. All I could do was to list a few general suggestions that could be adjusted ... This was the beginning of my eight years as the head of the sent-down youth office.[11]

County leaders were similarly daunted by the new set of responsibilities conferred on them. Jiang explained that many had no previous leadership experience, and those who had experience "were afraid to make mistakes." The counties did not have the resources to handle the sudden arrival of urban youth. As the vice head of Nenjiang county in Heilongjiang put it, "Locals are so busy. How could they find the leisure time to manage the sent-down youth?"[12]

---

[10] Jiang Danping, 39–40.   [11] Ibid., 39–40.

[12] Li Wenxiang 李文祥, "Nenjiang xianwei fushuji, Li Wenxiang tongzhi zai zhiqing gonzuo huiyi shang de jianghua" 嫩江县委副书记李文祥同志在知青工作会议上的讲话 (A Talk by Comrade Li Wenxiang, Vice Secretary of the Nenjiang Party Committee, about the

Even the initial task of transporting urban youth to their new rural homes required scrambling on the part of local officials, both to secure vehicles and to find viable routes. A bus driver summoned to transport Shanghai youth from Heihe to villages had to negotiate precarious roads that were closed for the season. Taking a narrow, rocky, muddy, and winding road, first the axle broke, and then the oil tank was punctured (which the driver repaired by plugging the hole with a piece of soap that he wrapped in a towel). Asked by a nervous Shanghai youth if he often traveled this road, the driver replied, "No! This is the season we do not normally drive and we would not be doing this if we had not been assigned to transport you."[13] In some parts of Heilongjiang, buses and trucks had to be obtained from distant areas, their drivers not having a clue how to get from the train station to specific villages. The village head of Sandaogou recalled riding his bike to Heihe to meet the Shanghai youth in order to direct the driver to the village.[14]

Transporting urban youth to villages was only the beginning of the challenges faced by local leaders, who immediately had to house and provide food for the new arrivals. As Jiang Danping explained, village dwellings in poverty-stricken rural Anhui were so crude that it was inconceivable "for them to have room to house sent-down youth, so it was common to have the urban youth live in barns, with two or three sharing a bed."[15] Similar problems were pervasive in Heilongjiang. Just across the Black Dragon river from Russia, the sparsely populated Xunke county received some 7,600 sent-down youth in 1969–1970, of whom 5,000 were from Shanghai.[16] At one production brigade in Xunke, five young urban women were sent to live with families, where they slept on the same *kang* (large heated brick bed) as the village couples.[17] At another brigade, twenty-two female youth slept in a single mud-roofed room.[18] In yet another, the dormitories housing sent-down youth were extremely crowded, the rooms small and often missing doors and windows, and

Sent-Down Youth Work), 1975, NJCA. Although dated 1975, this talk was describing problems with the sent-down youth movement from their initial arrival.

[13] Zhang Baoguo, "Xiaogou dadui huiyi" (Memories of the Xiaogou Village Production Brigade), in Zhongguo renmin zhengzhi xieshang huiyi Heilongjiang sheng weiyuanhui wenshi he xuexi weiyuanhui, ed., *Zhishi qingnian zai Heilongjiang* (Sent-Down Youth in Heilongjiang) (Harbin: Heilongjiang renmin chubanshe, 2005), 744.

[14] Interview with villagers in Sandaogou.   [15] Jiang Danping, 47.

[16] Lü Qiaofen and Xie Chunhe, *Heilongjiang sheng zhishi qingnian shangshan xiaxiang dashiji* (Chronology of Sent-Down Youth in Heilongjiang) (Harbin: Heilongjiang jiaoyu chubanshe, 2013), 42.

[17] Xunkexian diba weiwentuan san fentuan 逊克县第八慰问团三分团, "Diaocha baogao" 调查报告 (Investigative Report), July 8–31, 1970, XKCA.

[18] XKCOSY, "Zongjie: Zhiqing gongzuo he diaocha" 总结：知青工作和调查 (Summary: Sent-Down Youth Work and Investigation), October 20, 1970, XKCA.

the air smoky from unrepaired *kang* leaks.[19] In at least one case, instead of using money allocated for constructing housing for sent-down youth, the village assigned them to live in a remote abandoned dwelling. The youth, appalled by these conditions, all but destroyed it: they used one side of the building as a bathroom (refusing to walk to the public bathroom that they considered too far away); they used the door and window frames of that room as fuel for a fire; they also burned two beds. Finally, they threatened that if the brigade did not begin building them a proper dormitory, they would burn the gate to the dwelling and then set the whole building on fire.[20] At one village, sent-down youth were so enraged by the material conditions that they beat the head of the Party committee.[21]

Providing food for the sent-down youth was also challenging. At the Ganchazi commune in Heilongjiang, lunch consisted of only a plain steamed bun accompanied by "soup" made of boiled water with some salt and a few green onions. At one of the production brigades, youth were given moldy flour. Yet another did not have enough food to provide regular meals for the urban youth, provoking some to refuse to work in the fields and others to leave.[22] Inadequate food supplies caused conflicts at the sent-down youth dining hall. In one case in Huma, a sent-down youth, informed that he could not have steamed bread for lunch, poured his bowl of millet porridge over the head of the cook. The rest of the kitchen crew, enraged, refused to cook for the next two days, while the sent-down youth refused to work.[23] And at a production brigade in the Yuxi district of Yunnan, Shanghai youth complained that they could not swallow the food that locals cooked for them. Not knowing how to cook, how to get fuel or water, or how to light a fire, one pondered, "How can we survive here?"[24]

Not only did locals have to provide food and housing for the sent-down youth, but they also had to determine how to assign work to these city-bred youth who had neither farming skills nor the physical strength of villagers. Some locals articulated five "don't wants": youth with health problems, individuals with bad class backgrounds, those who were

[19] Heilongjiang sheng Xunke xian diba weiwentuan san fentuan 黑龙江省逊克县第八慰问团三分团, "Weiwen diaocha baogao" 慰问调查报告 (Visiting and Investigation Report), August 5, 1970, XKCA.
[20] XKCOSY, "Guanyu zhishi qingnian gongzuo jiancha baogao huibao cailiao" 关于知识青年工作检查报告汇报材料 (Materials on the Investigative Report Concerning the Work with Sent-Down Youth), August 1970, XKCA.
[21] Ibid.   [22] XKCOSY, "Zongjie," October 20, 1970, XKCA.
[23] XKCOSY, "Guanyu zhishi qingnian gongzuo de jiancha baogao huibao cailiao, 1969–1970" 关于知识青年工作检查报告汇报材料 (Materials on the Investigative Report Concerning the Work with Sent-Down Youth), June 22, 1970. XKCA.
[24] Chen Ping, 65.

immature or disobedient, and finally those who were female. "When it comes to work," members of a Heilongjiang commune explained, "three sent-down youth cannot match the abilities of one local. And two female sent-down youth cannot match the work of one male."[25]

Finding appropriate work for female sent-down youth was particularly challenging for locals. Not just physical strength, but also their "special characteristics," had to be taken into account in job assignments. A report from a county in Jilin noted that 70 percent of female sent-down youth were diagnosed with "female illnesses" caused by working in wet fields during their menstrual periods. The report blamed the female youth themselves for lacking health education and also criticized the local cadres for mindlessly assigning female youth the same jobs as their male counterparts.[26]

Most troubling for the local hosts was the presence of *liumang afei* (Shanghai youth characterized as hoodlums) in the ranks of sent-down youth. County leaders in Heilongjiang complained about some "inferior" individuals sent from Shanghai. The eighty-six Shanghai youth sent to the Ganchazi commune included some who had served time in Shanghai's juvenile hall when they were only eleven or twelve years old, and some with criminal records.

They fight and swear not only in their own village, but they also form gangs with youth in other villages. They carry knives and iron bars, steal, and cause trouble … In one incident they used a hot iron bar to burn a fellow Shanghai youth who had complained about their behavior.[27]

Residents of Ganchazi complained that solving these problems was beyond their capacity. And in the Bianjiang commune in Xunke, locals found themselves having to deal with some youth from Shanghai who "gamble, drink hard liquor, and have a carefree life-style." The *liumang* divided into two opposing gangs: on one occasion members of one gang used clubs to hit their opponents.[28] Not equipped to "educate" these youth and not wanting to spend time managing them, some brigade leaders were blamed for "just letting

[25] XKCOSY, "Ganchazi gongshe weiwentuan qingkuang huibao" 干岔子公社慰问团情况汇报 (Report by the *weiwentuan* at Ganchazi Commune), June 27, 1970, XKCA.
[26] Quoted in Lü Qiaofeng and Xie Chunhe, 97.
[27] XKCOSY, "Xunke xian shangshan xiaxiang zhishi qingnian daibiaohui cailiao huibian" 逊克县上山下乡知识青年代表会材料汇编 (Collected Materials on the Conference of Sent-Down Youth Representatives), 1973, vol. 2, XKCA.
[28] Xunke xian geweihui anzhi bangongshi diaochazu 逊克县革委会安置办公室调查组, "Bianjiang gongshe Bianjiang dadui zhishi qingnian jieshou pinxiazhongnong zai jiaoyu qingkuang baogao" 边疆公社边疆大队知识青年接受贫下中农再教育情况汇报 (Report on the Re-education by Poor and Lower-Middle Peasants of Sent-Down Youth on the Bianjiang Production Brigade of Bianjiang Commune), May 8, 1969, XKCA.

them do whatever."[29] Although the Anhui government had agreed to accept problematic youth, "considering the national interest," local residents were completely unprepared to cope with adolescents who had criminal records. These youth reportedly refused to work, roamed, stole chickens, killed dogs, and seized materials from local markets. According to Jiang Danping, head of the Anhui provincial Office of Sent-Down Youth, the villagers "hated them, but they were afraid to say anything."[30]

To rural residents, the project of educating urban youth may have seemed impossible. They spoke what to locals were incomprehensible dialects and had unfamiliar lifestyles.[31] Some had "bourgeois" bad habits: "they don't like to study, don't like to work, and just want 'free play.'" Some damaged equipment.[32] Villagers feared that their income would be reduced if they accommodated sent-down youth, as work points would have to be shared with them.[33] For these reasons, local reception of urban youth became less lavish over time. In one commune, leaders organized local residents to welcome the first group of youth with gongs, cymbals, and fireworks; when the second group arrived, the reception was reduced to a small meeting; and by the arrival of the third group, no one even waved red flags.[34]

Underlying all these issues was the vast gap between urban and rural China. The daily work routines that rural residents had performed most of their lives were completely unimaginable to sent-down youth. For example, one Shanghai youth, Zhang Liang, described getting up at 4 a.m. to work in the corn fields in Heilongjiang, walking two hours (hauling both a hoe and a canvas book bag holding Chairman Mao's little red book), working until the sun set at 8 p.m., and then walking back to the village. "This kind of routine was killing for us Shanghai people," he admitted, worse than the most menial job in Shanghai:[35]

---

[29] XKCOSY, "Xunke gongshe Sanhe dadui Shanghai zhishi qingnian jieshou zai jiaoyu qingkuang huibao" 逊克公社三合大队上海知识青年接受再教育情况汇报 (Report on the Conditions Of Re-education of Shanghai Sent-Down Youth on the Sanhe Production Brigade of Xunke Commune), July 1969, XKCA.

[30] Jiang Danping, 37–54.

[31] Zhonggong Xunkexian weiyuanhui 中共逊克县委员会, "1970 nian di sishi hao wenjian" 1970 年第四十号文件 (1970 document no. 40), January 15, 1970, XKCA.

[32] XKCOSY, "Zhiqingban baogao" 知青办报告 (Report of the Office of Sent-Down Youth), May 27, 1971, XKCA.

[33] XKCOSY, "Xunkexian geming weiyuanhui dui zhishi qingnian jinxing zai jiaoyu de jidian zuofa" (Some Methods of Conducting Re-education for Sent-Down Youth by the Xunke County Revolutionary Committee), January 19, 1970, XKCA.

[34] XKCOSY,"XKCOSY baogao" 逊克县知青办报告 (Report from XKCOSY), April 14, 1971, XKCA.

[35] Zhang Liang, 49–51.

In Shanghai, the lowest job was to pull a night-soil cart … This job required getting up really early, smells awful, and earned very little; only people in extreme poverty would be willing to do that. When we were in Shanghai we ridiculed this occupation … No one would ever consider doing anything like that. But when we were in the countryside, some youth said they would rather be hauling a night soil truck than working the land. No matter what you do, living in Shanghai is the biggest happiness. So you would probably understand how bad conditions in the countryside were at that time: worse than pulling a night soil truck.[36]

Zhang's perception of the gap between Shanghai and the countryside was echoed by another sent-down youth who described walking twenty *li* over snow-covered fields in Heilongjiang as "torture for us youth from Shanghai." "My jacket was like a piece of paper and the wind like a knife … My long underwear was frozen and felt like needles on my body … I was only fifteen at the time."[37]

Only when the urban youth arrived in the villages did they and their rural hosts realize how profound was the divide between the city and countryside, a divide that could not be reduced to geography. While urban officials were able to mobilize and relocate large numbers of youth to the countryside, turning them into ordinary "peasants" or even simply settling them in rural villages was far more challenging. Perhaps unexpectedly, the Shanghai government found itself becoming involved in multiple aspects of overseeing its youth in the countryside.

The Reach of the City

The involvement of the Shanghai government in managing its youth in the countryside took place partly through the nationwide system of sent-down youth offices that were created at the beginning of the movement. Under the State Council's All-China Office of Sent-Down Youth (*Zhonggong zhongyang guowuyuan zhishi qingnian shangshan xiaxiang bangongshi*), every major city that sent youth to the countryside established its own municipal office which co-ordinated the work of district branches. The initial charge to these urban offices was mobilization: persuading youth to join the movement, identifying rural destinations for them, and transporting them out of the city to new homes in the countryside. Throughout China, provincial, district, and county sent-down youth offices were also established. These offices had to mobilize their own urban youth to go to the countryside. Some also shouldered the

[36] Ibid., 117–118.
[37] Yan Qianzi, "Kegu minxin de kuayue" (The Unforgettable Cross), in Zhongguo renmin zhengzhi xieshang huiyi Heilongjiang sheng weiyuanhui wenshi he xuexi weiyuanhui, 238–244.

responsibility of receiving urban youth from major municipalities outside their province, primarily Shanghai, Beijing, and Tianjin, and assigning them to appropriate local districts and counties. Commune-level offices assigned educated youth to production brigades, and then to teams, and distributed government stipends during their first year. Once settled in villages, youth would be under the jurisdiction of their production brigades.

The Shanghai government may have assumed that once youth arrived in the countryside, it would not be responsible for them, particularly as they no longer held urban residence permits.[38] The overwhelming difficulties faced by rural communities now tasked with hosting and "educating" the youth, along with the profound dissatisfaction expressed by sent-down youth themselves and by their parents (still residents of Shanghai) about the harsh living and working conditions in the countryside, compelled Shanghai government agencies to assume a role in the administration of the program, particularly if they wanted (or were expected) to mobilize more youth to participate.

Reporting to the Shanghai Office of Sent-Down Youth, the *weiwentuan* sent to other regions provided the major connection between youth and the city. *Weiwentuan*, literally "comfort teams," were not a creation of the sent-down youth movement, as they had been sporadically organized to support Chinese soldiers during the Korean War and, more recently, to help Shanghai youth sent to army farms in Xinjiang in the 1950s and 1960s. The ones organized at the beginning of the sent-down youth movement were most likely intended to provide the same kind of symbolic support: delivering greetings, small gifts, money, and books. However, in the context of the sent-down youth movement of the Cultural Revolution, the *weiwentuan* assumed a far broader role as a link between youth, their urban families, and Shanghai government agencies.

The form, content, and composition of the *weiwentuan* varied, some comprising entirely urban cadres, and others including parents, teachers, and even Red Guards. In the case of those organized in Shanghai, members of the short-term *weiwentuan* spent only one to three months in the countryside; those on long-term *weiwentuan* stayed on production brigades with Shanghai youth for several years. *Weiwentuan* were not unique to Shanghai, as Beijing, Tianjin, Chongqing, and other major cities also

---

[38] This had, after all, been its experience when Shanghai youth were sent to Xinjiang in the 1950s and early 1960s. However, the youth sent to Xinjiang had gone to state-owned military farms, where the government guaranteed basic food and a stipend. The movement triggered by Mao's 1968 directive created an entirely different situation: although some urban youth still went to state and military farms, the vast number assigned to village production brigades was completely unprecedented.

organized teams to visit their own youth, and in some instances, provincial and county governments constituted *weiwentuan* to visit the sent-down youth.[39] The ones from Shanghai attended exclusively to the conditions of Shanghai sent-down youth: they not only visited the youth in the villages but also conducted investigations that formed the basis for detailed reports submitted to the Shanghai Office of Sent-Down Youth and other municipal government bureaus. The role played by these Shanghai *weiwentuan* was applauded by the State Council's Office of Sent-Down Youth, which in July 1971 organized representatives from seven provinces to learn from the Shanghai teams.[40]

The long-term *weiwentuan* from Shanghai had their origins in 1969 when thousands of urban cadres were sent to the countryside along with urban youth. During the Cultural Revolution, a large number of cadres working in Shanghai government agencies, schoolteachers, college professors, medical professionals, and other employees of state enterprises were sent to May 7th cadre schools to learn agricultural work on farms in the Shanghai suburbs.[41] This was partly to reduce what seemed an abundance of bureaucratic officials. These May 7th schools also became a destination for some high-ranking cadres not trusted by the new government. Zhang Chunqiao, head of the Shanghai Party Committee and one of the most powerful central government leaders of the Cultural Revolution, suggested in August 1969 that some of these cadres could lend support to the sent-down youth movement by accepting assignment to production brigades in remote regions.[42] Wang Chenlong, a member of the Shanghai revolutionary committee, elaborated: "Let's use this opportunity to send away some of the *laobao* [cadres loyal to the old Shanghai government] . . . That way these people won't act up and our offices will be more peaceful!" As an incentive, cadres who were on probation would be allowed to regain their Party membership and salaries if they volunteered to leave Shanghai and go to production brigades.[43] Eventually some 1,700 cadres were sent to Heilongjiang, where 160,000 Shanghai youth lived on production brigades.[44] Tan Guoxing, one of 400 Shanghai cadres assigned to Huma,

[39] Jin Dalu and Jin Guangyao, *Zhongguo xin difangzhi*, vol. 1 Also see Zhonggong Yunnan shengwei dangshi yanjiushi, *Yunnan zhishi qingnian shangshan xiaxiang yundong*, 102; *Renmin ribao*, May 22, 1970.

[40] Gu Hongzhang, *Zhongguo zhishi qingnian shangshan xiaxiang dashiji* (Chronology of China's Sent-Down Youth) (Beijing: Renmin ribao chubanshe, 2008), 90.

[41] Zheng Qian, "Wenhua da gemming zhong zhishi qingnian shangshan xiaxiang yundong wuti" (Five Issues Concerning the Sent-Down Youth Movement during the Cultural Revolution), http://history.sina.com.cn/bk/zqs/2014–02–18/153782759_2.shtml, accessed February 1, 2017.

[42] Jin Dalu and Lin Shengbao, 67.   [43] Ibid.

[44] Wan Xia, "Nanwang yu women tonggan gongku de Shanghai chadui ganbu" (The Unforgettable Sweetness and Woes That We Shared with the Shanghai Cadres),

described it as "like being exiled. We were people the Shanghai government did not want."[45] Tan spent six years in Huma, where he lived and worked closely with Shanghai sent-down youth. The plan to send more cadres in this manner was short-lived, but those like Tan who had already gone and were initially referred to as "Shanghai cadres" functioned as members of a long-term *weiwentuan*.

Like sent-down youth, members of the *weiwentuan* were disturbed by conditions in rural areas. In 1969, the Shanghai Jing'an district organized a fifty-six-strong *weiwentuan* of workers, parents, cadres, and teachers to go to Suxian, Anhui. At the first village, they stayed in a local's house, where two female sent-down youth had lived (both of whom had apparently already returned to Shanghai). "Outside it was raining," recalled Jiang Yue, head of the *weiwentuan*,

but the doors were wide open. Goats and pigs slept next to my bed. A cat curled on the pillow next to my head, keeping me cozy. I was awakened in the middle of the night because the peasant's child had diarrhea all over the ground. A dog came in and ate it up. The countryside has no hygiene at all![46]

The parent of a son assigned to Anhui, Jiang Yue was worried about the conditions for Shanghai youth. "Those Shanghai kids were the same age as my own child," she explained. "They were going to stay here their whole life. How could they endure this? My heart was heavy. They had to perform hard labor every day. In addition, they had no vegetables to eat. Every day they ate dried sweet potatoes, millet, and sorghum."[47]

Many sent-down youth perceived the cadres sent to "comfort" them as quasi-parental figures who could provide sympathy and material help. A sent-down youth in Heilongjiang recalled,

Around the second month we were in Heilongjiang, four cadres from the Shanghai Textile Bureau came to our village. They were about the same age as our parents … Passing our days in the village with these four cadres from Shanghai, we always felt that they were our support and that we could rely on them as family.[48]

January 6, 2012, http://dn.wanxia.com/fenxiang/show/1/645.html, accessed April 22, 2017.

[45] Tan Guoxing, "Huma chadui de qianqian houhou" (Some Recollections of Being Sent Down to a Huma Village), in Liu Shijie, *Huma zhiqing fengyunlu xuji*, 137–139.

[46] Qin Tingkai, "Dangnian Anhui zhiqing weiwentuan Jiang Yue de jingli" (The Experience of Jiang Yue as a Member of the Sent-Down Youth *weiwentuan* to Anhui), July 24–August 11, 2013, http://shzq.net/pjq/thread.asp?tid=12442, accessed July 28, 2017.

[47] Ibid.

[48] Wan Xia, "Nanwang yu women tonggan gongku de Shanghai chadui ganbu" (The unforgettable sweetness and woes that we shared with the Shanghai cadres), 6 Jan., http://dn.wanxia.com/fenxiang/show/1/645. html Accessed 22 April 2017.

Another Shanghai youth described the bond he established with one particular Shanghai cadre on the train to Heilongjiang in 1969. "The head of the group was a woman with gray hair, a pale face, and a soft voice," he recalled. Formerly a high-ranking cadre in the Shanghai Federation of Women, she had been assigned to work with sent-down youth in Heilongjiang. "She sat next to me and held my hand explaining that her own son had been sent to Inner Mongolia ... Please call me Auntie Shao," she instructed him. Assigned to the same village, she continually reminded him not to risk his life at work. When they went to a meeting together, she gave him a package of sugar (which he could not have obtained in the local market) and books. "I could not sleep that night because I knew she had prepared these things for me."[49]

The sent-down cadres sometimes went out of their way to make the lives of Shanghai youth more comfortable. Shen Longgen, a cadre from Shanghai's Xuhui district, was one of seven cadres sent to the Jinshan production team in Huma. In the dining hall, he heard sent-down youth repeatedly expressing their desire to have noodles. Some, from the Minhang Middle School in Shanghai, reported that the school had a noodle-making machine. Diagnosed with hepatitis, Shen was sent to a hospital in Shanghai. Once released, he went to the Minhang district offices, where coincidentally he had worked for some years. "Through connections with people in that office," he wrote,

I was able to negotiate a positive result: the noodle-making machine would be donated to the commune and the middle school would be responsible for shipping it as well. By the time I returned to Huma, the noodle-making machine had already arrived. I assisted with its installation and taught them how to produce noodles. Everyone was very happy.[50]

Cadres from Shanghai did more than provide sympathy and material goods, sometimes assuming the task of managing sent-down youth. In Huma, for instance, the number of urban youth in some villages far exceeded the local population, and the Shanghai cadres, for the first few years, shouldered the major responsibility for taking care of them. Ultimately, the Huma county government decided that every commune should have a full-time position for sent-down youth work, and almost always assigned Shanghai cadres to these jobs.[51] When Shanghai youth sent to Wudaogou refused to get off the truck, it was the Shanghai cadre who was summoned to help. Able to use Shanghai dialect,

[49] Li Weiliang, "Nanwang Huma guan'ai qing" (The Love and Care of Huma Is Unforgettable), in Liu Shijie, *Huma zhiqing fengyunlu xuji*, 251–252.

[50] Shen Longgen, "Zai Huma de yixie wangshi" (Some Memories about Huma), in Liu Shijie, *Huma zhiqing fengyunlu xuji*, 78–82.

[51] Cao Wensheng, "Shanghai ganbu zai Huma" (Shanghai cadres in Huma), in Liu Shijie, *Huma zhiqing fengyunlu xuji*, 610–614.

incomprehensible to locals, these cadres could connect and communicate with the arriving youth.[52] The cadres also actively promoted sent-down youth into local leadership positions. One Shanghai youth sent to Heilongjiang in 1969 recalled that it was these Shanghai cadres (not the locals) who mentored him to become a member of the CCP in 1971, and then become head of the production brigade.[53]

Technically under the jurisdiction of local governments, the *weiwentuan* might have been expected to adhere to their directions. However, partly because most of these cadres maintained their Shanghai *hukou* and remained on the Shanghai government payroll, they behaved more like delegates from Shanghai than as members of the local community, and they often advocated for the interests of sent-down youth. Tan Guoxin, a cadre sent to Huma, explained, "We tried to encourage the local government to help the sent-down youth."[54] So, for example, when urban youth in Huma believed they were not treated fairly in the allocation of work points, it was the cadres of the *weiwentuan* who argued on behalf of the sent-down youth, helping them get through what one described as "a [very rough] and confusing time."[55]

One advantage that the *weiwentuan* had in negotiating conflicts between sent-down youth and locals was their access to resources in Shanghai. For example, responding to concerns about widespread skin infections suffered by the Shanghai youth in Jiangxi, the Shanghai cadres requested that local leaders remove the sent-down youth from work in the wet rice fields. When they realized that in a rice-growing region, this could be tantamount to suggesting that the city youth not work at all, they turned to Shanghai for assistance. In the end, the Shanghai Health Bureau sent nineteen medical specialists to Jiangxi (some were also sent to Yunnan and Guizhou) to treat skin infections of sent-down youth.[56] In

[52] Ibid.

[53] Zhang Baoguo, "Xiaogou dadui huiyi" (Memories of the Xiaogou Village Production Brigade), in Zhongguo renmin zhengzhi xieshang huiyi Heilongjiangsheng weiyuanhui wenshi he xuexi weiyuanhui ed., *Zhishi qingnian zai Heilongjiang* (Harbin: Heilongjiang renmin chubanshe, 2005), 744.

[54] Tan Guoxing, 139.

[55] Yang Miaoxiang, "Rensheng daolu shang de liangshi" (A Good Teacher on the Path of Life), in Liu Shijie, *Huma zhiqing fengyunlu* (The Story of Sent-Down Youth in Huma) (Shanghai: Shangwu lianxi chubanshe, 2002), 404–405.

[56] SHMOSY, "Jiangxi sheng Le'an Yihuang Chongren xian chadui zhishi qingnian baifenzhi qishi huan guominxin piyanzhen" 江西省乐安、宜黄、崇仁县插队知识青年百分之七十患过敏性皮炎症 (70 Percent of the Sent-Down Youth in the Villages in the Counties of Le'an, Yihuang, Chongren Have Skin Infections), in *Qingkuang fanying*, July 1, 1969, SHMA. Also see Shanghai shi weishengju 上海市卫生局, "Jiangxi, Yunnan, Guizhou sansheng Shanghai zhishi qingnian pifu bing diaocha fangzhi qingkuang de huibao" 江西、云南、贵州三省上海知识青年皮肤病调查防止情况汇报 (Report on Preventing Skin Infections among Sent-Down Youth in Jiangxi, Yunnan, and Guizhou), November 1969, SHMA.

this case, resources from Shanghai, secured through the efforts of the *weiwentuan*, provided treatment for the infections suffered by its own youth, although they could not eliminate the cause of a problem that was part and parcel of life for peasants.

Although members of the *weiwentuan* worked to protect Shanghai youth in the countryside, their reception in the city by the parents of sent-down youth was mixed. When the 125-member *weiwentuan* returned from spending April to October 1969 visiting some 6,000 villages with Shanghai youth in Jiangxi, it presented a "very thorough" report to parents, who, in turn, "asked detailed questions." *Weiwentuan* members also visited individual families of sent-down youth and reported to the municipal government that some parents "were very nice and insisted we stay for a meal. But not all family members welcomed our visit," in at least one case refusing to greet the team members. Most parents recognized the visit by the *weiwentuan* as an opportunity to raise some specific grievances and express their anger at the movement itself.[57]

Like many sent-down youth, members of the *weiwentuan* were not always enthusiastic about their own assignment. A cadre from the Shanghai Housing Bureau sent to Jiayin county in Heilongjiang complained, "I could never understand why I was asked to relocate here!"[58] Like him, many cadres desperately wanted to be back in their Shanghai homes. Shanghai revolutionary committee leaders, having listened to a presentation by members of the *weiwentuan* sent to Yunnan, Guizhou, and Jiangxi in 1969, lamented that "some people are not willing to do long-term *weiwentuan* work. The main problem is that it is hard for them to adjust to the lifestyle in the countryside because they have never left Shanghai."[59] When some cadres who had spent five months in the countryside requested to return to Shanghai for a break, government leaders instructed them to wait.[60]

Nonetheless, members of *weiwentuan* commonly devised ways to spend as much time as possible in the city. One reportedly cited his wife's psychological problems and the deathly illness afflicting his elderly father-in-law as a pretext to return to Shanghai for a good part of a year. A diagnosis of high blood

---

[57] Shanghai fu Jiangxi xuexi weiwentuan 上海赴江西学习慰问团, "Fu Jiangxi sheng xuexi weiwentuan xiang geming jiazhang huibao xuanchuan huodong de qingkuang baogao" 赴江西省学习慰问团向革命家长汇报宣传活动的情况报告 (Jiangxi *weiwentuan* Report to the Revolutionary Parents about Its Propaganda Work), November 27, 1969, SHMA.

[58] Fu Jiayin xian Shanghai ganbu 赴嘉荫县上海干部, "Shanghai shi xiaxiang shangshan bangongshi" 上海市下乡上山办公室 (To Shanghai Office of Sent-Down Youth), October 15, 1969, JYCA.

[59] SHMOSY, "Shi geweihui lingdao tongzhi zai ting qu Yun, Gui, Gan san sheng xuexi weiwentuan huibao shi de tanhua jiyao" 市革委会领导同志在听取云贵赣三省学习慰问团汇报时的谈话纪要 (Notes on Speeches and Responses by Leading Comrades of the Shanghai Party Committee to the *weiwentuan* Sent to Yunnan, Guizhou, and Jiangxi), September 7, 1969, SHMA.

[60] Ibid.

pressure enabled him to extend his stay even longer.[61] Noting the number of cadres who had returned to Shanghai, one report complained, "there's nothing we can do."[62] Chen Jiang, a cadre from the Shanghai Institute of Economic Research, explained the joke shared among his colleagues about the meaning of May 7th cadre schools: "We interpreted the directive as meaning five months in Shanghai, seven months in Huma. Eventually we stayed in Huma for five months, and in Shanghai for seven."[63]

Even those who performed their tasks dutifully sometimes found themselves caught between the discrepant agendas of rural and urban governments. While local governments wanted reports that praised their achievements, the Shanghai government was more interested in whether its youth had been properly accommodated.

When a *weiwentuan* completed its three-month visit to Anhui, the provincial government instructed it that its report should focus on the positive aspects. The head of the Anhui provincial Office of Sent-Down Youth explained that "the backwardness of Anhui has its own long history. Of course, there have been mistakes and errors in our work, but the main point is that we have carried out Chairman Mao's revolutionary policy. In sum, we need to look at everything in a historical perspective." This instruction, stated the head of the *weiwentuan*, "set the tone, and so in our reports we focused on achievements."[64] Some members of the Shanghai *weiwentuan* were less compliant, actually accusing Anhui provincial report writers of distorting the truth. In one case a *weiwentuan* report revealed that only 20 percent of the sent-down youth had achieved the lowest standard of self-sufficiency, yet the provincial leaders insisted that 70 percent could support themselves. While the *weiwentuan* complained that the sent-down youth had been sent to the "most backward and poorest production brigades," the provincial leaders insisted they had been assigned to brigades "with great production potential."[65]

---

[61] Fu Jiayin xian Shanghai ganbu, "Shanghai shi xiaxiang shangshan bangongshi."

[62] Jiayin xian geweihui zhengzhibu zuzhizu 嘉荫县革委会政治部组织组, "Shanghai chadui ganbu de qingkuang huibao" 上海插队干部的情况汇报 (A Report on Shanghai Cadres), February 25, 1972, JYCA.

[63] Interview with Chen Jiang.

[64] Qin Tingkai, "Dangnian Anhui zhiqing weiwentuan Jiang Yue de jingli" (The Experience of Jiang Yue as a Member of the Sent-down Youth weiwentuan to Anhui), 24 July- 11 August 2013, http://shzq.net/pjq/thread.asp?tid=12442. Accessed 28 July 2017.

[65] Geng Changlan 耿昌兰, "Guanyu Anhui Chuxian diqu Fengyang xian dui xiaxiang qingnian anzhi jiaoyu gongzuo zhong de yixie wenti" 关于安徽滁县地区凤阳县对下乡青年安置教育工作中的一些问题 (Concerning Some Problems in the Settlement and Education of Sent-Down Youth in Fengyang County of Chuxian District in Anhui), April 25, 1974, SHMA.

Even *weiwentuan* members themselves recognized that "the locals didn't like the *weiwentuan* because we were always watching and reporting" and therefore did not welcome the dispatch of teams of Shanghai cadres to the countryside.[66] In the past, locals may well have dealt with officials representing various government bureaus, whose visits they could plan and orchestrate. The *weiwentuan* presented them with an entirely different situation: rather than confining themselves to hearing presentations prepared by local officials, they went to speak directly with the sent-down youth, who in turn were free to recount the problems they faced, ignoring the local cadres who accompanied them. Moreover, the reports of the *weiwentuan* not only were forwarded to the local and provincial governments, but also were directly addressed to the Shanghai government, which had no jurisdiction over the work in rural China but was too powerful to be ignored.

The prospect of long-term, as opposed to visiting, *weiwentuan* instilled even more anxiety among local officials. The problem first erupted in Heilongjiang with the arrival of 1,700 cadres following Zhang Chunqiao's instructions in 1969. These Shanghai cadres included some high-ranking government officials who had previously held far more prestigious positions than local county heads, and some veterans of the "revolutionary war" who had wide-ranging leadership experience. In Huma, county leaders treated these cadres with respect and "listened to their suggestions." They also "took good care of them," as some Shanghai cadres were already in their sixties and suffered poor health.[67] When the Shanghai government tried to transfer *hukou* and personnel files of the cadres to Heilongjiang, both local officials and the cadres themselves objected. For example, the Jiayin county government, which accepted 216 cadres, issued a report to the Shanghai revolutionary committee describing the Shanghai cadres' unsuitability for work in such a remote and harsh environment. "Some of them might be able to do light work in an office, but could not labor in this extremely cold region."[68] The report expressed the impossibility of hosting these cadres. Even if their *hukou* was transferred, it would be difficult to "regulate" cadres with higher ranks.[69] This reluctance of the local government to host urban cadres proved useful to the cadres themselves who did not want to give up their

---

[66] Zhu Bingxing, "Sishi nian hou you jian zhiqing weiwentuan" (Seeing the *weiwentuan* Forty Years Later), April 17, 2013, http://blog.sina.com.cn/s/blog_8727a5b00101icez .html, accessed December 30, 2016.

[67] Cao Wensheng, 610.

[68] Jiayinxian geweihui zhengzhibu zuzhi zu, "Shanghai chadui ganbu de qingkuang huibao."

[69] Ibid.

official affiliation with Shanghai, where their families remained. In their own communication to the Shanghai government, they invoked local reluctance in order to persuade the Shanghai government to refrain from transferring their personnel files to Jiayin. "This should not be rushed," the Shanghai cadres pleaded, "but instead wait for the situation to mature."[70] Ultimately, these cadres kept their urban *hukou* due to their resistance and the opposition of local and provincial governments in Heilongjiang.[71]

The Jiangxi government was more direct in its opposition to the long-term *weiwentuan*. When the Shanghai government was on the verge of sending a 300-member *weiwentuan* in October 1969, the provincial government protested, making it clear that it had its own teams to visit the sent-down youth and investigate problems. "Most of the problems have been or are in the process of being solved," Jiangxi government officials told the Shanghai delegates. According to the Shanghai Office of Sent-Down Youth, the Jiangxi government had declared that, if sent, these cadres would be incorporated into Jiangxi's own teams under the jurisdiction of the provincial government. "In future," the Shanghai delegates were told, "the short-term *weiwentuan* visits during festivals or holidays will be welcomed." "But if you are going to send long-term *weiwentuan*, they will be under our jurisdiction."[72] Based on this response, the Shanghai Office of Sent-Down Youth suggested to the municipal government that it should focus on sending short-term *weiwentuan* to "comfort and encourage" Shanghai youth but not to investigate local treatment of them.[73]

Regardless of the protests by both its own cadres and local receiving governments, the Shanghai government continued to station *weiwentuan* in the countryside to support the work of its sent-down youth. Reports by the *weiwentuan* about problems faced by sent-down youth became the most important source of information for the municipal government. At

---

[70] Kong Guangshou 孔光寿 and Kang Zhihua 康志华, "Guangyu jinyibu jiaqiang dui zai Jiayin xian chadui luohu de Shanghai ganbu jiaoyu guanli de qingshi baogao" 关于近一步加强对在嘉荫县插队落户的上海干部教育管理的请示报告 (Proposed Report on How to Take a Step Forward in Strengthening the Education and Management of the Shanghai Cadres in Jiayin County), July 20, 1970, JYCA.

[71] Cao Wensheng, 610–611. Although the *Shanghai shi qingnianzhi* states that the Shanghai cadres went to Heilongjiang with their *hukou* and grain and oil rations transferred, most cadres did keep their *hukou* registration in Shanghai. This is evident in both the written statement of Cao Wensheng, who worked in the Shanghai government office after returning from Huma, and also an interview with Chen Jiang, who worked as a cadre in Huma. See Shanghai qingnian zhi bianzhuan weiyuanhui, 556–557.

[72] SHMOSY, "Guanyu fu Jiangxi changqi xuexi weiwentuan de baogao" 关于赴江西长期学习慰问团的报告 (Report Concerning Sending Long-Term *weiwentuan* to Jiangxi), November 1, 1969, SHMA.

[73] Ibid.

the same time, local officials also found ways to take advantage of the connection to Shanghai provided by the *weiwentuan*. However, the fact that the Shanghai government sent its own cadres to oversee the livelihood of youth already in the countryside reflected its continued perception of them as its own citizens. It also suggests that from the beginning of the movement, the Shanghai government harbored doubts that villagers and rural officials could take care of its youth. Overstepping administrative jurisdictions, the work of *weiwentuan* exacerbated tensions between Shanghai and local and provincial governments, one that intensified the rural–urban divide and eventually contributed to the demise of the sent-down youth movement.

"The Problems Cannot Be Solved"

Extensive efforts by the central, provincial, and municipal govern-ments as well as by the *weiwentuan* and rural officials could at best only provide makeshift solutions to the settlement of urban youth in the countryside. *Weiwentuan* members, in particular, began to cast doubt on whether long-term solutions were possible. For them, the issue of self-sufficiency became the most significant indicator of the viability of sending urban youth to work on production brigades. No matter what locality *weiwentuan* considered, their reports almost always raised the question of self-sufficiency, which for them meant the ability of sent-down youth to support themselves economically without subsidies from the city. An early report from a *weiwentuan* in Jiangxi outlined three reasons that had made it difficult for urban youth to become self-sufficient. In many regions the value of work points was extremely low, so that even locals did not earn enough to cover grain or oil for their families. Female sent-down youth, even if they worked a full day, could only earn a fraction of the work points assigned to male laborers, and therefore had an even more difficult time supporting themselves.[74] Moreover, some sent-down youth were physically "too weak" to perform farm labor and therefore "cannot earn a living through work." The *weiwentuan* suggested that "the

---

[74] The disparity between work points earned by men and by women on rural production brigades extends back to the 1950s, partly a product of the value attached to jobs assigned based on gender. Typically, male laborers could earn a maximum of ten work points a day, women only seven or eight. The value of work points varied by location, depending on the relative wealth of the particular production team. See Kay Ann Johnson, *Women, the Family and Peasant Revolution in China* (Chicago: University of Chicago Press, 1983), 172–172; Emily Honig, "Iron Girls Revisited: Gender and the Politics of Work in the Cultural Revolution," in Barbara Entwisle and Gail E. Henderson, eds., *Re-drawing Boundaries: Work, Households, and Gender in China* (Berkeley: University of California Press, 2000), 104–106.

situation could be improved through advances in the local economy, ideological consciousness, and work skills of the youth." But it came to the pessimistic conclusion that even with these improvements, most sent-down youth still would not be self-sufficient.[75] Given that Jiangxi was generally considered to have a somewhat higher standard of living than many other provinces to which Shanghai youth were sent, this report may have been sobering to the Shanghai government. City agencies could provide temporary relief for sent-down youth; they could also donate some material goods and equipment to local villages, but this alone could not solve the underlying problem of rural poverty that made it inconceivable for sent-down youth to become self-sufficient.

The Shanghai Health Bureau reached a similarly pessimistic conclusion. When in 1969 the Shanghai government sent a medical team to Jiangxi, Guizhou, and Yunnan, its report promised that the city would provide treatment for widespread skin infections "at any cost." The Health Bureau, though, concluded that a solution would require locals to develop their own medicine, sent-down youth to refrain from scratching their infected skin, and the extermination of mosquitos and all other bugs, as well as leeches in the wet fields.[76] They specified that the extermination was "most critical," although from other campaigns to exterminate disease-carrying insects or snails spreading schistosomiasis, they may have known how massive a project this would be.[77] Although these conclusions concerned specific issues, such as self-sufficiency or health, they implied that urban people could not sustain lives in remote rural regions.

The phrase "this is a problem that cannot be solved" became a refrain in many of the *weiwentuan* reports sent to the Shanghai government during the first two years of the movement, casting doubt on the viability of *chadui luohu*, which represented the essence of the movement, since that was the only context in which sent-down youth would live with and like villagers. None of these reports specifically argued that *chadui luohu*

---

[75] SHMOSY, "Fu Jiangxi sheng xuexi weiwentuan xuexi weiwen gongzuo baogao" 赴江西省学习慰问团学习慰问工作报告 (Report on the Work of the *weiwentuan* to Jiangxi), December 10, 1969, SHMA. By the end of 1971, in Mengla, Xishuangbanna, only 42 percent of sent-down youth could support themselves. This was attributed to the poor working conditions, the low value of work points, and the amount of time the youth spent at home in Shanghai. Mengla xian zhiqingban 勐腊县知青办, "Dianhua huibao" 电话汇报 (Report of Telephone Call), 1971, JHDA.

[76] Shanghai weishengju geming weiyuanhui, "Jiangxi Yunnan Guizhou san sheng Shanghai zhishi qingnian pifu bing diaocha fangzhi qingkuang de baogao," November 1969, SHMA.

[77] For an excellent account of this campaign, see Gross.

was a mistake, but instead simply informed the government that practical solutions to some of these critical problems had not been found. As Bonnin points out, the "lack of enthusiasm" among "the grassroots cadres" contributed to the decline of the movement.[78]

The Shanghai government was not the only municipal government bombarded with reports detailing problems with the movement. In Beijing, some youth, especially children of high-ranking government officials, found ways to file grievances directly to the municipal government agencies and leaders of the central government.[79] When report after report informed the government that it was impossible to solve the problems resulting from the program, it became imperative to seek alternative ways to continue the movement.

Within two years of Mao's directive, the central government modified its policies about the work assignments of graduating urban students, allowing urban governments to change their practices. In February 1971, the National Planning Conference announced the creation of roughly 1.5 million factory jobs each year.[80] Although the conference affirmed that the sent-down youth movement must be continued, local governments could now assign middle school graduates to urban factory jobs. Unlike the previous two years when all graduates were required to go to the countryside, members of the 1970 class (receiving assignments in 1971) in Shanghai had the possibility of getting jobs in the city. Priority would go to those who had siblings already in the countryside, who were the family's only child, whose families had hardships, or who had health problems that would make them unsuitable for working in the fields.[81] By assigning some urban graduates to factory jobs this policy suggested that receiving peasant re-education was no longer necessary for everyone. Of the 210,000 students in this 1970 class in Shanghai, 95,000 were assigned factory jobs. The remaining 115,000, for whom there were not enough jobs, were to be sent to the countryside. As we shall see below, however, only a small percentage of these students were sent to production teams in remote regions.[82]

Shanghai was not the only city that changed its practices. Nationwide, the number of factory jobs created far exceeded the intentions of the National Planning Conference. Over the next two years, some 9.33 million industrial jobs were created, more than triple the government's projection. Meanwhile, the number of urban youth being sent to

[78] Bonnin, 86.
[79] For an account of problems of Beijing youth sent to Yan'an, see Liu Xiaomeng, *Zhongguo zhiqingshi*, 161; and Gu Hongzhang, 82–83.
[80] Gu Hongzhang, 87.   [81] Lü Qiaofen and Xie Chunhe, 86–87.
[82] Shanghai qingnianzhi bianzhuan weiyuanhui, 552.

the countryside decreased substantially.[83] When the State Council held a conference in Beijing from December 1971 to February 1972, Premier Zhou Enlai complained that the number of new industrial jobs was far too large, causing "serious problems for the national economy." This trend, he announced, needed correction. Although Zhou did not connect this problem directly to the sent-down youth movement, the excessive increase in urban jobs would allow cities to reduce the number of students sent to the countryside. Statistics for Shanghai are not available, but we know that in Beijing 77 percent of students in the classes of 1970, 1971, and 1972 were assigned nonagricultural jobs; only 14 percent went to the countryside, the majority to nearby state farms.[84] By 1973, Zhou Enlai once again expressed his concerns about what seemed to him an excessively rapid growth of factory jobs, this time emphasizing that over the next seven years, he wanted 10 million more youth sent to the countryside.[85]

The policy changes created even more challenges for urban officials who were assigned to continue mobilizing youth to go to the countryside. In 1972, the Putuo district of Shanghai assembled a 387-member study group (composed of members of the office of sent-down youth; street, alley, and factory cadres; and school administrators) to discuss mobilization. Officials in the study group expressed deep frustration with the new policies that effectively enabled some youth to stay in the city, making it extremely difficult for them to succeed in their task of mobilization. Some cadres argued, "If going to the village is so important, then why is it that now not everyone has to go? Our job would be a lot easier if everyone had to go."[86]

The Shanghai government not only assigned factory jobs to middle school graduates, but also devised a number of alternatives for those who would otherwise be sent to the countryside. The most prominent was the expansion of its own state farms in the Shanghai suburbs. State farms, including ones in proximity to Shanghai, had existed well before the Cultural Revolution. As noted earlier, many of the 1966 and 1967 graduates were assigned to these farms, an option that was all but eliminated when Mao issued his directive about sent-down youth, in part because of the limited capacity of the farms.[87] In the early 1970s, however, the

---

[83] Gu Hongzhang, 93.   [84] Liu Xiaomeng, *Zhongguo zhiqingshi*, 242.

[85] Gu Hongzhang, 93.

[86] PTDOSY, "Xiaxiang shangshan lingdao banzi chengyuan xuexiban de qingkuang zongjie" 下乡上山领导班子成员学习班的情况总结 (Summary of a Study Session of the Sent-Down Youth Leadership Members), July 25, 1972, PTDA.

[87] While some 56,107 Shanghai youth from the three years prior to the implementation of the sent-down youth policy were assigned to state farms, only 200 youth from the classes of 1969 and 1970 were sent. Shanghai nongkenzhi bianzhuan weiyuanhui, *Shanghai nongkenzhi* (Shanghai Agriculture Gazetteer) (Shanghai: Shanghai shehui kexueyuan chubanshe, 2004), 425.

Shanghai municipal government organized massive land reclamation projects in the nearby counties of Nanhui and Fengxian to expand state farms. According to the Shanghai agricultural gazetteer, 5,400 hectares of land were reclaimed, so that three state farms could be expanded to six and an additional four be established, in order "to satisfy the needs of [accommodating] urban educated youth." By 1972, Shanghai had thirteen farms under its jurisdiction, with 130,000 individuals on its payroll, of which some 34,415 were sent in 1972 alone. Most of these farms were located in Chongming, Baoshan, Nanhui, and Fengxian counties of Shanghai, with some in nearby Jiangsu and Anhui provinces.[88] The expansion continued in 1973–1974.[89] Assigning urban youth to nearby farms administered by Shanghai, as opposed to distant production brigades, was far more acceptable to Shanghai residents.

As state farms administered by Shanghai expanded, the proportion of Shanghai youth required to go to remote regions, particularly to production brigades, decreased substantially. This can be clearly seen in the statistics for Shanghai's Changning district. In the years 1968–1970, 15,300 youth from this district went to production brigades, and only 7,800 to state farms, all of which were in remote regions. From 1971 to 1977, out of a total of 28,300 youth who went to the countryside, only 4,141 went to production brigades and 1,794 went to state farms in distant provinces. While 1,508 students returned to their home villages in the suburbs, 20,897, an overwhelming majority, went to state farms administered by the Shanghai municipality.[90]

Conclusion

Although technically the sent-down youth movement continued throughout the 1970s, within two years of its inception not only did its implementation change dramatically, but also Mao's goal of having urban students receive "re-education from peasants" was honored mostly in official rhetoric. From this time on, Shanghai youth were sent to the countryside, but increasingly the "countryside" to which they were sent was state farms administered by Shanghai in the city's suburbs. By 1971, the practice of sending students to remote rural production team had come to an almost complete halt.

[88] Shanghai shi gewei hui jiaoquzu 上海市革委会郊区组, "Shi geweihui jiaoquzu baogao" 市革委会郊区组报告 (Report of the Suburb Group of the Shanghai Revolutionary Committee), May 12, 1972, SHMA.
[89] Shanghai nongkenzhi bianzhuan weiyuanhui, 22.
[90] Changning qu zhi bianzhuan weiyuanhui, ed., *Changning qu zhi* (Changning District Gazetteer) (Shanghai: Shanghai shehui kexueyuan chubanshe, 1999), 538.

That Shanghai government officials could adapt practices that departed from Mao's intentions reflects the reminder by recent scholars of the PRC that the Chinese state in the 1960s and 1970s was not monolithic, that its control was sometimes "limited and tenuous." Local officials, Jeremy Brown and Matthew Johnson point out, often subverted state policies, with local groups pursuing their own interests.[91]

While the change of policy in 1971 obviously enabled a significant portion of urban youth to avoid going to remote production brigades, it did nothing to address the predicament of those who had already gone. Having been told they had no options and that this policy would endure, these youth and their family members most likely felt betrayed by the teachers, neighborhood cadres, and work unit leaders who had pressured them to leave. The number of sent-down youth who filed grievances increased significantly.[92] The Shanghai government, unable to ignore their complaints, developed an increasing range of initiatives to improve the conditions of these sent-down youth, particularly those sent to village production brigades. As we shall see in the following chapters, some of its efforts not only benefited Shanghai youth in these regions, but also facilitated rural economic development, even if they could do little to close the gap between urban and rural China.

[91] Brown and Johnson, 1–3.
[92] XKCOSY, "Guanyu zhishi qingnian gongzuo jiancha baogao huibao," August 1970, XKCA.

3   The Unplanned Economy

When Huma county in Heilongjiang was assigned 6,000 youth from Shanghai in January 1970, its leaders, while dutifully expressing enthusiasm for the job of educating urban youth, also harbored serious reservations about their ability to accommodate so many of them. In a report to the provincial government, they expressed concern about the inadequacy of arable land, farm machinery, housing, and transportation, as well as the time away from farm work that would be required by villagers delegated to host and supervise the urban youth. Arguing that the county could host only half of the 6,000 youth, this report pleaded for material goods and financial resources that would be needed for the additional urban youth assigned, including forty new tractors (with attachments) to expand arable land, materials to build housing, as well as tools, fertilizer, and seeds. To cover these expenses, along with the cost of transporting youth from the train station to the villages, Huma officials proposed that the government issue 911 yuan in addition to the 370 yuan allocated for each Shanghai youth; they also requested that locals responsible for the youth be given financial compensation. The budget to cover the costs of all 6,000 youth from Shanghai came to more than several million yuan.[1]

The 1970 requests from Huma were issued before the actual arrival of Shanghai youth, indicating that many rural officials were worried about the potential financial burden they would face. At that point, probably few could envision the benefits of hosting youth from large cities. And yet, as it turned out, their arrival did bring some benefits, ones that extended beyond the scientific and technical knowledge brought by sent-down youth to the countryside that has been applauded in a number of recent

---

[1] Heilongjiang sheng Huma xian geming weiyuanhui shengchan zhihuibu wenjian 黑龙江省呼玛县革命委员会生产指挥部文件, "Guanyu jieshou anzhi 1970 nian waidi zhishi qingnian gongzuo anpai yijian" 关于接收安置 1970 年外地知识青年工作安排意见 (Ideas on the Arrangements for Receiving and Settling Sent-Down Youth from Other Places in 1970), January 31, 1970, HMCA.

studies.[2] The presence of Shanghai youth and the *weiwentuan* provided remote rural regions with connections to commercial and industrial agencies in Shanghai that were previously beyond the reach of most remote rural regions.

These connections proved important not only to acquire goods necessary for the support of urban youth, but also to fulfill the central government's mandate to develop rural industry. This state initiative coincided with the beginning of the sent-down youth movement, but it was an unfunded directive; the government did not provide the financial or material resources that would have made such rural industrial development possible. This chapter explores the relationship between the sent-down youth movement and economic development in rural China: the ways that sent-down youth themselves initiated improvements in rural life, and, more importantly, how rural officials used their presence to promote local economic development. Individual sent-down youth, their families, and both urban and rural officials, none of whom had a role in determining government policies, all identified and made use of resources that those policies unintentionally produced. In other words, behind the economic growth of this period is a tangle of complex connections binding the city to the countryside in unexpected ways through the bodies and social networks of urban sent-down youth.

Shopping in Shanghai

Sent-down youth from Shanghai found the extreme poverty of the countryside shocking, but probably very few understood it in the context of the state planning policies of the PRC. Large industrial cities, centers of state-owned enterprises, and expansive public infrastructure provided most urban residents lifetime employment, heavily subsidized housing, health care, education, and access to material goods unavailable in the countryside. At the same time, rural residents were required to supply cities with grain and other agricultural products. As historian Jeremy Brown puts it, "Over the course of the 1950s, 1960s, and 1970s, cities became privileged spaces while villages became dumping grounds. City-dwellers enjoyed special perks while villagers endured bitter sacrifices."[3] The strict residential registration system (*hukou*) prevented migration to the cities, and the

---

[2] See, for example, Schmalzer; Dongping Han, *The Unknown Cultural Revolution: Life and Change in a Chinese Village* (New York: Monthly Review Press, 2008).

[3] Brown, *City versus Countryside*, 1–2.

government's campaigns against private commerce in a centralized economy deprived rural residents of access to goods from other regions.[4]

In this context, an initial experience for almost all sent-down youth was confronting the gap in material goods available in urban versus rural China. One youth poignantly described this in a letter home following his journey from Shanghai to Ganlanba in Xishuangbanna, Yunnan. At Kunming, the provincial capital, he saw Shanghai-made merchandise in the fanciest stores, but learned that purchasing these items required government-issued coupons. When he arrived at Jinghong, the county seat, he found the stores completely empty, lacking even locally grown fruits. Customers had to stand in long lines to purchase dry biscuits and fermented tofu. The only thing he found to buy was an unwrapped flavorless popsicle. The availability of goods in local stores was even bleaker. In a letter home, he wrote that there was "nowhere to buy any daily necessities, let alone food products."[5] Another Shanghai youth, sent to northern Anhui, complained that the small store at his commune had only a few ceramic jars filled with wine, soy sauce, vinegar, and lamp oil, along with an extremely small supply of candy and cigarettes as well as a few towels, bowls, and pots.[6]

Almost all accounts by former sent-down youth are punctuated by references to the myriad goods they brought from Shanghai to the countryside, ranging from clothing and bedding to soap, metal washing bowls, and vacuum flasks. Food was most important, as meat, sugar, cooking oil, and other food products were hard to find in rural markets. Urban youth brought lard, biscuits, candy, noodles, dried meats, sausages, salted fish, canned foods, and milk powder to the countryside. A few managed to bring along luxury items such as musical instruments and radios.[7]

During their annual home visits, sent-down youth not only sought to replenish goods for themselves, but also secured items desired by local villagers. Those sent to Yunnan, for instance, discovered that Dai women, accustomed to producing dyes for their cloth from local plants

---

[4] A 1985 study of Chinese market concludes that political campaigns against private trade led to the decline of commerce. In a twenty-five-year period between 1953 and 1978, China's population increased from 507 million to 775 million, while rural markets reduced from 45,000 to 33,300. See William G. Skinner, "Rural Marketing in China: Repression and Revival," *China Quarterly*, 102 (1985), 393–413.

[5] Lu Rong, *Yige Shanghai zhiqing de 223 feng jiashu* (A Shanghai Sent-Down Youth's 223 Letters Home) (Shanghai: Shanghai shehui kexueyuan chubanshe, 2009), 3–8.

[6] Yang Jidong, "Xiaozapu" (A Little Convenience Store), in Fan Kangming, Yang Jidong, and Wu Hao, *Guntang de nitu*, 305.

[7] See, for example, Zhang Liang, 25, 105. Also see Fan Kangming, "Nanwang de rizi" (Days That Are Difficult to Forget), in Fan Kangming, Yang Jidong, and Wu Hao, 14.

and insects, treasured commercial dyes they could purchase in Shanghai. Visiting a factory in Shanghai, one youth spotted steel bars that could be used to fashion hunting guns. Stuffing a few into his duffle bag, he brought them back to the village in Yunnan to give his village friends.[8]

In many places, the presence of sent-down youth created new economic relationships, involving the exchange of gifts, buying, selling, and trading with locals. Villagers sometimes traded vegetables for candies and cookies from Shanghai, while youth brought Shanghai-made merchandise, especially soap bars, children's clothing, and candy, to express gratitude to locals who offered them rides or temporary accommodation, or tended to them when they were sick.[9] Dai villagers who in the past had grown bananas, pineapples, coconuts, grapefruit, and vegetables for their own consumption realized that sent-down youth were willing to pay cash for this produce, so they began to grow crops specifically for sale.[10] Increased demand drove prices up: the price of bananas in Xishuangbanna, for example, doubled in 1970 when a large number of Shanghai youth arrived.[11] In Huma, Oroqen hunters were able to sell wild pig and moose meat to Shanghai youth.[12] Youth also bought local goods to bring to their families in Shanghai, including wood ear fungus from Yunnan and Heilongjiang; bamboo shoots from Yunnan, Guizhou, and Jiangxi; camphor chests from Jiangxi; and many local varieties of herbal medicine. Often these products were not sold directly to the youth in stores, but instead by other locals who could earn some cash from the sale.[13]

The transport of goods by individual sent-down youth, whether for their own comfort and consumption or to share, trade, or sell, was only one aspect of a far broader traffic in material goods between cities and the countryside during the Cultural Revolution. For local officials— from leaders of production brigades to commune, county and district heads—the assignment of sent-down youth to their locales provided an opportunity to acquire resources from the cities that they would otherwise have not been able to access.

---

[8] Interview with Zhu Kejia.

[9] Shi Ruping "Qing yuan" (Sentimental Connection), in Liu Shijie, *Huma zhiqing feng-yunlu xuji*, 45; Lu Rong, 83, 343–344; He Jian, "Lanjiao monan" (The Torture of an Infected Foot), in Pei Yulin, Huang Hongji, Jin Dalu and Tian Dawei, *Lao zhiqing xiezhen* (Sketches of Former Sent-Down Youth) (Shanghai: Shanghai wenhua chubanshe, 1998), 211.

[10] Lu Rong, 7, 25.   [11] Ibid., 7.

[12] Yan Shaojun, "Huixiang dangnian de Shibazhan" (My Recollections of That Year in Shibazhan), in Liu Shijie, *Huma zhiqing fengyunlu xuji*, 124; Song Fulin "Heitudi de qinqing" (Feeling of Family in the Black Soil), in ibid., 223.

[13] Lu Rong, 32–33; Song Fulin, 223.

The individual connections provided by sent-down youth between rural areas and Shanghai were particularly important in the context of state economic planning and distribution of goods. For rural production brigades or communes, to purchase even the most basic materials as well as agricultural machinery such as tractors—even if they had sufficient funds—required approval by the commune, county, district, and province, a protracted process that could involve substantial delays, if not rejection because of limited supplies allocated by the state. The newfound connections provided by sent-down youth, however, created ways for these rural communities to circumvent state planning policies and obtain resources directly from large cities.

Local leaders almost immediately realized this potential value of sent-down youth. In 1971, production brigades in Hongqi commune in Jiangxi planned to install electricity, but they had no wire. While Shanghai residents could purchase it in neighborhood hardware stores, this luxury was not available to rural residents. The sent-down youth were thus dispatched to take a "business trip" to buy wire for their villages. As one woman recalled, hardware stores in Shanghai limited each purchase to fifty meters for home use. She and her family members went from one store to another throughout the city until they bought enough wire to fill her two duffle bags. All twelve youth in her village, along with classmates from neighboring villages, went as well, each bringing back two duffle bags full.[14] Whether or not the wire they acquired was sufficient to support the amount of electricity imagined by local officials, the project would have been inconceivable were it not for the youth who could go home to Shanghai, where they had a place to stay and family members they could enlist to maximize their purchases from hardware stores.

In some cases, local officials identified potentially useful connections of individual youth by scanning their personal dossiers. Held in the offices of sent-down youth, these personnel files provided a wealth of information, including parents' work units in Shanghai, their positions in those units, and their home address. Officials of a commune in Jiangxi, through the dossiers, found a sent-down youth whose father had a high-ranking position in Shanghai. The commune directed him to drive a "Liberation" truck from the commune to Shanghai in order to obtain certain equipment and materials. Unfortunately, it turned out that his connections were less useful than imagined, and he returned empty-handed.[15] But in many other instances such connections proved to be crucial for the local economy. Through connections of parents of several sent-down youth from Shanghai, Le'an county was able to obtain materials and skills to

[14] Interview with Wang Pei.   [15] Interview with Wang Yuan.

build an electric wire factory.[16] The county's automotive team hired one sent-down youth because her brother-in-law worked in the Shanghai Transportation Bureau, which could provide car parts and repair services.[17] In another instance, through the father of a Shanghai youth in Huma, a middle-rank cadre at the Shanghai Water Pipe Factory, the county succeeded in obtaining a water pump for irrigation and dispatched the youth for a "business trip" to Shanghai to take delivery.[18] One sent-down youth in Guizhou learned from conversations with local leaders that the tires on the one village tractor were damaged. As his father was a technician in the Shanghai Tire Repair Factory, he offered to use his father's connections to get help, and obtained four new tires for the village.[19]

Sent-down cadres often proved to have even more direct connections to sources of equipment than the urban youth. A certain Tian Feng, a cadre from the Shanghai Material Bureau sent to Jiayin county in Heilongjiang, used the occasion of visiting his family in November 1971 to purchase water pump machinery for the county irrigation department. A report from early 1972 notes that twenty-seven sent-down cadres from Shanghai were back in Shanghai helping locals purchase materials.[20] Huma county officials also made use of the sent-down cadres from Shanghai: in early 1970, the county sent two of them to Shanghai to help acquire equipment to build a papermaking factory, which they then shipped to Huma. The Shanghai cadres also helped out when the county government needed boat engines.[21]

The "Urgent Needs" of Sent-Down Youth

In addition to the individual connections of sent-down youth and cadres, local leaders utilized the administrative connection to Shanghai provided by the offices of sent-down youth that had been established at the outset of the movement. In petitioning the Shanghai office for goods and equipment, locals, commonly those staffing the rural offices of sent-down youth, invoked the ostensible needs of sent-down youth. Noting in late 1969 that "most of the youth had no shoes for cold winters," the Office of Sent-Down Youth in the Heihe district of Heilongjiang requested that

---

[16] Interview with Wei Min.   [17] Interview with He Hua.   [18] Shen Longgen, 81–82.
[19] Chen Jian, "Zhiqing yiyi" (The Significance of Sent-Down Youth), January 25, 2013, http://zhiqingwang.shzq.org/guizhouDes.aspx?ID=6793, accessed September 8, 2013.
[20] Jiayin xian geweihui zhengzhibu zuzhizu 嘉荫县革委会政治部组织组, "Shanghai chadui ganbu de qingkuang huibao," 上海插队干部的情况汇报 (Report on the Condition of Shanghai Cadres on Production Brigades), February 25, 1972, JYCA.
[21] Cao Wensheng, 613.

Shanghai immediately send 16,000 pairs of boots.[22] At about the same time, a district in Yunnan requested 10,000 to 20,000 pairs of plastic shoes and/or army shoes, as well as medicines for sent-down youth.[23]

In many cases, however, the requested goods were not entirely for the benefit of sent-down youth. In early September 1969, for example, the development office of the Heilongjiang provincial Office of Sent-Down Youth dispatched three comrades to Shanghai. The Shanghai Office of Sent-Down Youth reported that the visitors came "for the sole purpose of seeking support from our city for the allocation of materials required for sent-down youth," and that "they were asking us to give the maximum quantity possible."[24] The list of desired goods included items most likely for sent-down youth, such as socks, blankets, raincoats, scarves, and medicines. But it also included fifty-seven types of car parts, 140 types of tractor parts, thirty-three kinds of tools, and seventeen varieties of electrical materials, as well as stationery and textiles. The Shanghai Office of Sent-Down Youth assumed the role of mediator and conveyed this request to the appropriate government offices, only to learn that there was a shortage of most of these materials in Shanghai. "The amount of help we can provide is very limited," lamented the report. Of the 354 types of materials requested, the Shanghai office could secure only sixty. Although the Heilongjiang officials expressed appreciation for what they were given, they were not satisfied and "repeatedly conveyed that they needed the materials very urgently." Failing to get the desired response, they reiterated the needs of sent-down youth from Shanghai. "They [the youth] need the small tools and sheets of iron to build houses and stoves ... Please report this to the leaders of the Shanghai Party Committee."[25]

Eventually Shanghai sent some of the goods to Heilongjiang, but within two months Heilongjiang officials issued another request, once again invoking the needs of sent-down youth. "Some people from your area," reported the Shanghai Office of Sent-Down Youth, "wrote us to say that

[22] SHMOSY, "Guanyu jiabo 16,000 shuang mianjiaoxie gei Heilongjiang sheng Heihe diqu de qingshi baogao" 关于价拨一万六千双棉胶鞋给黑龙江省黑河地区的请示报告 (Proposal Concerning the Provision of 16,000 Pairs of Winter Shoes for Heihe District in Heilongjiang), November 17, 1969, SHMA.

[23] SHMOSY, "Guanyu dui Yun Gan Wan san sheng zhiyuan bufen jixu wuzi shebei de qingshi baogao" 关于云赣皖三省支援部分急需物资设备的请示报告 (Proposal Concerning Donating Some Materials and Equipment Urgently Needed by Yunnan, Jiangxi, and Anhui), November 14, 1969, SHMA.

[24] SHMOSY, "Guanyu Heilongjiang sheng yaoqiu Shanghai zhiyuan wuzi wenti de qingshi baogao" 关于黑龙江省要求上海支援物资问题的请示报告 (A Proposal Concerning a Request That Shanghai Donate Materials to Heilongjiang Province), September 1, 1969, SHMA.

[25] Ibid.

because the number of youth from Shanghai has increased, the supply of drinking water is now inadequate." Moreover, a number of urban youth were reportedly suffering from swollen joints due to the high concentration of minerals in the shallow wells. Officials in Heilongjiang thus asked the Shanghai government to provide them equipment to dig deep wells in order to ensure sent-down youth safe drinking water.[26]

Concerned with the health problems of sent-down youth, the Shanghai office immediately contacted the relevant municipal bureaus. When these bureaus replied that Shanghai did not have enough deep-well pumps to satisfy their needs, the office quickly pleaded with leaders of the Shanghai municipal government, which proved to be more responsive. Writing to Heilongjiang, the Shanghai office cheerfully conveyed that it would be able to send ten pumps right away and would strive to provide ninety the next year. "Please let us know the size and type you want," the letter concluded.[27]

Ultimately, in addition to medical and other supplies needed by youth themselves, Heilongjiang received a substantial amount of equipment from Shanghai. In response to the requests, the Shanghai Office of Sent-Down Youth, by 1971, had provided two buses, thirteen trucks, nine tractors, thirty-six hand-operated tractors, and several cars, with a total value of 1.06 million yuan.[28] While this amount might sound impressive, it in fact represented only a fraction of what Heilongjiang counties hosting sent-down youth estimated they needed.

Heilongjiang was not the only province utilizing the presence of sent-down youth to obtain equipment from Shanghai. The Yunnan provincial government, for instance, in 1972 submitted a request that the Shanghai municipal government supply some 14,000 items needed by the Kunming Iron and Steel Factory.[29] In addition to whatever goods the central government allocated, the provincial government now had a "back door" through which it could negotiate for additional goods from Shanghai, China's most prosperous industrial center.

Some districts imagined that resources from Shanghai might enable far-reaching regional economic development, which ultimately would benefit both sent-down youth and local residents. In October 1969, the

[26] SHMOSY, "Heilongjiang sheng geweihui" 黑龙江省革委会 (Letter to Heilongjiang Provincial Revolutionary Committee), November 21, 1971, SHMA.
[27] SHMOSY, "Heilongjiang sheng geweihui xiaxiang shangshan bangongshi" 黑龙江省革委会下乡上山办公室 (Letter to the Heilongjiang Provincial Office of Sent-Down Youth), November 17, 1969.
[28] SHMOSY, "Heilongjiang sheng geweihui," November 21, 1971, SHMA.
[29] Shi geweihui gongjiaozu 市革委会公交组, "Guanyu anpai zhiyuan Yunnan sheng suo xu shebei de tongzhi" 关于安排支援云南省所需设备的通知 (Announcement to Arrange Donations Needed by Yunnan Province), May 12, 1972, SHMA.

vice head of Jiangxi's Ganzhou district government sent a delegation of six people to Shanghai to plead for material support. Before their departure, the head of the Shanghai *weiwentuan* in Jiangxi wrote a letter of introduction to Mayor Ma Tianshui in Shanghai. After arriving in Shanghai, the delegation introduced the conditions of Ganzhou district, explaining its very weak industrial base and lack of equipment and technical expertise. The range of materials, equipment, and resources requested indicates that the district viewed its connection to Shanghai as crucial to its potential economic development. The delegation emphasized that both local residents and the 5,000 sent-down youth from Shanghai were eager to improve conditions and become self-sufficient. "In order to advance agricultural production," members of the delegation explained to Shanghai officials, "we need to build a new factory that can produce 300,000 sets of axles per year. We hope Shanghai will help us get the equipment for this." In addition to the axle factory, they requested that Shanghai contribute equipment for county-level factories to provide machine repair services, electrical supplies, a variety of machines, and stoves. They also wanted motors and water pipes for irrigation systems. Imagining ways to advance industrial and agricultural production, they envisioned establishing a cement factory and requested a full set of equipment—even a used one—for that. The district, they pointed out, would otherwise need 100,000 to 200,000 tons of cement shipped by truck every year, an enormous waste of energy that could be saved if Ganzhou could operate its own cement factory.[30]

This was only the beginning of their list of requests. Transportation was problematic in the hilly and mountainous parts of Ganzhou district, and members of the delegation hoped to be granted Jiaotong brand trucks and three-wheeled tractors produced in Shanghai. Supplies of high-quality seeds and superior breeds of pigs would enhance production, they said. And, finally, "in order to publicize Chairman Mao's thoughts," they urgently required supplies of cables and loudspeakers. They also conveyed their hope that any industrial units planning to relocate from Shanghai to other areas would consider Ganzhou.[31]

While members of the Shanghai Office of Sent-Down Youth engaged in negotiations with other government bureaus to acquire these goods, the six-person delegation from Ganzhou was anxiously waiting for an answer. "We took them to visit some communes near Shanghai,"

[30] SHMOSY, "Jiangxi sheng Ganzhou zhunqu yaoqiu Shanghai zhiyuan bufen gongye jichuang shebei he wuzi de baogao" 江西省赣州专区要求上海支援部分工业机床设备和物资的报告 (Report on the Request by the Jiangxi Ganzhou District for Shanghai to Provide Industrial Machinery, Equipment, and Materials), October 27, 1969, SHMA.
[31] Ibid.

explained the Shanghai office. "They could pick some seeds to take home. And we also took them to visit the Shanghai Axle Factory as well as the Shanghai Industrial Exhibition so they could get ideas for future development of factories in their district."[32]

While it is not clear how many of the goods requested by the delegation were eventually provided, it appears that their effort to acquire equipment for the cement factory was accomplished. They conveyed their willingness to take even the rusted machinery once used by the Shanghai Cement Factory that had sat unused for ten years. The Shanghai Industrial Bureau, however, informed the Shanghai Office of Sent-Down Youth that three sets of the polishing machines at the Shanghai Cement Factory had already been allocated to other places, and that the "baking machine" needed to be kept in the factory in case the other one broke. Having been persuaded that Ganzhou needed the machinery urgently, the Office of Sent-Down Youth still urged the municipal government to direct the bureau to give the machinery to Ganzhou.[33]

It was not long before the Shanghai Office of Sent-Down Youth realized that wherever sent-down youth resided, requests for goods from Shanghai could be expected. A 1969 office memo noted that several provinces had learned from the *weiwentuan* that Shanghai would provide material and merchandise. These provinces "have started to send people to Shanghai or ask the *weiwentuan* to convey their requests."[34] Quite a few districts, like Ganzhou, sent delegations or telegrams on their own. Soon the Shanghai office was juggling requests from numerous counties as well. "We feel that they have asked for too much, more than we could provide," the Shanghai office complained to the municipal government.[35] In some cases, the Shanghai office clearly found the requests outlandish, and conveyed disdain for requests issued directly to them by remote county-level officials. So, when the Tongzi County Office of Sent-Down Youth sent a request for motorcycles to the Shanghai Office of Sent-Down Youth in October 1969, the Shanghai office seemed annoyed. Its staff informed the Tongzi officials that motorcycles were allotted only by the central government, and that requests had to come from a provincial government. "If you desperately need these items," the response by the Shanghai office concluded, "and if your provincial government believes our assistance is necessary, then it may contact us and only then might we consider it."[36]

---

[32] Ibid.

[33] SHMOSY, "Guanyu dui Yun Gan Wan san sheng zhiyuan bufen jixu wuzi shebei de qingshi baogao."

[34] Ibid.   [35] Ibid.

[36] SHMOSY, "Tongzi xian zhiqing bangongshi" 桐梓县知青办公室 (Letter to Tongzi County Office of Sent-Down Youth), October 24, 1969, SHMA.

Requests for goods from Shanghai, which began in 1969, continued throughout the duration of the sent-down youth movement. Having received a request from several counties in Inner Mongolia in 1975, the Shanghai Office of Sent-Down Youth reported to the municipal government that "in order to do a better job related to sent-down youth," Shanghai should provide "four off-road vehicles and one two-ton-class truck."[37] That same year, Jiujiang district in Jiangxi repeatedly sent people to Shanghai to convey its urgent need for diesel engines. In considering this request, the Shanghai Office of Sent-Down Youth pointed out that "this area settles nearly 10,000 Shanghai sent-down youth," and therefore recommended that "two 120-horsepower diesel engines be supplied." "Looking forward to your approval," its report to the municipal government concluded.[38]

What we see in these accounts are requests for goods from rural areas being brokered between local offices of sent-down youth, communicating with the Shanghai Office of Sent-Down Youth, which in turn negotiated with relevant bureaus in Shanghai to make the deliveries. It is important to also highlight the active role of the *weiwentuan* in communicating these requests. Although, as we saw in the previous chapter, local officials complained about the ways in which the *weiwentuan* intervened in their administration, they also realized that the teams could provide a valuable connection to sources of goods in Shanghai. For instance, in December 1969, it was the head of the *weiwentuan* in Yunnan, Wang Qingyu, who phoned the Shanghai Office of Sent-Down Youth to say that the Simao district of Yunnan wanted Shanghai to immediately deliver the five to seven hand-operated tractors that they had already agreed to provide.[39] In a report addressed to the Shanghai Office of Sent-Down Youth, entitled "What the Sending Region Can Do for the Receiving Region," the *weiwentuan* in the Jinghong district of Yunnan articulated its own opinion on what should be sent. It reported the difficulties locals faced in their aspiration to develop local industry, and suggested ways in which bureaus in Shanghai should help. The *weiwentuan* described a local paper mill that employed 229 workers. Although the mill had equipment, it was only able to produce low-quality packing paper. Conditions at a different paper mill in Mengla, according to the same report, were extremely backward, producing low-quality toilet

[37] SHMOSY, "Baogao" 报告 (Report), June 28, 1975, SHMA.
[38] SHMOSY, "Shi geweihui" 市革委会 (Letter to Shanghai Revolutionary Committee), January 10, 1975, SHMA.
[39] SHMOSY, "Yunnan sheng Simao zhuanqu yaoqiu zhiyuan shoufu tuolaji de baogao" 云南省思茅专区要求支援手扶拖拉机的报告 (Report on a Request from Simao in Yunnan for the Donation of Tractors), December 20, 1971, SHMA.

paper. For these reasons, the *weiwentuan* suggested that Shanghai bureaus help by providing bleaching materials and more technology.[40]

In parts of Heilongjiang as well, members of *weiwentuan* played a critical role in helping counties negotiate materials from Shanghai. A report from Jiayin notes that a number of production brigades actually assigned cadres on the *weiwentuan* to purchase goods in the city. It described one such cadre who originally worked for the Shanghai Materials Bureau before going to Nenjiang. When he went to Shanghai to visit his family, he helped the county irrigation department purchase the water pump machinery that they needed. At that time, there were twenty-seven cadres from Nenjiang in Shanghai "helping locals purchase materials."[41] Often the Shanghai Office of Sent-Down Youth arranged donations to be sent to the countryside based on suggestions of the *weiwentuan*.[42] When supplies were inadequate, the *weiwentuan* also had to explain the problem to local governments.[43]

In addition to the Shanghai cadres and *weiwentuan*, Shanghai youth who had been promoted to prominent positions in the local government also joined the effort to negotiate with Shanghai for the transfer of goods to their local communities. Zhu Kejia, a national model sent-down youth in Yunnan who was also appointed to provincial and central government positions, "constantly called and wrote letters to the Shanghai Office of Sent-Down Youth asking for agricultural equipment such as tractors." Citing Zhu Kejia's request, the Shanghai office recommended sending thirty walking tractors and fifty Fengshou brand tractors to "settlement areas of sent-down youth."[44]

One might wonder why administrative bureaus in Shanghai—when bombarded with requests for goods from the offices of sent-down youth and the *weiwentuan* in rural areas—frequently acquiesced and provided equipment. An obvious explanation has to do with the sheer number of

---

[40] Shanghai shi fu Yunnan sheng xuexi weiwentuan Xishuangbanna fentuan 上海市赴云南省学习慰问团西双版纳分团, "Dongyuan diqu jixu yao wei anzhi diqu zuoxie shenme" 动员地区继续要为安置地区做些什么 (What the Sending District Could Continue to Do for the Receiving District), November 23, 1974, JHDA.

[41] Jiayin xian geweihui zhengzhibu zuzhizu, "Shanghai chadui ganbu de qingkuang huibao," February 25, 1972, JYCA.

[42] SHMOSY, "Anhui sheng zhishi qingnian shangshan xiaxiang bangongshi" 安徽省知识青年上山下乡办公室 (Letter to the Anhui Provincial Office of Sent-Down Youth), December 12, 1969, SHMA.

[43] SHMOSY, "Guanyu dui xiaxiang qingnian zhiyuan wuzi de luoshi qingkuang baogao" 关于对下乡青年支援物资的落实情况报告 (A Report on Donations to the Sent-Down Youth), June 23, 1975, SHMA.

[44] SHMOSY, "Shanghai shi geming weiyuanyui gongjiaozu" 上海市革命委员会公交组 (Letter to Shanghai Revolutionary Committee Transportation Team), November 20, 1975, SHMA.

the city's high school graduates sent to remote rural areas. Even if providing material support was not their initial charge, all these government agencies were involved in the mobilization of sent-down youth and thus shared a sense of responsibility for the welfare of the youth and for making them self-sufficient, both of which were crucial to the stability of urban society. To improve the conditions of its sent-down youth, it was imperative for Shanghai to establish friendly relationships with these regions.

This is reflected in instances when the Shanghai Office of Sent-Down Youth not only responded to requests from rural areas, but on some occasions actually initiated the donation of goods. In mid-1971, for example, the Shanghai Office of Sent-Down Youth wrote to the Yunnan Labor Bureau,

From the time the youth of our city responded to the call of Chairman Mao to go to the countryside, your province accepted and settled large groups of youth from Shanghai to settle in the countryside and receive the re-education of the peasants. To thank you for the massive support by your province, our city plans to give you another 150 hand-operated tractors. Please allocate them to areas where there are Shanghai sent-down youth. Please also give priority to poor communes and brigades.[45]

This type of allocation continued over the next few years.

Shanghai officials seemed particularly eager to provide broadcast equipment for rural areas with sent-down youth. In many remote regions where radio reception was poor, broadcasting through loudspeakers served as the primary means for youth to hear regional and national news. Perhaps even more important, from the perspective of Shanghai officials, were the nonagricultural jobs created by the installation of broadcast stations. Having learned to speak Mandarin in urban schools, sent-down youth were more suitable for positions in broadcasting stations than local residents. So, when Xishuangbanna received equipment for installing fifty broadcast stations, the government announced that each station would assign sent-down youth to be news announcers.[46] "If they have problems installing broadcast cables," the report conveyed, "Shanghai will provide support."[47] The importance of broadcast

---

[45] Yang Xinqi, "Yunnan sheng zhishi qingnian shangshan xiaxiang yundong zongshu" (Comprehensive Accounts of the Sent-Down Youth Movement in Yunnan), in Zhonggong Yunnan shengwei dangshi yanjiushi, 25.

[46] Zhongguo gongchangdang Xishuangbanna daizhu zizhizhou weiyuanhui zuzhibu 中国共产党西双版纳傣族自治州委员会, "Guanyu xuanba xishou zhou guangbo diantai gongzuo renyuan de tongzhi" 关于选拔州广播电台工作人员的通知 (An Announcement Regarding Recruiting District News Announcers), January 15, 1976, JHDA.

[47] SHMOSY, "Guanyu waisheng yaoqiu Shanghai zhiyuan guangbo qicai wenti de baogao" 关于外省要求上海支援广播器材问题的报告 (A Report about Equipment Donation Requests from Other Provinces), October 25, 1969, SHMA.

equipment to the Shanghai Office of Sent-Down Youth is manifested in
its inclusion even when not requested by local officials. For example, the
office reported that in order to increase agricultural production, the
Huaibei region of Anhui, where a large number of sent-down youth
from Shanghai were located, had requested that Shanghai provide
2,000–3,000 electric or gas-operated motors for their newly constructed
irrigation system. "We think this is very urgent," the report advised. "If
we cannot allocate that many at once we should give them gradually. We
should also give them some broadcast speakers."[48] A subsequent letter in
December from the Shanghai Office of Sent-Down Youth to its counterpart in Anhui conveyed that it had "squeezed out" 100 motors from the
city's factories and also had three broadcast speakers to donate.[49]

Expanding Rural Factories

While initially most of the goods acquired by rural counties were to
support agricultural production, it became clear that Shanghai officials
hoped to create nonagricultural job opportunities for sent-down youth, as
suggested by their eagerness to supply equipment for broadcast stations.
This meant that local governments most likely could get what they
requested if they promised jobs for sent-down youth. Some communities
thus began to request agricultural machinery and other materials to
establish rural industries in the name of creating nonagricultural jobs
for sent-down youth.

At the beginning of the Cultural Revolution in 1966, Mao had issued
a directive that rural residents "should collectively run small plants."
Counties and communes were encouraged to develop "five small industries": iron and steel, cement, chemical fertilizer, machinery, and power
for self-reliance and national defense.[50] However, rural regions were
expected to accomplish this goal by raising most of the funds necessary
for these enterprises themselves.[51] The central government did not allocate resources, leaving rural areas on their own to acquire the machinery,

---

[48] Ibid.   [49] Ibid.
[50] Carl Riskin, "China's Rural Industries: Self-Reliant Systems or Independent
Kingdoms?" *China Quarterly*, 73 (1978), 77–98. This was by no means the first time
that Chinese leaders had called for the development of rural industry. From the establishment of the People's Republic in 1949, in order to promote self-reliance and close the gap
between cities and countryside, the government had encouraged the construction of
factories in rural areas. The Great Leap Forward was the first nationwide attempt to
achieve rural industrialization, establishing approximately 250,000 small industries run
by counties and communes. Suffering from poor planning and organization, these
enterprises failed to produce quality goods and most of them had closed by 1962.
[51] Christine P.W. Wong, "The Maoist 'Model' Reconsidered: Local Self-reliance and the
Financing of Rural Industrialization," in William Joseph, Christine P.W. Wong, and

Photo 3.1 Shanghai youth He Xinhua anchors at the broadcast station at Huxi commune in Le'an, Jiangxi. It was common for rural communities to recruit urban youth to work in these stations.
Photo courtesy of He Xinhua.

technical equipment, and skilled labor that would make the development of these rural industries possible.[52] And so, for remote rural areas that were far from industrial centers, developing these industries would be an almost insurmountable task. Although it was not the intended goal of the sent-down youth movement, in some cases, the presence of sent-down youth and the administrative offices that accompanied them provided new connections for rural officials to access the equipment and skilled

David Zweig, eds., *New Perspectives on the Cultural Revolution* (Cambridge, MA: Harvard University Press, 1991), 183–196.
[52] Dwight Perkins, *Rural Small-Scale Industry in the People's Republic of China* (Berkeley: University of California Press, 1977), 6–7.

labor that was crucial for rural industrial development. And, from the perspective of the Shanghai government, providing support for the rural industrial development was a way to create nonagricultural jobs for its sent-down youth.

This is illustrated by the Le'an Industrial Bureau's use of sent-down youth connections to Shanghai. In April 1970, Shanghai youth Wei Min was assigned to the Shanhe production brigade where, along with eleven classmates, he worked in the fields with villagers. Less than a year later, in March 1971, he was summoned to the commune office, where the Party secretary informed him of his selection for a job under the county's industrial bureau. He was pleasantly surprised. County industrial units belonged to the state system, which would provide job security, health insurance, an eight-hour day working indoors, and other fringe benefits not available to villagers. At that point, no other youth were recruited by the county, and Wei Min could not fathom why he had been singled out for this privilege. He collected all his belongings without hesitation and reported to the industrial bureau, which informed him of employment at the county's Radio and Electrical Wire Factory. The factory was still in the preliminary phase of construction.[53]

Only then did Wei Min realize the reason for this assignment. Having learned of his family background from his dossier, the factory head, accompanied by another local official, took a trip to Shanghai to visit Wei's father, the head of a Shanghai electric wire factory. Instead of going to the factory for a business visit, they went directly to Wei's home in Shanghai. The visit was apparently successful: the factory would provide basic materials for the production of wires that were unavailable in Le'an. Moreover, a number of retired "master workers" would go to Le'an to help organize the county factory. While it was common for retired skilled workers in Shanghai to assist factories elsewhere, they were in high demand in suburban areas and would, under ordinary circumstances, not have gone to help in remote places like Le'an.

Like Wei Min's father, most parents in Shanghai were perhaps more than willing to help negotiate these arrangements if they had the means to do so. Besides sending packages of food and other goods, there was little the parents could to do to alleviate the harsh reality of working and living in the countryside for their children. Securing permanent jobs in county factories meant their children would no longer be required to work in the fields. In Wei Min's case, the benefits of such arrangements proved to be even greater. Along with a number of other Shanghai sent-down youth whose parents also provided services to the county industrial bureau, he

[53] Interview with Wei Min.

was assigned to three months of training in his father's factory in Shanghai. Over the next few years, Wei Min was sent back to Shanghai a number of times for further training and other assignments.

While Wei Min and his parents must have appreciated the opportunities for him to take long business trips to Shanghai, the Le'an factory also benefited from this. Without skilled or trained technicians, the material supplied by the Shanghai factory would have been useless. For the county to send local workers to Shanghai for training would have been far more complicated and costly than relying on an urban youth like Wei Min, who could live and eat at home, speak the local dialect with workers in the Shanghai factory, and navigate Shanghai with ease.

The Le'an Radio and Electrical Wire Factory solved at least one other impediment to production through sent-down youth connections to Shanghai. The factory's production of circuit boards for radios (in addition to electric wires) required fabrication of an alloy composed of copper and gold, a production process beyond local means. The officials, however, identified and recruited a sent-down youth whose father worked at a mint in Shanghai. They were then able to get the metals synthesized in Shanghai and transported back to Le'an. Sent-down youth subsequently had frequent "business trips" to Shanghai both for technical training and to process metals.[54]

Over the next few years, particularly following the 1974 Zhuzhou experiment (see Chapter 5), the Shanghai government provided enthusiastic support for the development of rural factory workshops that promised to provide nonagricultural employment for sent-down youth in commune or production brigade collective enterprises. For example, leaders at the Menghun commune in the Jinghong district of Yunnan proposed to establish a wood products factory. Because it would provide jobs for Shanghai youth, the commune leaders requested that the Shanghai government provide the materials necessary to build the factory. Their request for support from Shanghai began by announcing their two goals: "first, to support Chairman Mao's sent-down youth program; and second, to develop commune-based industries to consolidate the socialist collective economy."[55] Noting that forty out of the fifty prospective workers would be sent-down youth from Shanghai, they listed the items they wanted Shanghai to provide. "We will get the wood locally and do our best to solve the problems that we can," they stated. For everything

---

[54] Ibid.

[55] Menghai xian Menghun gongshe geweihui 勐海县勐混公社革委会, "Guanyu yi Shanghai zhishi qingnian weizhu chengli sheban jiti muqishe de baogao" 关于以上海知识青年为主成立社办集体木器社的报告 (A Report on Establishing a Woodwork Factory Consisting Primarily of Shanghai Sent-Down Youth), December 4, 1976, JHDA.

else, they planned to submit requests to the county government and the Shanghai *weiwentuan*. The request to Shanghai stated, "If we do not have enough initial capital and equipment, as well as transportation vehicles and tools, we expect to get a loan and a full set of equipment, all to be shipped here." Perhaps to ensure that none of the necessary goods would be withheld, they cautioned, "We will wait for all the equipment to arrive before installing any of it." The officials also requested Shanghai's assistance in technical training. Of the forty Shanghai youth, their report complained, only two had the basic carpentry skills to make simple furniture and "the rest know nothing." "We suggest that Shanghai contribute two or three skilled technicians in the area of architecture and furniture-making to provide training for three years."[56]

The presence of sent-down youth, in this case, provided an otherwise unlikely possibility of building a factory in a remote rural community. With nothing but forested jungle, a commune such as Menghun, populated primarily by Dai tribes, was not equipped to build a factory at the time. But connections with the nation's most prosperous city put this remote commune in an entirely different position. It could now expect equipment furnished by Shanghai to be shipped and delivered to the factory site, a loan to cover potential expenses, and urban technicians assigned to help set up and train the workers to make fashionable furniture.[57]

In all these cases, the equipment provided by Shanghai was not necessarily new, but instead sometimes consisted of discontinued or used goods. In 1975, the Municipal Industrial and Transportation Group announced that thirteen bureaus under its jurisdiction would collect used and clearance equipment to "support regions with sent-down youth of our city." Accordingly, these bureaus agreed to contribute 440 machines and 30,000 engines for this purpose.[58] With a supply of surplus and clearance materials in hand, the city government was able to satisfy requests from other provinces. In August 1976, the Shanghai Office of Sent-Down Youth notified its counterpart in Jilin province, the Jilin Provincial Office of Sent-Down Youth, that Shanghai had decided to donate a total of 135 tractors and other equipment from its "surplus materials" to the province and provide an interest-free loan of 100,000

---

[56] Ibid.

[57] See Feng Xiaoping, "Nanwang de 84 muqichang" (The Unforgettable No. 84 Woodwork Factory), in Liu Shijie, *Huma zhiqing fengyunlu xuji*, 182.

[58] Shanghai shi geweihui gongjiao zu 上海市革委会公交组, "Guanyu zhiyuan benshi zhishi qingnian shangshan xiaxiang diqu de jishu gengxin yong jichuang, dianji de tongzhi" 关于支援本市知识青年上山下乡地区的技术更新用机床、电机的通知 (An Announcement about Providing Machines and Engines for Technological Improvement in Regions of Our City's Sent-Down Youth), September 24, 1975, SHMA.

yuan.[59] When the Shanghai Office of Sent-Down Youth learned that one of its third-front factories (industries developed in China's interior provinces for defense purposes during the 1960s and 1970s) in Anhui province were about to replace existing Rome Jeeps with vehicles suited for mountain roads, it immediately requested that six to seven of the discontinued ones be transferred to the office, which it hoped to then send to regions hosting Shanghai youth.[60]

Shanghai was by no means the only city engaged in supplying materials and equipment to rural areas where urban youth were sent. Records of the Beijing Office of Sent-Down Youth indicate that it also co-ordinated the transfer of a large quantity of goods, such as diesel engines, water pumps, trucks, three-wheeled motorcycles, cars, hand-operated tractors, sewing machines, and books to Heilongjiang, Liaoning, Shanxi, and Inner Mongolia, where large numbers of Beijing youth were sent.[61] A proposal drafted by the Beijing Office of Sent-Down Youth in late 1973 recommended that the municipal government give goods worth 13,740,000 yuan during the 1974 fiscal year to areas with Beijing youth and attached a long list of cars, tractors, electric engines, and agricultural machinery for rural communities and some goods and medicine for the youth.[62] A subsequent proposal by the Sent-Down Youth Office, in March 1974, however, revealed the difficulties securing goods that even a city like Beijing faced. Admitting that the initial proposal had been unrealistic, the second one apologized that "we are not experienced in this, and therefore do not have a clear understanding of how much local areas with sent-down youth need and how much we are able to provide. Now we plan to study the material support experience of other cities." "This is new work," the proposal concluded, "and we need experience."[63] By August, the office reported that it had not delivered materials worth 6.3 million yuan intended to be sent to rural areas and confessed that "some of our plans are unrealistic. Because we do not have specialized knowledge, we just listed items and

[59] SHMOSY, "Jilin sheng zhiqing ban" 吉林省知青办 (Letter to Jilin Province Office of Sent-Down Youth), August 17, 1976, SHMA.

[60] SHMOSY, "Shi jidian shebei gongyin gongsi" 市机电设备供应公司 (Letter to the municipal Electromechanical Equipment Supply Corporation), January 23, 1976, SHMA.

[61] BJMOSY, "Guanyu jinyibu zuohao dui wai sheng qu de wuzi zhiyuan gongzuo de qingshi" 关于进一步做好对外省区的物资支援工作的请示 (A Proposal Regarding Further Material Support to Other Provinces and Districts), August 26, 1974, BJMA.

[62] BJMOSY, "Guanyu 1974 nian zhiyuan shangshan xiaxiang zhishi qingnian wuzi jihua de qingshi" 关于 1974 年支援上山下乡知识青年物资计划的请示 (A Proposal Regarding 1974 Material Support to the Sent-Down Youth), December 20, 1973, BJMA.

[63] BJMOSY, "Qingshi baogao" 请示报告 (Proposal), March 9, 1974, BJMA.

numbers. We need more careful investigation before developing our next plan."[64] This may have also reflected resistance by relevant units and bureaus in Beijing to the requests for goods from other regions. As a result, instead of donating the specific items proposed by the Sent-Down Youth Office, which presumably reflected the requests from rural areas, the office's revised proposal listed surplus equipment available in the city.[65]

The decade following the arrival of sent-down youth witnessed a vast expansion of the local economy in some parts of rural China. At the time sent-down youth first arrived, a large part of Huma county, Heilongjiang, had no paved roads, electricity, or telephones. During the time sent-down youth were there, the county built several power plants, irrigation systems, and paper-making and wood factories, utilizing connections with Shanghai as well as skills and labor provided by sent-down youth. The number of tractors in Huma increased from forty-eight in 1968 to 280 in 1979.[66] In one production brigade, Sanhe, Shanghai youth brought hand-operated tractors, an oil-processing machine, and a threshing mill for wheat and rice. In addition, they are credited for paving roads and for building houses and a public recreation hall.[67]

Conclusion

No matter whether given new, surplus, or used equipment, some counties with sent-down youth were able to mechanize agriculture and develop rural industry to an extent inconceivable in the past. Lacking even the most basic raw materials such as plastics and metal, and with no means of technical training, it would have been difficult for a county such as Le'an to plan, or even imagine, building an electrical wire factory. It was only through having connections to parents of sent-down youth in Shanghai that such a project could become conceivable.

The extent of agricultural and industrial development in these regions varied greatly and it would be misleading to imply that all remote counties with sent-down youth experienced such substantial improvement. However, the development that did take place challenges the image of

---

[64] BJMOSY, "Guanyu jinyibu zuohao dui wai sheng qu de wuzi zhiyuan gongzuo de qingshi," August 26, 1974, BJMA.

[65] Ibid.

[66] Zhonggong Huma xian weiyuanhui, *Huma xianzhi* (Huma County Gazetteer) (Heilongjiang: Huma xianwei, 1980), 363–378. The gazetteer also points out that in 1978, Huma output value had increased 281 percent from 1968. Also see Xu Feng, "Zongshu" (Comprehensive Accounts), in Liu Shijie, *Huma zhiqing fengyunlu xuji*, 7–8.

[67] Wang Shicheng, "Sanhe cun de zhiqingmen" (The Sent-Down Youth in Sanhe Village), in Liu Shijie, *Huma zhiqing fengyunlu*, 214–215.

rural economic stagnation implied by many studies of the Cultural Revolution.[68] The few studies that acknowledge rural economic growth during these years see it as a mere footnote to advances during the subsequent post-Mao economic reforms, and attribute it to state policies and plans. Dali Yang, for example, points out that from 1972 to 1976 rural industry grew dramatically, while agricultural production declined. Yang attributes this growth in rural industry to a national planning conference in February 1970, at which leaders advocated the "vigorous construction of local 'small industries.'"[69] While responding to government policy may help account for rural industrial growth, something more complex must have been involved, for, as noted above, the government did not accompany this initiative with a provision of funds and an allocation of equipment that would have made compliance possible. Although it is impossible to demonstrate a clear connection between the sent-down youth movement and the rural economic development of these years, it is also difficult to ignore the obvious, albeit unacknowledged, correlation between the rise and decline of local industry and the arrival and departure of sent-down youth. In this context, the sent-down youth movement may represent a hidden aspect of the economic history of the Cultural Revolution, while the transportation of material goods and equipment engaged in by individual youth and negotiated by the bureaucratic structure that supported them may represent a previously hidden history of the sent-down youth movement.

Both accounts by sent-down youth themselves and the plethora of conversational back-and-forth of reports found in local archives make it clear that sent-down youth played a significant role in local rural economic development, particularly in areas far from major cities like Shanghai that otherwise had no access to the goods they needed to improve economic conditions. In many cases, the personal connections provided by the presence of sent-down youth were the main resource they had. What emerges most clearly in the archival record is the extent to which local leaders actively, persistently, and often creatively made use of these personal connections, as well as the ones now available through the bureaucratic infrastructure that accompanied the sent-down youth program. All of this bridged the vast gap between large cities such as Shanghai and the remote rural regions to which urban youth were sent.

---

[68] See, for example, Zweig, 46. He observes that throughout the 1960s and 1970s, impoverished rural production brigades could not obtain equipment that was not allocated through the state distribution system because its cost far exceeded what they could afford.

[69] Dali Yang, *Calamity and Reform in China: State, Rural Society and Institutional Change since the Great Leap Forward* (Stanford: Stanford University Press, 1996), 116. Also see Wong, "The Maoist 'Model' Reconsidered."

All of a sudden, officials from these remote regions were not only issuing written requests to offices in Shanghai, but in many cases traveling to Shanghai themselves in order to pursue their efforts to acquire resources.

At the same time, largely because of the vast number of the city's youth sent to the countryside, Shanghai government bureaus assumed responsibility for providing economic assistance to remote rural areas. According to its gazetteer, Shanghai provided materials worth 16 million yuan to places where Shanghai youth were sent, as well as tractors, cars and trucks, water pumps, and engines worth 55 million yuan.[70] The quantity of goods and funds officially distributed by the Shanghai municipal government is probably dwarfed by the materials sent by individual factories, shops, street committees, and schools in Shanghai that were negotiated through the personal connections established between sent-down youth, their parents, members of the *weiwentuan*, and rural officials and peasants. These connections were a source not only of material goods, but also of the skill, training, and technical support that was crucial for rural industrial development at a time of strong central planning that often excluded remote rural localities from the allocation of resources.

None of these activities were part of central planning, in which local communities could only receive goods allocated by the central government. Here we see goods going directly from Shanghai to remote rural communities in Jilin, Heilongjiang, Anhui, Jiangxi, Inner Mongolia, Yunnan, and Guizhou. This represents one of the major ways that Shanghai government bureaus and industrial units maintained strong connections with the sent-down youth whose urban registration had been transferred to remote counties. However, it also reflects the ways in which, by invoking the need to ensure the welfare of urban youth, Shanghai and rural officials collaborated to transfer materials for agricultural and industrial development to the countryside. The total quantity of these goods may seem relatively small, but to remote counties such as Huma, which could never hope to have priority to obtain goods from the government, the sent-down youth movement enabled acquisition directly from Shanghai, thereby making possible local industrial development. In this context, sent-down youth, sometimes unwittingly and sometimes intentionally, created connections that transcended the rural–urban divide of Maoist China and subverted the restrictions on interregional exchange prescribed by centralized state economic planning.

---

[70] Shanghai also issued loans worth 5 million yuan to those regions, all of which were ultimately treated as donations. Shanghai qingnianzhi bianzhuan weiyuanhui, 555.

4   Inappropriate Intimacies

The economic connections between Shanghai and remote villages created by the sent-down youth movement may have partially bridged the urban–rural gap, but did very little to change the fundamental belief that urban and rural residents belonged to entirely distinct and separate categories. Nowhere was this belief more evident than in the context of personal relationships: dating, love, marriage, and sexual encounters. Although the movement called on urban youth to receive re-education by peasants, and, ideally, to plant roots in the countryside, in the realm of private life, it intensified boundaries between the urban and the rural.

This contradiction can be found from the very beginnings of the sent-down youth movement, evidenced most clearly in discussions of early versus late marriage. In June 1969, a paragraph of an editorial in the *Renmin ribao* advocating that urban youth set down roots in the countryside was immediately followed by one emphasizing the importance of late marriage.[1] A year later, a *Renmin ribao* article about the movement boasted that "the poor and middle peasants are educating the sent-down youth to deal correctly with marriage issues and persuade them to marry late. Late marriage must be understood as part of class struggle. The instances of early marriage reflect class enemies trying to undermine the movement."[2] The promotion of late marriage, as Bonnin suggests in his study of sent-down youth, might have been a product of concerns about family planning and the cost of housing a married couple in the countryside.[3] However, it can also be read as conveying the message that, in spite of the ideals of the movement, urban youth should *not* set their roots in the countryside, and should instead uphold the boundary between urban and rural identity. Part of an urban identity, in this context, was to resist the rural practice of marrying at a young age.

The intensification of boundaries between urban youth and rural residents is most dramatically manifested in official management of sexual

---

[1] "Guanghuo tiandi, da you zuowei," *Renmin ribao*, June 26, 1969, 1.
[2] *Renmin ribao*, July 9, 1970.   [3] This explanation is discussed in Bonnin, 110.

relationships and sexual assault involving female urban youth. The issue of sexual abuse of female sent-down youth looms large in literature, films, artwork, journalistic accounts, and academic studies of the sent-down youth movement.[4] In these accounts, the culprits are invariably powerful male cadres. One typical dramatized tale, appearing in multiple publications under the title "A Pervert Loose in the Rubber Plantation," describes an idealistic girl from Shanghai assaulted by a brigade leader on a military farm in Yunnan who, having offered to help her cut trees, proceeded to "invade her," "like a ravenous animal eating a helpless creature." Before walking away, he promised he would arrange for her to join the youth league, and be promoted. She, according to this account, was his eighth victim; after the tenth he was executed.[5] This story, like almost all others, is constructed around a vulnerable and helpless urban girl, and a powerful local cadre who had control over her work and, most importantly, over her prospect of leaving the countryside to enroll in college or obtain an urban job. These accounts have emerged as part of a post-Mao discourse condemning the sent-down youth movement not only for depriving a generation of educational opportunities, but also for having destroyed the innocence and virginity of young girls. Their deployment as retrospective critique does not obviate the occurrence of sexual harassment, assault, and rape during the sent-down youth movement. In fact, there are probably far more incidents than will ever be known, for all the common reasons that most assaults of women go unreported. In the context of the sent-down youth movement, young urban women, away from parents, family, and home in the city, could be particularly vulnerable to sexual assault.

Instead of exposing and detailing cases of sexual assault, this chapter revisits the issue from a new and different perspective. Official reports in local archives make it clear that sexual relations of all kinds, including ones that were considered assault or rape, deeply concerned almost everyone involved in the administration of the movement, as well as public security bureaus and the central government. These reports make it possible to examine the issue of sexual abuse through the eyes of the state: why it became concerned with sexual assault of female sent-down youth, how it expressed its concern, and the consequences of its intervention in this issue. The reports reveal a political dynamic that has been previously unrecognized: that the collecting, reporting, and processing of cases of molestation was a product of a government directive and

---

[4] See, for example, Ba Shan; Deng Xian, Bonnin, 296–300. Also see the popular movie *Xiu Xiu: The Sent-Down Girl.*

[5] Ba Shan, 58. This is one of the most commonly circulated stories about the rape of female sent-down youth. Also see Deng Xian.

campaign instigated in 1973, one that mobilized local officials to expose, investigate, and criminalize male villagers who had sexual relationships with female sent-down youth.

The incidents of sexual assault that were recorded in archives differ in many ways from the better-known ones represented in the literature described above. They do not involve powerful cadres, but instead relatively ordinary male villagers, most of whom engaged in agricultural labor on production teams. Reports show local officials anxiously responding to the central government's directive; they reveal local residents fearful that any interaction with sent-down youth could subject them to charges of criminal behavior and investigation; they show accusations of rape invoked to describe what to many must have been a confusing set of physical intimacies in the countryside and which sometimes concealed other problems; they reveal the simultaneous dense web of connections and rift between the city and the countryside that the sent-down youth movement produced.

Love and Caution

Almost as soon as sent-down youth arrived at production brigades, their romantic activities attracted the attention of local offices of sent-down youth and the *weiwentuan* sent to inspect local conditions. Perhaps because the first groups of urban youth were adolescents, free from parental supervision, these cadres may have felt a particular responsibility to monitor their behavior, which included sexual relationships that would have been far harder to undertake in their urban homes. Official attention to romantic activities most likely also represented an extension of a more pervasive regulation of private life that, as Neil Diamant argues, characterized Maoist China, one in which political and sexual virtue became intertwined.[6]

From the earliest years of the sent-down youth movement, romantic and sexual liasons among sent-down youth were one of the main topics, alongside impoverished material conditions, that local sent-down youth office cadres and members of the *weiwentuan* wrote about. "There are unusual male and female relationships and it is serious," one *weiwentuan* sent to Hanjiang county in Heilongjiang warned in 1970,[7] stating that

---

[6] Neil J. Diamant, *Revolutionizing the Family: Politics, Love, and Divorce in Urban and Rural China, 1949–1968* (Berkeley: University of California Press, 2000). For a discussion of the role of the Maoist state in regulating and transforming private life in the PRC, see Yuxiang Yan, *Private Life under Socialism: Love, Intimacy, and Family Change in a Chinese Village, 1949–1999* (Stanford: Stanford University Press, 2003).

[7] Hanjiang is a fictitious name for a county in Heilongjiang, used in this chapter to protect the anonymity of individuals involved in criminal investigations.

some youth (one of whom had brought a record player from Shanghai) were "playing and singing love songs as well as dating too early."[8] In one brigade, the *weiwentuan* warned, "Some boys and girls are lying together; they talk, laugh, and have a good time."[9] Another report complained that some girls spent time knitting instead of working, while boys visited them in their dormitories; they were dating among themselves, with some boys and girls living together. "This is a serious problem," the report cautioned.[10] In one commune, officials identified sixteen couples of Shanghai youth "openly dating" and making no secret of sleeping together on their *kang* under mosquito nets. Officials suspected that many others were dating or sleeping together "less publicly."[11] And perhaps to bolster the legitimacy of these concerns, some officials punctuated reports with references to the impact these liasons had on local villagers. "The peasants are upset," one report noted, suggesting that dating couples were less willing to go to work in the fields, "creating a negative impression."[12]

Dating among sent-down youth was one of the main topics discussed at meetings of cadres working in local sent-down youth offices. At one such meeting in Nenjiang county, Heilongjiang, in March 1971, officials from the communes took turns identifying couples: one reported a pair of sent-down youth engaged in sexual relations (*fasheng nannü guanxi*); a second reported four pairs of sent-down youth dating; a third reported one pair living together, the girl several months pregnant; the fourth reported two pairs of youth dating; the fifth reported a villager having a relationship with a sent-down youth who took money and food from him and another local man dating (*gao duixiang*) a sent-down youth. A final commune noted pairs of sent-down youth who seemed "close."[13] Likewise, the Le'an (Jiangxi) County Sent-Down Youth Office expressed alarm that

---

[8] Hanjiang xian weiwen jiancha tuan 寒江县慰问检查团, "Hanjiang gongshe Shanghai zhishi qingnian jieshou zai jiaoyu qingkuang huibao" 寒江公社上海知识青年接受再教育情况汇报 (Report on Sent-Down Youth Receiving Re-education at Hanjiang Commune), July 1969, HJCA.

[9] Ibid.; Hanjiang xian weiwen jiancha tuan 寒江县慰问检查团, "Hanjiang xian weiwen jiancha tuan gongzuo huibao tigang" 寒江县慰问检查团工作汇报提纲 (Outline of Report of the Hanjiang County *Weiwen* Team), July 1970, HJCA.

[10] Hanjiang xian weiwen jiancha tuan 寒江县慰问检查团, "Hanjiang gongshe weiwen jiancha qingkuang huibao" 寒江公社慰问检查情况汇报 (Report on the *Weiwen* and Investigation Situation at Hanjiang Commune), July 27, 1970, HJCA.

[11] HJCOSY, "Hanjiang xian zhiqingban zongjie" 寒江县知青办总结 (Summary of Hanjiang County Office of Sent-Down Youth), October 20, 1970, HJCA.

[12] Hanjiang xian weiwen jiancha tuan, "Hanjiang gongshe Shanghai zhishi qingnian jieshou zai jiaoyu qingkuang huibao," July 1969.

[13] NJCOSY, "Gongshe nongchang zhishi qingnian gongzuo huiyi jilu" 公社农场知识青年工作会议记录 (Meeting Minutes for the Work of Sent-Down Youth in Communes and State Farms), March 10, 1971, NJCA.

there is a "prevalent phenomenon of wanton love" (*luan tan lian'ai*) among the Shanghai sent-down youth. In one production brigade that consisted of four villages, seven pairs of sent-down youth were dating, including three team leaders. In a different commune, one local resident was reported getting close to an urban youth, considered a serious problem primarily because the man was the son of a rich landowner, one of the five enemy categories at the time.[14]

The close attention paid to these romantic liaisons reflects challenges they posed for the sent-down youth movement. In their urban homes, such pre-marital relationships would have been considered immoral. In the context of being sent to villages, a number of young women became pregnant, which could impact their future marriage and job prospects. In some cases, women kept their pregnancy secret and tried to self-abort, a risky proposition that caused some deaths. Local communities had inadequate facilities and were often unwilling to meddle in abortions for sent-down youth. One commune clinic in Micang county refused to perform an abortion on a Shanghai youth because she was ninety days pregnant and this was her second pregnancy.[15] She had to get permission from county leaders to have the operation at the county hospital.[16] Having an abortion in urban hospitals posed fewer physical risks, but acquiring permission to do so meant surrendering privacy and suffering stigmatization. Babies born to unmarried sent-down youth in the countryside also created a confusing set of issues: cadres did not know how to handle their household registration and grain ration, let alone the provision of health care and nutrition for the unwed mothers. "These are problems we must resolve," reported an inspection team at a commune in Heilongjiang that contended with two cases of births by unwed sent-down youth in 1970.[17]

During the early years of the movement, officials were concerned not only by relations among sent-down youth, but even more by those between sent-down youth and locals. The ones they reported did not involve relations between male sent-down youth and women villagers,

---

[14] LACOSY, "Chadui Shanghai zhishi qingniang qingkuang huibao" 插队上海知识青年情况汇报 (Report of Sent-Down Youth on Production Brigades), August 21, 1969, LACA.

[15] Micang is a fictitious name for a county in Jiangxi, used in this chapter to protect the anonymity of individuals involved in criminal investigations.

[16] Micang xian wuqi bangongshi 米仓县五七办公室, "Guanyu zhishi qingnian XX huaiyun qingkuang jieshao" 关于知识青年XX 怀孕情况介绍 (Report on the Pregnancy of Sent-Down Youth XX), May 30, 1973, MCCA.

[17] Hanjiang gongshe xuanchuan jiangyong Jianchazu 寒江公社宣传讲用检查组, "Gongzuo qingkuang fanying" 工作情况反映 (Work Report), October 20, 1970, HJCA. Dating among sent-down youth was also common on state and army farms. See Liu Xiaohang, 85.

but instead ones involving Shanghai female youth whom officials identified as having "hoodlum tendencies." In a single commune in Hanjiang
county, one where apparently the assigned Shanghai youth included
a contingent recently released from a center for juvenile delinquents,
five women "hoodlums" among the sent-down youth were identified.[18]
One allegedly had sexual relations with more than ten men and wanted
their money. A second was described as a "notorious woman hoodlum"
accused of having no desire to improve and had sexual relationships with
multiple local men. A third reportedly never went to work but instead had
sex with many men and asked for payment. After becoming pregnant she
went to Shanghai and never returned. A fourth was described as a "very
bad" "female hoodlum" who was "always seducing guys" and wanted
money.[19] One declared her desire to establish a "hoodlum commune"
and a "production brigade of sluts" (*la san* in Shanghai dialect).[20] During
the early years of the movement, village men involved in these relationships were not punished. And some reports praised locals who provided
"good education" to help the problematic youth improve while criticizing
those who did not provide proper supervision.[21]

While the term *liumang* could be invoked to describe any young woman
considered "loose" in her sexual behavior, most of those from Shanghai
involved in sexual relations with local men were not labeled "hoodlums."
Accusations of sexual assault and/or rape filed by female urban youth
often resulted in investigations that involved the county public security
bureau, the county government, and the office of sent-down youth. One
case in Micang county was initiated in Shanghai in early 1973 by a sent-
down youth, surnamed Chen, who had returned home to obtain an
abortion, and filed an accusation of rape against the vice head of her
production team, Li. He was aged thirty-one, classified as a villager whose
household included his mother, wife, and two daughters. The county
police report initially suggests that Li had made multiple attempts to
befriend and "cultivate closeness" with female sent-down youth by

[18] HJCOSY, "Hanjiang xian shangshan xiaxiang zhishi qingnian daibiao dahui wenjian
huibian" 寒江县上山下乡知识青年代表大会文件汇编 (Document Collection of the
Sent-Down Youth Representatives Conference in Hanjiang County), 1973, HJCA.
[19] Hanjiang xian weiwen jiancha tuan, "Hanjiang xian weiwen jiancha tuan gongzuo huibao
tigang," July 1970; HJCOSY, "Hanjiang gongshe jieji douzheng wenti de baogao" 寒江
公社阶级斗争问题的报告 (Report on Problems Regarding Class Struggle at Hanjiang
Commune), November 17, 1972, HJCA.
[20] HJCOSY, "Weiwen jiancha tuan gongzuo huibao tigang" 慰问检查团工作汇报提纲
(Outline of the Work Report of the *Weiwen* and Investigation Team), August 5, 1970,
HJCA.
[21] The terms that they used were *er xiancai* and *la san*. HJCOSY, "Weiwentuan jiancha
qingkuang baogao" 慰问团检查情况报告 (Report of the *Weiwen* and Investigation
Team), August 5, 1970, HJCA.

offering them gifts, in one case a heater. He had often invited Chen to his home to eat, helped her with her personal vegetable plot, and assisted her in obtaining grain stipends.[22]

The public security bureau report goes to some lengths to present detailed evidence that their relationship was consensual and Li therefore not guilty of rape. It noted that Chen helped do chores at Li's home, and brought him medicine when he was sick. The report cites the commentary of local villagers, who had allegedly said, "they often work together, fool around, and say indecent things for fun ... They were stuck together like sticky rice." The police investigators argued that although they "had indecent carnal relations," this was "after obtaining the absolute consent from the woman."

The issue of consent in this case is perplexing. The public security bureau, with no questioning of Li's defense, reported that in June 1972, Li had "attempted to test her attitude by flirting and rolling around together on the ground in the production team warehouse, with the doors closed. Rather than resisting, Chen complied with a smile." From then until November, after "obtaining her consent," Li had "indecent carnal relations with Chen on her bed, on top of the stove in Li's kitchen, in the fields, and while the two were on a team trip." The response to the public security report, written by the Micang County Revolutionary Committee, endorsed the original findings, expressing skepticism about Chen's accusations, adding that the time and place of the incidents in Chen's account were identical to Li's, and that although Chen described them as rape, the specific circumstances would have made it impossible to have forced her into a sexual relationship. Had he raped her on the stove, this report argues, Li's wife would have heard noise if Chen had resisted or struggled.

It is not possible to evaluate the veracity of the characterizations of the relationship between Li and Chen. The archival reports do not include a response by Chen to the police or revolutionary committee reports, nor do they include her original accusation. As will be seen in some later cases described below, it is possible that locals—both villagers and officials staffing the respective bureaus—were rather more inclined to defend members of their community than an outsider from Shanghai. Most likely her pregnancy, and the fact that the bottles of "Ten Drop Water" secured by Li failed to affect an abortion, led her to file charges. Ultimately, he was

---

[22] Micang xian gong'an ju 米仓县公安局, "Guanyu Hanjiang gongshe Li XX jianwu xia-xiang zhishi qingnian Chen XX de diaocha qingkuang baogao" 关于李XX奸污下乡知识青年陈 XX 的调查情况报告 (An Investigative Report on the Case of Li XX Having Molested Chen XX), March 17, 1973, MCCA.

found guilty of adultery, not rape, and required to confess. His position as assistant production team captain was revoked.[23]

This case reflects broader trends of how cases of romantic and sexual relationships between sent-down youth and locals were handled during the early years of the sent-down youth movement. Intimacies between sent-down youth and locals, such as the ones between Chen and Li, were subject to suspicion, investigation, criticism, and administrative punishment, but compared to what happened beginning in mid-1973, only rarely were those found guilty of adultery sent to jail. Only a few months after the case between Chen and Li was resolved, the government launched a nationwide campaign to investigate and punish individuals who sexually assaulted female sent-down youth. Had Chen filed her accusation during the campaign, Li would almost certainly have been issued a jail sentence.

Launching a Campaign

A palpable, if not dramatic, change in official handling of sexual relations took place in 1973. First, beginning that year, officials at almost all levels suddenly began to focus their attention on relations between youth and their rural hosts, more specifically those between urban women and local men. Second, when local men had sexual encounters with female sent-down youth, their behavior was subject to being deemed criminal. This was reflected in a shift in vocabulary: from reports that in the past referred to possibly consensual male–female relations (*nannü guanxi*), living together (*tongju*), dating (*tan lian'ai* or *gao duixiang*) to terms that clearly connoted criminality. This included labels ranging from rape (*qiangjian*), gang rape (*lunjian*), and attempted rape (*qiangjian weisui*) to adulterous sex (*tongjian*), luring into sex (*youjian*), seduction/molestation (*weixie*), and flirtation (*tiaoxi*), the last having a far more negative and pejorative connotation at the time than the English translation suggests.[24] The most significant change in vocabulary is the insertion of the word *jian*. For example, sex between two individuals who were not a married couple, an

---

[23] MCCOSY, "Guanyu Micang xian Li XX jianwu xiaxiang zhishi qingnian Chen XX de chuli qingkuang baogao" 关于米仓县李 XX 奸污下乡知识青年陈 XX 处理情况报告 (Final Report on the Situation of Li XX Having Molested the Sent-Down Youth Chen XX), April 12, 1973, MCCA. "Ten Drop Water" is the name of a product.

[24] Yang Bin and Cao Shuji interpret *tiaoxi* and *weixie* as follows: "touching and fondling a woman's body. What distinguishes *weixie* from *tiaoxi* is that the former perhaps refers to touching a woman's genitals or breasts, while *tiaoxi* generally refers to verbal harassment. Neither of them, however, refers to sexual intercourse." Yang Bin and Shuji Cao, "Cadres, Grain, and Sexual Abuse in Wuwei County, Mao's China," *Journal of Women's History*, 28, 2 (Summer 2016), 36.

extramarital affair, would have been described as inappropriate in the past. But when it was described as *tongjian* (adultery), the act became deceitful and malicious, objectionable on legal grounds. By far the most frequently invoked crime was *jianwu*, most literally sexual violation, molestation, or assault, but now applied to any sexual relationships involving urban women.

This criminalization of sexual relations was largely due to intervention by the central government and its promulgation of new directives addressing "harm to sent-down youth."[25] The first, referred to as Document 21, accompanied the circulation of the famous December 1972 letter to Mao from Li Qinglin, a schoolteacher in Fujian, complaining about the intolerable material conditions faced by his son, a sent-down youth. Lacking the personal connections or a "back door" believed necessary to obtain an urban job, Li feared his son would be doomed to stay in the countryside for the rest of his life. "How could he survive when he could no longer receive support from his family?" Li asked the chairman of the Communist Party in despair. The following April, Mao, to the surprise of many people, not only replied to the letter but also sent Li 300 yuan. In his response, Mao acknowledged the prevalence of similar problems throughout the country, declaring, "Please allow us to solve these problems in a planned way."[26] Two days after Mao's letter, Zhou Enlai convened a meeting of the top leadership to discuss problems of the sent-down youth movement, stating, "We must do this work well and not let the Chairman worry anymore."[27]

Li's letter had focused on the depravity of material conditions in the countryside and the abuse of power by cadres who used the "back door" to secure jobs for their own children, but Document 21 framed the problems of the sent-down youth movement in the context of class struggle, commanding punishment of class enemies guilty of

---

[25] There was an earlier government directive issued in May 1970. Commonly known as Document 26, it specified that forcing or luring sent-down youth into marriage and/or raping female sent-down youth both constituted undermining the movement. The former would be subject to criticism, the latter to criminal charges. It appears that this document was not widely implemented. As will be seen below, a number of reports directly address the palpably different climate that resulted from the 1973 directives. During the pre-Cultural Revolution program of sent-down youth, the central government had also issued a directive (1964) specifying that fraudulent and forced marriage, as well as "insulting women" (*wuru*) should be punished. See Ding Yizhuang, 321.

[26] Zhonggong zhongyang bangongshi, "Zhonggong zhongyang tongzhi" (Announcement of the CCP central committee), June 10, 1973, CCRD. For an account of Li Qinglin, see Elya J. Zhang, "To Be Somebody: Li Qinglin, Run-of-the-Mill Cultural Revolution Showstopper," in Joseph W. Esherick, Paul Pickowicz, and Andrew Walder, eds., *The Chinese Cultural Revolution as History* (Stanford: Stanford University Press, 2006), 211–239

[27] Gu Hongzhang, 101.

undermining the movement. Although it did not specify what constituted undermining the movement, it triggered a full-fledged campaign replete with government directives, meetings, conferences, and demands for exposing, reporting, and punishing guilty individuals. As in other political campaigns since the 1950s, officials who responded quickly and forcefully received praise and publicity as positive models; those who responded sluggishly were criticized and instructed to improve their efforts. To implement the campaign, provincial and district governments ordered rural officials to mobilize both villagers and the sent-down youth.

The Heilongjiang provincial government monitored progress of the campaign and pressured locals to produce criminal cases. Following its order, the district government overseeing Hanjiang called each county, asking for detailed information about how many people had been reached and when they could have "everyone," including women and the elderly, mobilized for this campaign. The government also wanted information about what had been done to implement the campaign, praising officials with an exemplary performance while demanding the names of those with "ideological problems."[28]

Initially, not all local officials responded to the campaign as enthusiastically as the government might have expected. Reports transmitted back to the provincial government complained, "Some of the cadres made it clear they were not at all interested . . . Some commune heads did not treat the campaign seriously: they just read the documents and had discussions but did not go down to investigate. Some leaders did not pay attention to it at all."[29] One commune official was described as having a "very bad attitude" when commanded to submit criminal cases of abuse, saying, "You want those reports? We do not have anyone in the commune who can do that for you. How about you come and do it yourself?" A second commune head was described as very impatient when the county phoned to ask him to compile reports. At a third commune, a leader assigned to conduct investigations had done nothing after a week. At a fourth commune, the Party head refused to answer the phone. At yet another, the Party secretary sounded resentful and confrontational, unwilling to budge or do anything to implement Document 21 in spite of the myriad problems with sent-down youth on his commune. He was quoted as saying, "If the sent-down youth are willing, they can stay; if not, they can leave

---

[28] HJCOSY, "Diqu zhiqingban zhuanda shengwei dianhua huiyi" 地区知青办转达省委电话会议 (The District Sent-Down Youth Office Conveys the Provincial Government Conference Call), July 24, 1973, HJCA.

[29] Hanjiang xian chuanda 21 hao wenjian xuexi bangongshi, "Qingkuang huibao," August 13, 1973, HJCA.

right away."[30] One report to the county revealed that some people worried that the recruitment of cadres to do this work would create a deficit of production leaders. Others were "scared" of making mistakes and "just waited."[31] Bad attitudes of local cadres who did not treat the campaign seriously were also reported to the provincial government, such as a village head quoted as sarcastically saying to sent-down youth, "You guys wrote to Mao and got 300 yuan; I could write a letter too and perhaps he would send 3,000 yuan!"[32]

Local officials soon learned their superiors would not tolerate failure or refusal to implement Document 21. Worried about potential criticism, the Hanjiang county government in late July ordered commune and village leaders to hurry up: "The document needs to be widely propagated and thoroughly implemented; all wrong attitudes need to be corrected right away!"[33] The county head insisted that meetings be convened at "all levels to correct this 'wrong direction'" to expose "anything that can be exposed," stating that "this should be done as soon as possible and proactively."[34]

At the same time that local officials faced pressure to identify individuals believed to be undermining the movement, the central government convened a six-week (June 20 to August 10, 1973) National Working Conference on Sent-Down Youth in Beijing. At this conference, the issue of "harm to sent-down youth" became the focus of attention. This was not the first time this issue was addressed in a government directive, as so-called Document 26, issued in 1970, included a section on "harm to sent-down youth." Although it referred to rape in its list of "harms," it was acts of beating, hitting, and tying up sent-down youth that were most frequently punished.[35] The 1973 conference, in contrast, focused attention on sexual assault. The reasons for the emphasis on sexual behavior are not entirely clear. It may be partly related to what Neil Diamant, in his study of the family in Maoist China, calls "the sexualization of political critique": the sexual nature of crimes attributed to political enemies.[36] Quite

---

[30] Hanjiang xian chuanda 21 hao wenjian xuexi bangongshi, "Guanyu chuanda guanche zhongyang 21 hao wenjian de qingkuang baogao" 关于传达贯彻中央 21 号文件的情况报告 (Report on Circulating and Implementing Document Number 21 of the Central Government), July 31, 1973, HJCA.

[31] Ibid.

[32] Hanjiang xian chuanda 21 hao wenjian xuexi bangongshi, "Qingkuang huibao," August 13, 1973, HJCA.

[33] Hanjiang xian chuanda 21 hao wenjian xuexi bangongshi, "Guanyu chuanda guanche zhongyang 21 hao wenjian de qingkuang baogao," July 31, 1973, HJCA.

[34] Hanjiang xian chuanda 21 hao wenjian xuexi bangongshi, "Qingkuang huibao," August 13, 1973, HJCA.

[35] See Jin Dalu and Jin Guangyao, *Zhongguo xin difangzhi*, vol. 4, 2235–2236.

[36] Diamant, 285–294.

possibly, this sexualization of politics became particularly acute in the early 1970s, when, as problems with the sent-down youth movement became increasingly troublesome, it was easier to issue accusations of sexual crimes than confront underlying problems.

The emphasis on sexual behavior may be more directly attributed to reports on two major incidents of sexual assault, one in Yunnan, the other in Heilongjiang.[37] A month before the conference, Zhou Enlai, having read the report on sexual molestation of female sent-down youth by two cadres on a military state farm in Yunnan, declared, "These fascist behaviors must be dealt with immediately!" More specifically, he ordered the central government, the Yunnan provincial government, and the military to dispatch a joint investigative team to encourage "the masses" to make accusations. Those found guilty would be removed from leadership positions and forced to confess, their crimes to be announced at a public assembly. Zhou Enlai also ordered that the report on sexual abuse in Yunnan be circulated to all participants in the national conference, requesting that they return to their provinces and conduct a thorough investigation of sexual assault of sent-down youth on state farms, military farms, and commune production brigades.[38] While the Yunnan report prompted investigations of sexual harassment, the report on Heilongjiang addressed potential punishments. Responding to information that two cadres at a military farm were accused of sexually seducing and assaulting several dozens of sent-down youth, government leaders began speaking in terms of capital punishment. Zhang Chunqiao declared that these two cadres should be sentenced to death, with Ye Jianying adding, "Killing one would teach a lesson to hundreds and thousands of people." Wang Hongwen urged that if these criminals were not punished, parents would be extremely worried about sending their daughters to the countryside.[39]

Given the attention paid to sexual abuse, it is not surprising that the final conference report, circulated on August 4, 1973, as Document 30, provided a much more explicit and forceful directive about this issue. Article Five of the report most specifically addressed issues of rape and marriage:

---

[37] Guowuyuan zhongyang junwei, "Guanyu Huang Yantian, Li Yaodong jianwu pohai nü zhishi qingnian anjian de tongbao" (Circular of the State Council and the Central Military Commission on the Case of Huang Tiantian and Li Yaodong Raping and Harming Female Sent-Down Youth), August 11, 1973, CCRD.

[38] Gu Hongzhang, 104–105.

[39] Liu Xiaomeng, *Zhongguo zhiqingshi*, 229–230; Liu Xiaomeng, *Zhongguo zhiqing shidian*, 512–513.

The masses must be mobilized to forcefully fight against criminal activities that are undermining the sent-down youth movement. Those criminals who have cruelly harmed sent-down youth and who have used fascist means to rape female youth must be punished according to the law. Criminals who have threatened victims or have retaliated against accusers in order to conceal their own crimes shall be given harsher punishments. Individuals given a death sentence to assuage public wrath for their most heinous crimes should be publicly condemned before their execution. The death penalty should be controlled to avoid excesses. Leniency shall be given to those who confess and plead guilty. The reputation and safety of the victims should be protected. Proper courtship and marriage among youth must be protected. Forced marriage is strictly forbidden. We must resolutely distinguish two types of contradictions and guard against class enemies who attempt to undermine our front line.[40]

A week after the promulgation of Document 30, the State Council and Central Military Commission publicized the execution of the two cadres from the Heilongjiang military farm accused of sexual abuse. The State Council announcement of the execution pointed out, "Some of our comrades do not have an adequate understanding of class struggle, and treat sexually assaulting female sent-down youth as a 'petty incident of life'." This problem cannot be solved, the document stated, unless it is treated very seriously.[41] Almost every county with sent-down youth held sentencing rallies, such as one in Jinghong, Yunnan, that boasted 23,000 participants, including representatives from different districts, counties, cities, and military farms, to hear the announcement of the death sentence for five cadres guilty of abusing urban girls.[42]

Although Document 30 specified punishment of rape (using the term *qiangjian*), the central government did not confine investigations and punishments to cases that fit the literal definition of rape. In fact, the charge against the two Heilongjiang cadres who were executed was sexual molestation (*jianwu*) and seduction (*weixie*), not rape per se. Following this example, provincial governments also interpreted Document 30 as referring to *jianwu* as well as rape. A sent-down youth conference held in Yunnan issued a directive to its districts and counties stating that in addition to exposing and executing rapists, cases of *jianwu* must be investigated and punished.[43] A conference of district chief judges in Jiangxi, held in 1973, affirmed that rape should be punished, adding

---

[40] Zhongguo zhongyang guowuyuan guanyu quanguo zhishi qingnian shangshan xiaxiang gongzuo huiyi de baogao, August 4, 1973, CCRD.
[41] Ibid.
[42] Yang Xinqi, "Yunnan sheng zhishi qingnian shangshan xiaxiang yundong dashiji" (The Great Return to the City by State Farm Sent-Down Youth in Yunnan), in Zhonggong Yunnan shengwei dangshi yanjiushi, 413.
[43] Zhonggong Yunnan shengwei, "Pifa 'Yunnan sheng zhishi qingnian shangshan xiaxiang gongzuo huiyi jiyao'" (Circulation of "Summary of the Yunnan Province Conference on

that "in the context of the sent-down youth movement *jianwu* should be punished identically to rape."[44] When confronted with the task of investigating cases, local officials expanded the range of punishable offenses even further, to include seduction and flirtation. Even sexual relations that occurred in the context of marriage could be the subject of criminal investigation. In cases involving forced or lured marriage, the husbands could be charged and sentenced for sexually abusing and destroying the virginity of their wives.

The implementation of Document 30 produced a continuation of the campaign triggered by Document 21, with an intensified focus on exposing and punishing sexual relations involving sent-down youth.[45] The Hanjiang county government in Heilongjiang, for example, established an office to lead the campaign and appointed sixteen cadres to take charge at the communes. In a period of six weeks, county leaders held three meetings to study the government directives and convened eight countywide conferences.[46] The pressure on rural officials to not simply expose, but also punish, is exemplified by a report in Heilongjiang. In December 1973, four months after the instigation of the campaign, the head of the provincial office of sent-down youth summarized the accomplishments of his province, which included 1,701 cases under investigation, in 1,173 of which sentences had already been passed. Many counties and cities had already held "sentencing mass rallies, educated the masses, and cracked down on class enemies." However, he pointed out,

those cases are still not enough … In some investigations, people were not sentenced or punished, including more than thirty serious cases. There is not enough protection given to the youth who have suffered injury and social stigma. We need to do more … We need to speed up our management of cases of abusing sent-down youth.[47]

the Work of Sent-Down Youth), in Zhonggong Yunnan shengwei, *Yunnan zhishi qingnian shangshan xiaxiang yundong*, 332–337.

44 Jiangxi sheng difangzhi bangongshi, *Jiangxi sheng fayuanzhi* (Jiangxi Province Court Gazetteer) (Jiangxi: Fangzhi chubanshe, 1996), 102.

45 In many locations, cases of sexual assault of female sent-down youth became the overwhelming majority of incidents of "harm to sent-down youth." Statistics of the Shanghai courts indicate that beginning with the promulgation of Document 30 in 1973, some 90 percent of cases of "harm to sent-down youth" involved molestation of female youth. See Jin Dalu and Jin Guangyao, *Zhongguo xin difangzhi*, vol. 4, 2235–36.

46 Hanjiang xian chuanda 21 hao wenjian xuexi bangongshi 寒江县传达中央 21 号文件学习办公室, "Qingkuang huibao" 情况汇报 (Report on Conditions), August 13, 1973, HJCA.

47 HJCOSY, "Sheng zhiqingban zhuren Lu Fu zai ge di shi xian zhiqingban zhuren he caikuai renyuan zuotan huiyi shang de zongjie" 省知青办主任鲁夫在各地市县知青办主任和财会人员座谈会议上的总结 (Closing Remarks by Lu Fu, Head of Provincial Office of Sent-Down Youth, at the Workshop for District, City, and County Sent-Down Youth Office Heads and Financial Officials), December 10, 1973, HJCA.

Finally, he told officials from districts and counties that the government was losing its patience and explained how he would deal with cadres whose performance was inadequate: "We will push them once, twice, and after the third push if they have not sentenced people, we will summon the responsible Party secretary to report to the provincial government in person!"[48]

When counties were unable to produce enough punishable cases, local officials searched for incidents from the past, and many of the cases exposed in the aftermath of the 1973 promulgation of Documents 21 and 30 consisted of events that had taken place years earlier. In Hanjiang locals were pressured to revisit and reinvestigate older cases, with individuals previously punished with criticism for "inappropriate" or "immoral" behaviors now facing criminal charges and jail sentences.[49] A report by the Hanjiang Party Committee for the district sent-down youth conference observed that

90% of the cases exposed during the campaign took place before 1973, but ... they had not been dealt with properly. So, when we implemented Documents 21 and 30, the county Party committee mobilized the entire county's population for the work of exposing, reporting, and reinvestigating cases of harm to sent-down youth. We held public sentencings for major cases and mass rallies to criticize and humiliate abusers. We achieved the goal of educating the masses, while shocking and terrorizing the enemies. In 1973, twenty-seven cases of sexual abuse were sentenced, of which only two took place that year.[50]

In Micang, a doctor was found guilty of having, in 1969, used anesthesia to immobilize two sent-down youth and rape (*qiangjian*) them, as well as sexually abusing (*jianwu*) and flirting (*weixie*) with three others. At least one of his victims became pregnant and had an abortion. It was not until the 1973 campaign that this case was exposed and investigated by the Public Security Bureau, which found him guilty and sentenced him to death.[51] Similarly, in Nenjiang, county officials in 1973 sentenced one male villager to life in prison for actions committed in November 1970: sexual abuse of three female sent-down youth, seduction of and flirtation

[48] Ibid.
[49] HJCOSY, "Shangshan xiaxiang zhishi qingnian zaoshou pohai anjian baogao biao" 上山下乡知识青年遭受迫害案件报告表 (Tables of Abusing Sent-Down Youth Cases), February 5, 1974, HJCA. HJCOSY, "Jianwu pohai zhishi qingnian tongji mingxibiao" 奸污迫害知识青年统计明细表 (Detailed Statistical Tables of Sexually Abusing and Harming Sent-Down Youth), May 22, 1975, HJCA.
[50] Zhonggong Hanjiang xianwei 中共寒江县委, "Zai diwei zhiqing gongzuo huiyi shang de huibao" 在地委知青工作会议上的汇报 (Report to the District Sent-Down Youth Work Conference), no date (1974), HJCA.
[51] MCCOSY, "Guanyu jiefa chu gezhong anjian tongjibiao" 关于揭发出各种案件统计表 (Statistical Table of Exposed Cases), August 21, 1973, MCCA.

with two others.[52] And in Hanjiang, the charge against a villager for *jianwu* was later changed to *qiangjian* in 1973—he had engaged in sex with the sent-down youth in her dormitory from October 1969 to March 1970. The sexual relationship was reportedly stopped in April of that year, when a work team of cadres came to the village. At that time, the "great masses" of sent-down youth "raised their class consciousness" and exposed the relationship, criticizing the peasant with a revolutionary big-character poster. Although the problem was then solved, the case was reinvestigated in 1973 and he was sentenced to two years in jail.[53] In Huichun county (Jilin), local officials "exposed and reinvestigated" forty-two cases in which guilty individuals had been criticized in the past and found that sixteen of them clearly warranted jail sentences.[54]

The campaign expressed a clear message that unwanted sexual advances would no longer be tolerated. For example, a local man in Hanjiang county found guilty of "attempted" sex had, on three occasions, sought out a Shanghai female youth who worked in the barn. He reportedly kissed her, touched her breasts, dragged her down onto the sacks on the ground, pulled down her pants, and attempted to have sex, but she refused. He also "disgustingly" exposed himself and asked her to touch him. She again refused. The fact that this man was able to make such attempts repeatedly most likely was because he saw little consequence to such behavior. Not until 1973 was he investigated and sentenced to three years in jail for "attempted rape."

On the surface, the investigation (or reinvestigation) of cases of sexual misconduct and the resurrection of old cases might seem to resemble the exposure of past incidents of sexual misconduct in more contemporary efforts to contend with issues of harassment, molestation, and rape in many parts of the world. The cases involving sent-down youth discussed here, however, are somewhat different. Document 30 may well have offered protection and recourse to young urban women who, far from home, were particularly vulnerable; it may have also contributed to

---

[52] Nenjiang xian geweihui 嫩江县革委会, "Guanyu panchu jianwu nü zhishi qingnian fan XX wuqi tuxing de qingshi baogao" 关于判处奸污女知青犯 XX 无期徒刑的请示报告 (Life Sentence Informational Report Concerning XX, Sexual Abuser of Female Sent-Down Youth), December 28, 1973, NJCA.

[53] HJCOSY, "Shangshan xiaxiang zhishi qingnian zaoshou pohai anjian baogao biao," February 5, 1974, HJCA.

[54] Huichun xian geming weiyuanhui wuqi bangongshi, "Huichun xian xiaxiang zhishi qingnian gongzuo diaocha baogao" (Report on Work with Sent-Down Youth in Huichun County), June 1, 1973, in Xu Zhigao, *Wenge shigao: Wuchan jieji wenhua da geming* (Historical Documents of the Cultural Revolution: The Great Proletarian Cultural Revolution) (Beijing: Shijie huayu chubanshe, 2016), 271.

a more sympathetic environment for victims of sexual assault, prompting some women to issue charges they would have feared raising in the past. Such charges may have been welcomed by local officials, now under pressure to produce cases of sexual assault. Yet the records only occasionally identify who initiated the accusations, and so it is not possible to understand this as a story of individual women now emboldened to accuse sexual abusers. Surely some did. However, we also find women on occasion coerced into issuing charges of assault by local officials required to produce as many cases as possible.

Criminal Intimacies

Although the problem of sexual misconduct was only one part of the category "harm to sent-down youth," it was singularly criminalized. For example, Micang county reported forty-four individuals guilty of "tying up and beating sent-down youth." Of them, only four were punished with criticism and "education," those who were Party members were issued warnings, and two cadres were transferred. None faced criminal charges or sentences; none were subject to public humiliation. The rest, mostly locals who tried to discipline rebellious youth, received no punishment at all. In one case a production team head had tied up a sent-down youth and left him overnight in a cow shed (the youth had tried to evict his roommates so he could have sex with a female sent-down youth). For having harmed a sent-down youth, the village head was simply criticized. In contrast, locals who were intimately involved with female sent-down youth faced criminal investigations and far more serious punishments, most receiving jail sentences.[55] The ten Micang county locals found guilty of sexual activities with female sent-down youth lost their jobs and/or Party membership, and faced public humiliation, arrest, jail sentences, and, in one case, the death penalty.[56] Similarly, in Hanjiang

---

[55] MCCOSY, "Anjian huiji" 案件汇集 (Compilation of Cases), September 11, 1973, MCCA.

[56] MCCOSY, "Guanyu pohai zhishi qingnian anjian cailiao" 关于迫害知识青年案件材料 (Materials Concerning Cases of Harm to Sent-Down Youth), 1973, MCCA. The sentences issued to those found guilty of inappropriate intimacies were wildly inconsistent, with almost no discernible relationship between the specific crime and its punishment. In Hanjiang county, the five men found guilty of rape (*qiangjian*) were sentenced to two, eight, and twelve years in jail, with two sentenced to death. Those guilty of sexual abuse (*jianwu*) of sent-down youth had sentences ranging from one year's probation to fifteen years in jail. Of the men found guilty of hoodlum behavior (*shua liumang*), one was labeled a "bad person" (*huai fenzi*) in an enemy category, one was subjected to criticism and education, and others were sentenced to jail for seven months to seven years. Hanjiang xian zhiqingban, "Jianwu pohai zhishi qingnian tongji."

county, most of those found guilty of sexual abuse received jail sentences, and in two cases the death penalty.[57]

Even when a rural man and female sent-down youth had a seemingly consensual relationship, the man could find himself the subject of investigation and criminalization. For example, a young man in Huma, Cui Shushan, was found guilty of having sexually abused his girlfriend and sentenced to three years in jail. The report's assertion that she was his girlfriend is suggested by the fact that as soon as he was released from jail, the woman, who had by then returned to Shanghai, went back to Huma to marry him. The local government eventually conceded that Cui had been wrongly punished.[58]

Sexual relations that occurred in the context of marriage could also be subject to criminal investigation and punishment. Document 30 specified that "proper dating among sent-down youth must be protected," but it granted no protection to marriages between locals and sent-down youth, raising questions as to whether such relationships should be considered "proper." One male villager in Micang county, who had married a sent-down youth from Shanghai, was subject to investigation in 1973 for having had a sexual relationship with this woman starting in 1969. When they became engaged, her parents protested. She refused to change her mind, however, declaring to her fiancé, "Even if all the seawater is drained and rocks shattered, my heart will not change!" They did get married, but during the 1973 campaign he was accused of having lured her into marriage by promising that she would not have to work. Her production team leader reportedly worked tirelessly to persuade her to "fight against enemies" until she finally agreed. The man was then found guilty of sexually molesting the woman and sentenced to three years in jail.[59] In another case in the same county, a local villager and a female sent-down youth had begun to date in October 1972 and married in December. As soon as her parents in Shanghai learned about this, they sent her a telegram with twenty-five yuan and a brief message: "Mother ill! Return immediately!" When she refused, her mother and brother traveled to the countryside to try to subvert the marriage. During the 1973 investigation, the man was arrested, charged with "seduction," "luring into sex" (youjian), and forced marriage (bihun). The investigation concluded that he had used "small gestures of kindness" to poison the mind of this sent-down youth and eventually lure her into sex, adding

[57] HJCOSY, "Shangshan xiaxiang zhishi qingnian zaoshou pohai anjian baogao biao," February 5, 1974.

[58] Zhang Jie, "Beiji mohe yu xin ren" (Nurturing the young in the Far Northern Mohe), in Liu Shijie, ed., *Huma zhiqing fengyunlu*, 77–80.

[59] MCCOSY, "Guanyu pohai zhishi qingnian anjian cailiao," 1973.

that he had sex with her when she had her period, thereby "seriously damaging her health."[60]

Only rarely do retrospective accounts reveal the pressure experienced by individual sent-down youth to accuse men they were dating or to whom they were engaged of sexual assault. One, authored by a woman sent to a production team in Anhui, reports having "fallen in love" with a local young man who worked as the brigade accountant, and who, after the 1973 directive, was accused of having sexually molested her and arrested. According to her account, she immediately ran to the commune headquarters to meet with the head of the Office of Sent-Down Youth. "I repeatedly told him that we were dating," she reported. "But he pretended not have heard and encouraged me to issue an accusation that he had raped me ... I went everywhere to say he had not raped me." The investigators subsequently went to meet with her parents in Shanghai, encouraging them to issue accusations. Eventually he was charged with rape and given a jail sentence. Her account of these events concludes with a cynical point that sent-down youth who married villagers and "set down roots" had been models, but in this new political context, the husbands of these models became criminals.[61]

Although reports of criminal cases focus on the conduct of the campaign in rural areas, these last few cases indicate the often less obvious role of Shanghai residents in the promulgation of Document 30. Parents of sent-down youth could use this directive to prevent any kind of intimate relationships, let alone marriage, between their daughters and rural residents. This sometimes created an additional burden on local officials, who now not only had to confront the government's pressure to produce criminal cases, but also had to contend with Shanghai residents seeking to control their children's behavior at a distance. In some cases, it was only due to the interference of urban family members that investigations of potential abusers were initiated. This is evident in a case in Micang county involving a sent-down youth and a county cadre stationed on her production team. In a letter to her brother in Shanghai in 1973, she complained that he had touched her face and then put his arms around her when opening the courtyard gate for her one evening. The letter triggered an investigation that ultimately found the cadre guilty of flirtation and

[60] MCCOSY, "Guanyu XX dui XX youhun bijian de qingkuang huibao" 关于 XX 对 XX 诱婚逼奸的情况报告 (Report on XX Luring Sent-Down Youth XX into Marriage and Forcing Her to Have Sex with Him), December 13, 1973, MCCA.

[61] Fan Zi, "Yi wenge zhuming yuan'an: 'qiangjian nü zhiqing an' shimo" (The Full Story of Remembering the Famous Case of "The Rape of a Female Sent-Down Youth"), *Fenghuang wang lishi*, October 13, 2011.

seduction. The county government then issued a letter to the young woman's father in Shanghai:

About your daughter: she was seductively flirted with (*tiaoxi*) on the evening of March 23 by Yuan Sheng. After investigation by both our office and the comrades in the office of sent-down youth, we concluded that what happened is close to what your daughter described. As a state cadre, this is rather serious ... We hope that you, respected parents, will express whether these consequences are appropriate.[62]

Most likely, were it not for the initial letter to her family in Shanghai (and presumably their expression of concern), this incident would not have become the subject of investigation.

Interventions by Shanghai residents did not always override local management of cases, such as when the parents of a female sent-down youth challenged the three-year jail sentence given to a village cadre who had been accused of sexually molesting their daughter. Insisting that he had seduced, flirted with, and abused as many as twenty-four women (one of whom became pregnant), the parents requested that the Putuo District Office of Sent-Down Youth in Shanghai demand a heavier sentence. But ultimately, the Micang Office of Sent-Down Youth concluded that the original sentence was appropriate and would not be changed.[63]

It is not always evident how these accusations, investigations, and jail sentences affected local communities. At least one report from a local office of sent-down youth describes the confusion and fear created among villagers. Cadres did not understand why the county public security bureau was suddenly churning up "these old things" and conducting investigations of them. "People are concerned and afraid," the report stated, "and there are lots of rumors."[64] Some case reports reveal the contradictory perspectives of local residents, officials, and sent-down youth. A village driver in Hanjiang was accused of raping a Shanghai sent-down youth, one of several he had invited to live in his house when there was a shortage of dormitory rooms for the urban young women. She became pregnant and went to Shanghai for an abortion. The Public Security Bureau, called to investigate, "forced him to confess." Details

[62] MCCOSY, "Hua Ying diaocha cailiao" 华英调查材料 (Hua Ying Case Investigation Materials). This file includes a statement by Hua Ying, an investigation report, a confession by Yuan Sheng, and a letter from MCCOSY to Hua's father in Shanghai, September 12–October 15, 1973, MCCA.

[63] PTDOSY, "Xiaxiang qingnian anjian jianbaobiao," 下乡青年案件简报表 (Table of Sent-Down Youth Cases), July 13, 1973, PTDA; MCCOSY, "Putuo, sheng, di xiang-ban" 普陀、省、地乡办 (To Putuo, Provincial, and District Office of Sent-Down Youth), December 14, 1973, MCCA.

[64] Hanjiang xian chuanda zhongyang 21 hao wenjian bangongshi, "Guanyu chuanda guanche zhongyang 21 hao wenjian de qingkuang baogao."

in the account suggest conflicting assessments: the driver is first described, most likely by the official handling the case, as having a reputation for flirting and "talking filthy" with sent-down youth. The writer complains that in the past, leaders paid no attention. When the Public Security Bureau forced him to confess, local cadres were apparently sympathetic to him and believed that a confession was sufficient punishment. "He works hard, has a wife and children," local cadres are reported to have argued. "So, we hope he can be treated leniently." Others, however, declared that "the guy is not good, but the woman is not good either." Local residents also sympathized with the driver and were dubious about the charges, reportedly insisting that the sexual relationship had been consensual and that "consensual sex was very common in the village." Finally, his production brigade wrote to investigators lamenting that he was an unfortunate victim of the new government directive.[65] In other words, had this case been handled before Document 30, the driver might have received the relatively light "administrative punishment" given to the villager described earlier in this chapter.

In this case, we see villagers who are most likely relatives or long-time neighbors or coworkers having to confront an issue that arose because of the presence of an outsider, the sent-down youth. The sent-down youth, having returned to Shanghai because she was pregnant, might herself have filed an accusation, or it might have been filed by her parents, who surely did not want the reputation of their daughter to be tarnished. Meanwhile, the Public Security Bureau had obviously dispatched an agent to investigate this local affair, while officials at a higher level were experiencing pressure to produce criminal cases.

In rare cases, local challenges to accusations prevailed, such as when a twenty-four-year-old Shanghai youth wrote to the Micang County Public Security Bureau stating that she had been raped by a villager. Although he was deemed morally corrupt, evil, and guilty of sexually abusing a Shanghai youth, he received a very light punishment: removal from his position as production brigade head and public criticism. The investigation concluded that the two behaved "like magnets," very close, always touching each other, joking, flirting, and engaging in sex many times.[66] Another youth who had become pregnant and went to get an

---

[65] HJCOSY, "1973 nian gongzuo zongjie" 1973 年工作总结 (1973 End-of-Year Work Summary), February 3, 1974, HJCA; also see letter from Hanjiang XX production brigade, August 21, 1973, HJCA; HJCOSY, "Shangshan xiaxiang zhishi qingnian zaoshou pohai anjian baogao biao," HJCA.

[66] Micang xian gong'an ju and MCCOSY 米仓县公安局和米仓县知青办, "Guanyu dui XX jianwu Shanghai xiafang nü zhishi qingnian XX de qingkuang baogao," 关于对 XX 奸污

abortion in Shanghai also accused a villager of having had unwanted sex with her. The investigators, however, sided with the villagers as well as other sent-down youth who described the two as spending a lot of time together. Some also speculated that the woman filed the accusation only because she needed an explanation for her pregnancy. The case was eventually ruled "inappropriate male–female relations" (*bu zhengchang de nannü guanxi*); the alleged abuser was removed from his position as Party secretary of the production brigade and required to undergo criticism. The light sentence can also be attributed to the fact that the accused man was able to produce letters from the woman proposing ways to keep their relationship secret.[67]

Over the course of the campaign, complaints that locals minimized the seriousness of incidents of sexual assault became the subject of concern at higher levels. A 1975 investigative report by the Ministry of Public Security (labeled "secret") first praised those who were "cracking down on criminals who are destroying the sent-down youth movement, and protecting the safety of the youth." However, the report acknowledged, some local officials were reluctant to interfere. The cases deemed most serious in the report all concerned sexual assault. In some districts, officials classified cases of rape and sexual assault of female sent-down youth as "adultery" (*tongjian*), as having "lifestyle problems" (*shenghuo zuofeng wenti*), or as "ordinary male–female relations" (*yiban nannü guanxi*). The report observed that many locals would challenge rape charges lodged against village men, declaring, "You can only say it's rape if they had sex just once. If they had sex more than once, then it's *tongjian*."[68]

Far more often, men accused of sexually abusing female sent-down youth did not escape criminal sentences. "Now cases of abuse are being exposed everywhere," a production brigade leader complained.[69] In the name of protecting sent-down youth, the campaign imposed yet another burden on villagers who now had not only to host and manage sent-down

---

上海下放女青年 XX 的情况报告 (Investigation Report on XX Sexually Abusing Shanghai Female Sent-Down Youth XX), December 31, 1973, MCCA.

[67] MCCOSY, "Guanyu dui XX jianwu Shanghai xiafang nü zhishi qingnian XX de diaocha baogao" 关于 XX 奸污上海下放女青年 XX 的情况调查报告 (Investigation Report on the Sexual Abuse of the Shanghai Sent-Down Youth XX by XX), March 27, 1974, MCCA.

[68] Gong'an bu 公安部, "Jianjue daji cuican pohai Shanghai xiaxiang zhishi qingnian de jieji diren" 坚决打击迫害上山下乡知识青年的阶级敌人 (Resolutely Cracking Down on Class Enemies Who Abused Sent-Down Youth), *Gong'an gongzuo jianbao* 公安工作简报 (18), April 16, 1975, AHCA.

[69] HJCOSY, "1973 nian gongzuo zongjie"; "Shangshan xiaxiang zhishi qingnian zaoshou pohai anjian baogao biao." There is also a letter from the involved production brigade dated August 21, 1973, HJCA.

youth but also to contend with public security agents and local officials commanded to expose and issue jail sentences for a wide range of romantic and sexual relationships.

Abusers and Victims

The campaign was not simply a crusade against sexual assault, and involved something more than the criminalization of sexual relations between villagers and sent-down youth. More than what kinds of sexual relationships were deemed criminal or the types of punishments issued was a consideration of *who* committed such crimes and who was victimized by them. When it came to determining guilt and issuing punishments, it was local men who were found culpable; the innocent victims in the investigations were invariably female, all of them sent-down youth. Male sent-down youth who engaged in sexual relations with female sent-down youth or with village women were largely immune from criminal investigations. Although sexual abuse must have also caused harm to village women, they were not among the victims identified in this campaign. Much like the widespread obsession in the post-Civil War United States with sexual liaisons between white women and African-American men, one that resulted in what historian Martha Hodes has called "the terrorization of black men,"[70] the campaign to expose cases of sexual assault by male peasants against female urban youth in China's sent-down youth movement produced social categories that were profoundly different and unequal.

The nature of the social categories instilled by this campaign—that between male peasants and female urban youth—is highlighted by a comparison to earlier moments in PRC history when sexual misconduct, including rape, attracted public and state attention. Yang Bin and Cao Shuji's research on an Anhui county in the early 1960s documents the extent to which male cadres (brigade heads, county leaders, Party secretaries) subjected peasant women (as well as

---

[70] Martha Hodes, "The Sexualization of Reconstruction Politics: White Women and Black Men in the South after the Civil War," *Journal of the History of Sexuality*, 3, 3 (January 1993), 402–417. For brief summary of the discourse on lynching in the United States, see Leon Litwack, "Hell Hounds," in James Allen, Hilton Als, John Lewis, and Leon F. Litwack, eds., *Without Sanctuary: Lynching Photography in America* (Santa Fe: Twin Palms Publishers, 2017), 8–37; and Angela Davis, *Women, Race and Class* (New York: Vintage Books, 1981). There are myriad contexts in which accusations of rape are analyzed as a crucial element in the creation of unequal racial and national categories. See, for example, Caitlin Carroll, "The European Refugee Crisis and the Myth of the Immigrant Rapist," *Europe Now*, July 6, 2017, www.europenowjournal.org /2017/07/05/untitled, accessed July 15, 2018.

saleswomen, telephone operators, cooks, and housewives) to sexual abuse. In the context of the severe famine that followed the Great Leap Forward, male cadres used the potential provision of grain to lure local women into sexual relationships. "While food was the most powerful tool during the food shortage period," Yang and Cao add, local cadres also used "jobs, promotions, household registration, and Party or league membership" to victimize women.[71] "Not a single 'corrupted' cadre was investigated or punished on the basis of their sexual misconduct," Yang and Cao lament. If they faced administrative punishment, it was for political and economic errors, not for allegations about their sexual behavior. Pointing out that CCP economic campaigns to move women from households to labor in the public sphere made them particularly vulnerable to sexual abuse, Yang and Cao note other studies that reveal the sexual abuse of rural women by powerful male cadres, including William Hinton's account of Long Bow village in Shanxi as well as Edward Friedman, Paul Pickowicz, Mark Selden, and Kay Ann Johnson's study of Raoyang county in Hebei.[72]

The campaign launched in the context of the sent-down youth movement differs in several ways. First, the reports and records of sexual misconduct were the product of an actual government campaign, one that specifically targeted these categories of abuse (in contrast to incidents of sexual assault described by Bin and Cao, in which these problems were revealed in the context of investigations of political wrongdoing). Second, and most significant here, is that the perpetrators of abuse in these reports were rather ordinary local men, rarely ones who served as cadres or had positions of power. Finally, the women identified as victims in these reports were all sent-down youth; abuse of rural women, which surely took place, was not subject to investigation or reporting.

In contrast to popular and scholarly literature that portrays the "abusers" during the sent-down youth movement as powerful cadres who lured young urban women into sex in exchange for urban jobs or college admission, the overwhelming majority of rural men accused of abuse during the campaign were poor villagers who had no power whatsoever. In Hanjiang county, where the Public Security Bureau classified the forty-one accused individuals, thirty-two were "poor peasants," two had *danwei* (work unit) jobs as workers, one did road maintenance in the collective

---

[71] Yang and Cao, 40.

[72] Citing Bonnin, they also describe the urban educated girls sent to villages and state farms who were raped by local cadres, including ones who "had to sleep with cadres to be granted return to cities." Yang and Cao, 51.

sector, and the only four cadres were all at the village level; two were Party members, one of whom served as village Party secretary.[73]

Unlike the powerful cadres who could lure young urban women into providing sexual favors by the promise of arranging a return to the city or admission to college, the male perpetrators in the case reports had what, on the surface at least, might seem only the most meager of resources to offer. One poor villager in Hanjiang county, for instance, was reported as having "corruptly lured" a sent-down youth by treating her like a goddaughter and giving her wood ears, bean thread noodles, beans, flour, and candy.[74] Another report described a truck driver who "used the convenience of his work to offer [a Shanghai youth] small favors" such as giving her rides. "From joking to hugging, kissing, touching ... he 'had relations' with her."[75] Other "lures" included offering a meal to a female sent-down youth, instruction on riding a bike, helping purchase a bus ticket, helping carry baskets of rice back from the fields, and accompaniment back to a dormitory.[76] It is impossible to determine how sent-down youth assessed these offerings. But they can be understood, to invoke the parlance of the contemporary Me Too movement, as grooming: the engagement in acts of generosity or kindness that may well have made adolescent girls, far away from their own families and relatives, feel cared for, protected, and willing to please in return.

One might wonder how and why a campaign triggered by reports of sexual abuse committed by high-level cadres on state farms became, instead, an investigation of relatively powerless local men. It is possible that in the context of sent-down youth on production brigades, there were far fewer occasions for contact with high-level officials than would have been the case on state or military farms, neither of which were populated by locals. It is also possible that male villagers were being scapegoated for the powerful cadres accused of sexual assault, cases of which were likely more numerous than the highly publicized ones who were executed. Finally, given that this all took place in the context of a state campaign that mandated local officials to produce numerous cases, even if they were not issued quotas, quite probably those officials would seek the least powerful and vulnerable individuals to fill their lists of perpetrators. Such officials were hardly likely to list themselves, which would help account for the absence of powerful cadres in the ranks of abusers charged and punished in this campaign.

[73] Hanjiang xian gong'an ju Hanjiang 寒江县公安局, "Guanyu 1969 yi lai daji pohai xiaxiang qingnian de qingkuang" 关于 1969 年以来打击迫害下乡青年的情况 (Case Files of Cracking Down on Sent-Down Youth Abuse since 1969), 1974, HJCA.
[74] Hanjiang county case no. 51, reported on March 20, 1973, sentenced on April 21, 1973.
[75] Hanjiang county case no. 50.   [76] Hanjiang county case nos. 65, 67.

If, in the context of this campaign, male villagers were the majority of those found guilty, the women identified as victims were invariably sent-down youth. This is most conspicuous in the cases involving female sent-down youth who had been labeled in *weiwentuan* reports as "hoodlums," who in some instances engaged in sex work, receiving monetary payment from locals in exchange for sex. These attributes are absent in the actual case reports on sexual misconduct, which instead focus on the multiple male villagers by whom they were sexually abused. One youth was identified as the victim of three men who received jail sentences of ten, four, and three years. Another female sent-down youth was deemed the victim of four sexual abusers: two received a sentence of five years in jail, one received one year, and one received probational education. A third female sent-down youth was the subject of investigations involving three local men, one of whom was sentenced to death. The fourth woman was victimized by at least two local men, who were sentenced to five and seven years in jail. And the fifth was reported as having been abused by two men, one sentenced to two years in jail, the other seven. A last woman was deemed victim of two men, who received jail sentences of ten to fifteen years. Most of these criminals were not charged with rape, but with sexual molestation (*jianwu*) of sent-down youth or of luring them into sex (*youjian*), in each case multiple times.[77] Although the earlier reports had identified some of these women as asking for money from the village men with whom they had sexual relations, in the 1973 criminal investigation the local men were now accused of luring these women into sex.[78] And in the one case that noted that the sent-down youth had a reputation as a "loose woman," county leaders concluded she had been "seduced by class enemies" and transferred her to a different village for "ideological education."[79]

Although these women are not typical of all the women involved in cases of sexual relationships, they highlight that those labeled as victims in this campaign were always female sent-down youth. As historians, our point is not to endorse the views of some members of the *weiwentuan* or of other sent-down youth who had suggested that some of these women should be the subject of punishment. Instead, these cases highlight that *who* mattered more than the nature of the "crime" during this campaign. While in the earlier stages of the sent-down youth

[77] HJCOSY, "Jianwu pohai zhishi qingnian tongji mingxibiao." Also see HJCOSY, "Shangshan xiaxiang zhishi qingnian zaoshou pohai anjian biao."

[78] "Hanjiang xian weiwen jiancha tuan gongzuo huibao tigang," 寒江县慰问检查团工作汇报提纲 (Outline of Work Report of the *Weiwen* and Investigation Team), July 1970, November 17, 1972, HJCA.

[79] HJOSY, "Jianwu pohai zhishi qingnian tongji mingxibiao" and "Hanjiang xian zhiqing ban baogao" 寒江县知青办报告 (Report of Hanjiang County Office of Sent-Down Youth), 1974, HJCA.

movement, report writers (especially *weiwentuan* members from Shanghai) were careful to not tarnish the image of the "poor and lower-middle peasants" in their reports, during the 1973 campaign, when the movement aimed to protect urban youth from sexual assault by rural men, the accounts now demonized the rural men.

Male sent-down youth who engaged in sexual relations with female sent-down youth or village women were exempted from criminalization. The few whose activities were exposed rarely received serious punishment. In Micang county, one male youth from Shanghai was accused of having had sex with a number of sent-down youth. He confessed to relations with two, one becoming pregnant. He insisted that the sexual relationships had been consensual, but admitted that assuming responsibility for obtaining an abortion was a mistake, one that violated the law and reflected his moral bankruptcy. Unlike locals who would have been sentenced to jail, this male sent-down youth was not subject to any criminal charges, but simply transferred to a different brigade and required to "study" for two months and submit a written confession. In the end, he was actually praised by a local official who declared that his determination to "start all over" should "be welcomed."[80] The double standard is also evident in another case in the same county. Two male sent-down youth had sexual relationships with one female sent-down youth, resulting in her becoming pregnant twice. Although this attracted the attention of local officials and the youth were labeled abusers, they were not treated as criminals. The county sent-down youth office, in a note to Shanghai's Putuo district office, justified this leniency, stating that the case "is absolutely not rape at knifepoint."[81] Had the men been peasants, whether or not they used a knife to have sex would have been irrelevant; the fact that she became pregnant both times would have most likely ensured severe criminal punishment.

Even young men labeled "hoodlum-types" from Shanghai seemed exempt from criminalization for sexual exploits. A seven-page report from some cadres visiting in Micang county described such male "hoodlums" as "especially dangerous to female sent-down youth." The report stated that some of the urban women abused by these hoodlums were afraid to report their experiences and therefore returned to Shanghai and never came back.[82] Although this report was forwarded to the county head, there is no indication that these sent-down youth "hoodlums" were

[80] Statement by XX, July 22, 1973, MCCA.
[81] MCCOSY, "Guanyu pohai zhishi qingnian anjian cailiao," July 22, 1973, MCCA.
[82] The letter was dated August 14, 1973, during the campaign and was forwarded to the head of the county. MCCA.

ever investigated or punished.[83] These incidents involving male sent-down youth, few and far between, suggest that the target of the 1973 campaign was not to identify criminals per se, but to criminalize rural males who had intimate relations with sent-down youth.

The group of victims most conspicuously absent in investigation reports during the campaign are village women, who could also have been subjected to unwanted sexual advances. Instead, the few accounts that include any references to female locals portray them as quasi-abusive. One, after discovering her carpenter husband having sex with a Shanghai sent-down youth, is said to have grabbed a knife, gone to the village where the Shanghai youth lived, and slashed her face.[84] One of the few other village women who appears in investigative reports was sentenced to five years in jail for having "undermined the sent-down youth movement" by encouraging a female sent-down youth to marry her brother who was serving a jail sentence for sexually abusing the youth, perhaps with the hope of having his sentence reduced.[85]

Adulterous sexual relations between male and female villagers, as well as rape, were probably far more frequent than between local males and female sent-down youth. Investigative reports inadvertently reveal that some of the accused local men had records of having engaged in sex outside marriage prior to the arrival of sent-down youth, such as one, described as having a reputation as a "womanizer," who had been criticized and "educated" for his "improper" relationships with five village women, one only seventeen years old. His "erroneous" behavior was never criminalized until 1973, when he was exposed not for these past problematic encounters, but for having sex with a female sent-down youth, for which he was sentenced to four years in jail.[86] To whatever extent male villagers or male sent-down youth subjected local women to inappropriate sexual relations, no one was criminalized for such incidents in the campaign. Nor are the complaints of local women recorded in the investigative reports.

---

[83] Of all the cases of abuse compiled in 1973 by Hanjiang county office of sent-down youth, only one involved a male sent-down youth who received a jail sentence. He was described as a *liumang* before being sent to Hanjiang in March 1969. He had a record of being arrested for theft in Shanghai as well as in Hanjiang for stealing goods from local stores and pickpocketing at the train station and at movie theaters. He also had sex with at least four female sent-down youth. He was sentenced to five years in jail, although it is unclear when he was arrested and whether this was for stealing or for the sexual relationships (or both). HJCOSY, "Shangshan xiaxiang zhishi qingnian zaoshou pohai anjianbiao," February 5, 1974, and "Jianwu pohai zhishi qingnian tongji mingxibiao," May 22, 1975, HJCA.

[84] HJCOSY, "Jianwu pohai zhishi qingnian tongji mingxibiao," May 22, 1975.   [85] Ibid.

[86] HJCOSY, February 5, 1974. "Shangshan xiaxiang zhishi qingnian zaoshou pohai anjianbiao."

The 1973 campaign did offer some modicum of protection to female sent-down youth who might be subjected to unwanted sexual advances and abuse. Before 1973 there were women who screamed, fled, and said "no" when confronted by male villagers who grabbed them, tried to kiss them, touched their breasts, flirted, exposed themselves, and sometimes attempted to rape them. At most, male villagers might have been subject to criticism for these acts. But the 1973 directive and campaign issued a clear message that such assaults would be criminalized and punished by jail sentences.

Conclusion

Both scholarly and popular accounts of the sent-down youth movement often dwell on the sexual abuse of female sent-down youth as symbolic of the victimization of women, if not the suffering of all Chinese people, during the Cultural Revolution. But both the extent and the nature of sexual abuse in the sent-down youth movement have a profoundly different meaning when we recognize that administrative reports of abuse were the product of a political campaign. Like almost all campaigns during the first three decades of the PRC— land reform (1947–1952), the anti-rightist movement (1957), and the Four Cleanups campaign (1964)—the 1973 campaign was a top-down project initiated by the central government, employing the dispatchment of work teams, pressure on individuals to confess, and the punishment of guilty individuals. Under these circumstances, local communities and law enforcement agencies conflated criminal and immoral behaviors. County records reveal a dizzying range of sexual interactions, including flirtation, seduction, affairs, sexual harassment, and assault, all of which were subject to criminal charges and punishment.

Our point is not to deny, or even minimize, the extent to which rape and assault took place in villages where sent-down youth were sent. However, the incidents we are able to hear about are from accounts generated under very particular circumstances. One thing obscured in all of this is a shifting power dynamic: urban young women were undoubtedly vulnerable to assault in the countryside, but many rural men (not necessarily the assaulters) were vulnerable to victimization by the state in the course of a cleanup campaign. It was most likely easier to incarcerate rural men than to contend with the impoverishment of the countryside or admit that the sent-down youth program was a systemic failure. This means that we will never know the true extent of sexual assault during the movement, and that the record we do have tells us more about state priorities than it does about who was sleeping with/dating/assaulting/harassing/raping whom.

As the sexual victimization of female sent-down youth became symbolic of the bankruptcy of the movement, the demonization of male peasants became emblematic of the impossibility of crossing the divide between urban and rural China. While the campaign may well have provided protection for female sent-down youth from the sexual advances of rural males, it simultaneously reinforced the divide between urban and rural residents. All the investigations, charges, and punishments served as a constant reminder that sent-down youth and peasants were entirely different. They aimed to quell the potential for intimate, let alone abusive, relationships between urban youth and locals, and the equally disturbing possibility that urban girls might be encouraged to marry rural men, thereby committing themselves to permanent rural residence. And so, although the ideal of the sent-down youth movement was to bridge the gap between city and countryside, between urban residents and peasants, the investigations of sexual assault of female sent-down youth had the result of both reifying and perpetuating that gap. Regardless of its intent, the campaign reinforced both class and gender hierarchies, while generating the only contemporaneous record we have.

5   Urban Outposts in Rural China

The directives of 1973 and the campaign to criminalize abusers of sent-down youth raised serious questions about the principles of the sent-down youth movement: the wisdom of having urban youth live in close proximity with villagers and the role of villagers as their educators. As discussed in Chapter 2, from 1971 on, mobilization of sent-down youth in Shanghai no longer aimed to send urban youth to live in remote rural villages with locals, but instead focused on assigning them to state farms administered by Shanghai. In subsequent years, the city also intensified efforts to help those still on rural production teams. In addition to providing material goods that would facilitate the construction of small factories and sent-down youth stations, it launched projects to promote education and technical training for these youth to position them for skilled positions in rural communities. Although these programs were ostensibly initiated to support the sent-down youth movement, they inadvertently contributed to the separation of sent-down youth and villagers, and to the creation of a class of educated and skilled rural residents who, for all intents and purposes, constituted quasi-colonial outposts of Shanghai in the countryside.

"Shanghai Barbarians"

The rationale for the sent-down youth movement was for peasants to "re-educate" urban youth and for urban youth to live with and like peasants. Many sent-down youth fondly recall skills they learned from their rural hosts. One youth sent to Huaibei remembered learning to till the extremely hard soil, harvest wheat, build houses, and carry heavy loads:

At first, when I carried water [on a shoulder pole], I would fill the two buckets only halfway but still could not stand up. My body would be bent over and it was very painful. All the peasants laughed at us. But eventually I could carry 120 *jin* of grain from the field to the storage shed.[1]

---

[1] Fan Kangming, "Jieshou zai jiaoyu" (Receiving Re-education), in Fan Kangming, Yang Jidong, and Wu Hao, 47. One *jin* is 500 grams.

Another youth admitted suffering, but having had "a lot of fun" and learning a lot from the locals in northern Heilongjiang:

I learned to collect pine nuts, cut soy, drive the horse cart, build houses with lumber, and raft lumber for transport ... In those days we admired the people in the countryside: they were extremely capable and could do all kinds of jobs perfectly. When I first arrived, I didn't even know how to fetch water from a well.[2]

Another Shanghai youth described the joy of learning from locals how to catch fish in the river using hooks, flies, and nets, by digging holes in the ice in winter and building small dams in the summer.[3] Another was especially proud of learning to milk cows: locals taught her how to use warm towels to clean the teats, massage them, and avoid being kicked by cows annoyed by mosquitos. "Learning to milk cows was not easy," she explained, expressing gratitude to the villager who helped and encouraged her.[4]

Even though some youth pledged to make the countryside their permanent home and eventually mastered some skills in agricultural labor, locals perceived them as foreigners. As Jeremy Brown points out, individuals in Mao's China, based on clothing, food, language, and skin color, could be recognized as urban or rural "at first glance."[5] It is therefore not surprising that rural residents laughed at the physical awkwardness of urban youth, or jokingly referred to them as strange outsiders. Living in a Huaibei village, one sent-down youth recalled, "Whenever they saw Shanghai youth walking, even from very far away, they could tell we were not locals and would yell, 'The barbarians are coming!'"[6] This hardly offended the urban youth, who desperately clung to their identity as Shanghainese. Their closest bonds were with other youth from Shanghai, as they befriended those whom they discovered had grown up in their neighborhood, had gone to the same school, and spoke the same dialect. When some eventually obtained jobs in the commune or county seat, they would offer meals and lodging to other youth from Shanghai. And when sent-down youth faced difficulties, it was other Shanghai youth to whom they turned for help or comfort. Even villagers recognized the importance of this shared background, so when three

---

[2] Chen Jianhua, "Zhiqing shengya zaji" (Life as a Sent-Down Youth), in Liu Shijie, *Huma zhiqing fengyunlu*, 321–325.

[3] Cheng Yunting, "Puyu lixianji" (Fishing Adventures), in Liu Shijie, *Huma zhiqing fengyunlu*, 174–176.

[4] Chen Liming, "Niu yuan" (My Destiny: Cows), in Liu Shijie, *Huma zhiqing fengyunlu*, 180.

[5] Brown, "Spatial Profiling."

[6] Fan Kangming, "Shanghai manzi" (Shanghai Barbarian). In Fan Kangming, Yang Jidong, and Wu Hao, 49–53.

youth from Shanghai refused to speak, eat, or open their luggage upon arrival in Huaibei, locals sought nearby Shanghai youth to help. Hearing the familiar Shanghai dialect, these "three barbarian girls" stopped crying.[7]

The bonds sent-down youth formed among themselves were accompanied by a refusal to surrender their identity as educated urbanites. They noticed almost every aspect of their physical appearance as distinct from that of villagers. "It was extremely easy to distinguish sent-down youth from locals just by looking at how they dressed," one Shanghai youth recalled.

Sent-down youth wore tailored clothes, fashionable styles ... Even worn-out clothes with patches were elegant. Peasant clothes were simple and had no style. It didn't matter whether male or female; they dressed in black, gray, and blue. Some of their clothes were made of home-woven cloth ... If you pass through a village, you could tell from the laundry hanging outside whether there were sent-down youth.[8]

Daily routines also manifested differences between sent-down youth and locals. After work, many villagers would immediately go to work on their private plot. Sent-down youth, in contrast, would wash, put on clean clothes if possible, and rest. When they had free time, they might entertain themselves by playing chess, cards, or musical instruments; by playing soccer, table tennis, or basketball; by reading, listening to the radio, and writing letters to family and friends. In some places, they would go to local schools or offices to read the newspaper.[9]

For sent-down youth, difference was accompanied by a sense of their own superiority, reflected in their skepticism about whether villagers were qualified to provide them with an education. One youth, assigned to make brick-like patties of mud mixed with wheat stalks that were used to construct buildings, wondered how this was supposed to constitute the re-education they were to receive from peasants. He complained that "we left our families and what we confronted was poverty, backwardness, and ignorance. Re-education returned us to a backward age."[10] A woman sent to Yunnan complained, "The Dai people were still in the Stone Age. They just planted the seeds and waited until it was time to

[7] Ibid.
[8] Zheng Yahong, "Zhiqing yi: Shangshan xiaxiang shi kan yizhuo chayi qufen zhiqing yu nongmin" (Reflections of a Sent-Down Youth: Differentiating Sent-Down Youth and Peasants by Their Clothing), April 24, 2014, http://history.sohu.com/20140424/n3987 46630.shtml, accessed 20 July 2016.
[9] Xu Feng, 51.
[10] Fan Kangming, "Di yi ci chugong" (The First Time I Went to Work), in Fan Kangming, Yang Jidong, and Wu Hao, 30–32; Fan Kangming, "Jieshou zai jiaoyu," 43–48.

harvest."[11] Losing their urban identity and superiority was sometimes disturbing to sent-down youth, as described by one assigned to feed horses and cows with an old deaf man in Huaibei. "After about three months," he recalled, "I did not have even a whiff of a Shanghai smell."[12]

This sense of urban identity among sent-down youth was reinforced by the Shanghai *weiwentuan*, whose efforts focused specifically on those from Shanghai. The *weiwentuan* advocated for Shanghai youth, urging locals to promote them, give them job opportunities, or recommend them for college admission slots. One Shanghai cadre who spent seven years in Huma did not think his time in remote Heilongjiang was wasted, as he and his colleagues protected the Shanghai youth from being bullied by the locals.[13] The presence and work of the *weiwentuan* conveyed to sent-down youth that they still belonged to Shanghai and were different from rural dwellers as well as from sent-down youth from other regions.

One way for sent-down youth to maintain their identity as educated urbanites was to position themselves as the educators of their rural hosts, often manifested by a determination to introduce new farming methods. In this context, they participated in what Sigrid Schmalzer calls "socialist China's rural scientific experiment movement." She rightfully points out that, although for some, engaging in experiments may have been an "amusing diversion" from the hardship of life on a production brigade, for many it was "both revolutionary and intellectual" and offered them an opportunity "to accomplish something important."[14] While her focus is on the contradictions youth confronted between book learning and the experience-based wisdom of rural farmers, we are more concerned with the ways in which attempts by sent-down youth to improve farming methods both reflected and contributed to their identity in villages as an educated elite, as well as with the critical role of their families and institutions in Shanghai in their ability to engage in these endeavors. In a production brigade in Anhui, Shanghai youth Zhang Ren found that the locals tended to be suspicious of new crop varieties. To overcome their

[11] Interview with Chen Sheng.
[12] Yang Jidong, "Zui manchang de yige dongtian" (The Longest Winter), in Fan Kangming, Yang Jidong, and Wu Hao, 319–322.
[13] Interview with Chen Jiang.
[14] Schmalzer, *Red Revolution, Green Revolution*, 23–24, 196–197. She asserts that roughly one-third of sent-down youth participated in scientific experimentation. In addition, she points out that when urban youth went to production brigades following Mao's 1968 directive, they joined "a 'revolutionary movement' already in progress: rural, returned youth," who were active participants in scientific experiments in the countryside. See Sigrid Schmalzer, "Youth and the 'Great Revolutionary Movement' of Scientific Experiment in 1960s–1970s Rural China," in Brown and Johnson, *Maoism at the Grassroots*, 156.

ignorance, she experimented with new varieties of cotton and rice on her own small plot of land, demonstrating the potential benefits of these new plants. Her efforts persuaded villagers to adopt new crops, which, by her own account at least, significantly increased productivity.[15] In Heilongjiang, where the growing season was short and farmers specialized in potatoes, turnips, onions, and cabbages, sent-down youth from Shanghai brought the seeds of southern vegetables and grew Chinese mustard greens (*xuelihong*) and cauliflower. They also successfully introduced a new strain of soybean to the village, enabling the youth and the locals to enjoy their own soy milk, tofu, and cooking oil, and generating a substantial income for the village as well.[16] One youth recalled forming a "scientific experiment team" with four of her classmates in Huma: "Our parents, from faraway Shanghai, sent us the materials we needed for these experiments." The team developed new varieties of wheat and soy on its experimental plot before villagers eventually adopted them to grow in the regular fields.[17]

Regardless of the fact that northeast China lacked wet fields, was covered with snow in winter, and had a very short growing season, some Shanghai youth determined that nothing would prevent them from growing rice, the staple of their southern diet. Most of these efforts failed. In spite of strong winds, thin soil, and early frosts, several youth at the Yixiken commune in Huma in 1972 began to experiment with rice cultivation on a half-*mu* of allocated land close to a pond and carried buckets of water to irrigate the field.[18] An unexpectedly early frost in August destroyed their crop. The next year, however, they began again. This time they acquired the most early-maturing and cold-tolerant seeds and recorded the plants' daily development. To keep the soil warm, they used pig waste instead of horse and cow manure and mixed in grass and wood ashes when sowing the seeds. They even kept the land wet at night and dry during the day to promote root growth. This extremely labor-intensive approach to agriculture, which produced 219 *jin* of rice that year, was praised and supported by commune leaders and highly publicized.[19] Stories such as this may well have been part and parcel of government propaganda that celebrated instances of individuals or

[15] Zhang Ren, "Wo zhege ren xihuan xinxian" (I Like to Try New Things), in Liu Xiaomeng, ed., *Zhongguo zhiqing koushu shi* (Beijing: Zhongguo kexue chubanshe, 2004), 22–55.
[16] Wang Shicheng, 214.
[17] Wang Jian, "Mobudiao de jiyi" (The Memory That Could Not Be Wiped Out), in Liu Shijie, *Huma zhiqing fengyunlu xuji*, 130–136.
[18] One *mu* is 0.16 acres.
[19] Li Xinquan, "Beiguo daoxiang: Huiyi Shanghai zhishi qingnian zai gaohan diqu shizhong shuidao chenggong de gushi" (A Story of Recalling the Shanghai Sent-Down Youth Who

collectives accomplishing the seemingly impossible. They nevertheless attest to the determination of sent-down youth to demonstrate their superior scientific knowledge (although the impossibility of cultivating rice in most parts of Heilongjiang would soon be recognized).

Barefoot Teachers and Doctors

It did not take long for locals to recognize that an urban upbringing and education made these "barbarians" potentially useful to them in ways beyond agricultural labor. Many youth possessed skills and tools that might have seemed ordinary in Shanghai but were uncommon and welcomed in villages. Their presence enabled many children in remote areas to have education. One Shanghai youth had been sent to a Jiangxi village where most of the 200 residents were illiterate. Village leaders assigned her to teach, even though there was no classroom. Instead, she taught twenty students in an outdoor field, and when it rained, they would relocate to a villager's home. Another Shanghai youth in Anhui taught in a mud hut; some students brought their young siblings who played in wooden buckets next to them.[20] Shanghai youth Zhu Kejia, a nationally publicized model sent-down youth, recalled that when he worked in a production brigade in Xishuangbanna in Yunnan, the head of a nearby Aini village beckoned him to go there to teach. Because no teacher was willing to live in the isolated mountain area, children in the village had no education at all until Zhu arrived, and his students included six- to seven-year-olds as well as teenagers. Having brought hair-cutting equipment with him from Shanghai, he served as a barber for the locals and also made furniture for schoolchildren. He was recognized by the locals as a teacher who brought "culture and knowledge" to the countryside.[21]

Sent-down youth with even the most rudimentary knowledge of medicine were often selected as barefoot doctors and thereby spared the hardship of full-time field labor. Before leaving for Yunnan, for example, one Shanghai youth, whose father was a doctor, learned from him how to give inoculations. He also gave her painkillers, fever reducers, antibiotic drops and cream, and bandages to take with her to the countryside. "This," she explained, "enabled me to become a barefoot doctor."[22] At a production brigade in Xunke, one woman was selected as a barefoot doctor because her mother taught

Succeeded in an Experiment with Rice Cultivation in a High-Altitude and Cold Region), in Liu Shijie, *Huma zhiqing fengyunlu xuji*, 680–685.
[20] Pei Yulin et al., 17, 19.   [21] Interview with Zhu Kejia.   [22] Interview with Xiao Qing.

Photo 5.1 Zhu Kejia (left), a model sent-down youth, was a schoolteacher in a remote Aini community in Xishuangbanna. He is pictured here with Mi Nei, who provided the Shanghai youth with maternal care, and Mi Po, Zhu's pupil, who later taught with him. Photo courtesy of Zhu Kejia.

Photo 5.2 Zhu Kejia during an interview with the authors in Kunming.
Photo by Zhao Jianchang.

at a medical school in Shanghai. When she left for college, her
younger sister inherited the position.[23]

In some cases, the skills and equipment brought from their urban
homes enabled sent-down youth to generate cash income. One
Shanghai youth, a schoolteacher in Le'an (Jiangxi), for example, traveled
to villages with his camera on his day off. Many of his clients had never
had a picture taken until then, although at that time making money on

---

[23] Chen Xiaofang (untitled), in Pei Yuling et al., 12.

one's own was frowned upon and his colleagues at the school thought he should focus on teaching.[24] Another youth in the same county made a living repairing sewing machines and scales, a skill he learned from his father while in Shanghai. With tools and hardware supplies brought from Shanghai, he traveled from one commune to another, fixing scales for branch divisions of the county's grain bureau. A few neighboring counties also called on him for services from time to time. This skill allowed him to make a living in the countryside.[25] Two youth in Heilongjiang brought from Shanghai a machine to pop rice and corn. Instead of working in the fields, they went from village to village, earning more than ten yuan every day, a substantial amount at the time.[26]

More than anything else, it was the education urban youth had received in Shanghai that immediately distinguished them from their rural hosts, most of whom were almost illiterate. Even with no formal technical training, literate and educated youth provided an asset that rural areas would not ordinarily have had. This problem was most apparent in regions with low literacy rates. The Aini village in Xishuangbanna had purchased a sewing machine but no one knew how to use it until a sent-down youth from Shanghai arrived two years later.[27] All the efforts to acquire machinery and tools might prove useless without individuals who could read technical manuals. For precisely this reason, many communes and production brigades used sent-down youth to drive tractors or trucks or operate machinery. For example, the transportation team in Huma was composed primarily of sent-down youth. Transporting goods on narrow mountain roads in the long snowy winter season required not only good driving skills but also an ability to repair trucks in remote areas.[28] A Shanghai youth recalled the selection of sent-down youth for technical jobs when a flood-control project was launched in 1971:

We were in the class of 1969 and had had only six years of elementary education when the Cultural Revolution began. But in the Huaibei countryside, local youth had even less education and most were illiterate. So, the county irrigation bureau ordered each commune to provide a technician. Commune leaders believed that Shanghai youth had the most education so we were the ones selected.

[24] Interview with He Xinhua.   [25] Ibid.
[26] HHDOSY, "Zhiqing gongzuo zongjie baogao" 知青工作总结报告 (Summary Report for Sent-Down Youth Work), April 7, 1975, HHDA.
[27] Interview with Zhu Kejia.
[28] Wang Zelin, "Nanwang de di'er guxiang Shijiuzhan" (Remembering My Second Home Village in Shijiuzhan), in Liu Shijie, *Huma zhiqing fengyunlu xuji*, 83–85.

After two weeks of training, his job on the project involved issuing instructions to the workers.[29]

Their basic literacy marked sent-down youth as advantageous not only for jobs requiring technical knowledge, but also for staffing clerical and administrative positions in government offices. And in some cases, their artistic talents and athletic abilities made them desirable for other types of nonagricultural jobs. By scanning personal dossiers or through word of mouth, local officials identified those who had records of accomplishment as athletes, musicians, dancers, and actors. For instance, when some 1,000 Shanghai youth arrived in Lichuan county in Jiangxi in 1969, the county culture ensemble recruited twelve of them to work as performers, stage designers, and playwrights. Their participation enabled the county to organize full-length performances instead of the short skits of the past.[30] In addition to stage performances, sent-down youth were recruited for local sports teams, creative-writing groups, painting workshops, and broadcasting crews.

Rural regions aspiring to develop industry were especially interested in recruiting sent-down youth who had technical training. When officials in Huma learned that 104 graduates of technical schools in Shanghai had been sent to Inner Mongolia in 1969, they immediately went out of their way to negotiate with the Shanghai municipal government and the provincial government for their transfer to Huma. They succeeded in arranging for ninety-three to move. When the official from Huma met them, he explained that, situated at China's northern border, Huma had only a few very small factories and needed not just laborers but "talented people" to build national defense. "You are going to be the major force in Huma," he pronounced, "And we very much welcome you." Upon arrival, they were immediately sent to provide technical support and labor for the fledgling enterprises.[31] For example, when the Huma Yiziquan Electrical Power Plant was first established, the steam engine did not work efficiently and the boiler had to be cleaned by hand. Two Shanghai youth, one of whom had graduated from the Shanghai Chemical Industry Technical School, developed a solution that could be used to clean the boiler. To solve a problem with the water-softening process, a Shanghai youth read and translated material from a manual, based on which he built a new water-softening system that enabled the factory to produce water that exceeded

---

[29] Wu Hao, "Zai Huaibei shenghuo de rizi" (Days Living in Huaibei), in Fan Kangming, Yang Jidong, and Wu Hao, 368–370.

[30] N.a., "Chadui luohu shi Lichuan wengongtuan zhiqing de naxieshi" (Lichuan Performing Troupe during the Time of the Sent-Down Youth), www.redgx.com/hongse licheng/wenge/13553.html, accessed July 16, 2017.

[31] Feng Xiaoping, 182.

established quality standards. The same youth also designed a device to control the water level in the factory's water tank to prevent overflow.[32] Although these might appear to be minor projects, in remote regions lacking equipment and technical support, the presence of sent-down youth made a substantial impact on rural development.

Distance Learning

To assuage the discontent of city families whose sons and daughters were in the countryside and thereby deprived of educational opportunities, the Shanghai government, in the mid-1970s, instituted educational and technical training programs for its youth still on production brigades. One of the earliest types of programs consisted of training courses offered to Shanghai youth during their home visits. For example, from early 1974, the Yangshupu Power Plant offered short-term workshops to provide sent-down youth training in electronics.[33] According to a report, the one-month training class, which met for seven hours per day, had already been offered three times, with a total of 141 participants. Students learned how to install lighting circuits used in the countryside, switches of various types, and alternating-current motor connections. "When the sent-down youth finished the short-term training class," the report explained, "the power plant would mail written reports about their achievements to their communes and *weiwentuan*, so that local communities can be informed of their training in Shanghai and make best use of their skills." The program offered by the Yangshupu Power Plant was only one of many courses provided for sent-down youth. The Shanghai television station and the bureau of education sponsored a joint lecture series for youth on home visits to Shanghai. Some sixteen universities in Shanghai, co-ordinating with neighborhood committees, offered lectures in philosophy, political theory, literature, history, and science. They also offered training sessions in electrical work, carpentry, machinery repair, pesticide use, medicine, sewing, and hairdressing.[34]

---

[32] Pan Zhigen, "Wo wei dianchang zuo gongxian" (I Contributed to the Electric Power Plant), in Liu Shijie, *Huma zhiqing fengyunlu xuji*, 50–52.

[33] Shanghai shi geweihui gongjiaozu mishuzu 上海市革委会公交组秘书处, "Jiji zhichi zhishi qingnian shangshan xiaxiang zheyi xingshen shiwu, Yangshupu fa dian chang renzhen banhao huihu zhiqing diangong duan xun ban" 积极支持知识青年上山下乡这一新生事物，杨树浦发电厂认真办好回沪知青电工短训班 (Pro-actively Supporting the New Element of Sent-Down Youth: The Yangshupu Power Plant Offered Electronics Training Workshops for Sent-Down Youth Who Returned to Shanghai), *Gongjiao qing-kuang* 公交情况, 48, January 29, 1975, SHMA.

[34] Ibid.

These training courses in Shanghai were extremely popular, with some 200,000 sent-down youth enrolling during their home visits in 1974.[35] This overwhelming response is indicative of how almost any opportunity to acquire books and listen to radio broadcasts of course material, let alone participate in a class, was coveted by urban youth whose formal education had terminated at the beginning of the Cultural Revolution in 1966. Even if these training courses were narrow in scope and focused on subjects related to agricultural development, the opportunity to read texts and study represented an extraordinary privilege at that time.

As a result of the enthusiasm of sent-down youth to participate in workshops during their vacation time at home, institutions in Shanghai began to export classes of similar types to the countryside for the city's sent-down youth. These were ostensibly geared to address specific problems. "We learned," according to one report by the Shanghai Bureau of Education,

> that there is a shortage of people who can repair tractors. When a tractor broke, it had to be towed a long distance to the county to be repaired. Some areas do not have any understanding of scientific farming. They not only waste fertilizer and pesticides, but also fail to increase productivity. Some places need irrigation, but no one understands how to design the systems.[36]

With sent-down youth eager for educational opportunities, 200 teachers from Shanghai went to investigate five rural regions, on the basis of which they prepared course outlines and textbooks.[37] A number of academic institutions in Shanghai then began to offer workshops in rural areas. Jiaotong University offered a class on rubber tree cultivation in Xishuangbanna, a course on agricultural diesel engines in Heilongjiang and Jiangxi, and a meteorology class in Jingganshan (Jiangxi). Tongji University offered classes on agricultural irrigation in Anhui. In Wuyuan county, Jiangxi, the Shanghai No. 1 medical school offered a pharmaceutical class, while the Shanghai Traditional Chinese Medicine Academy offered a training program to sent-down youth in Jilin. And the liberal-arts Fudan University offered a course in political economy, aiming to integrate theory with practical problems in the countryside.[38]

[35] "Hanshou jiaoyu shi women de zeren," *Renmin ribao*, November 11, 1974.   [36] Ibid.
[37] Ibid.
[38] Guowuyuan kejiaozu 国务院科教组, "Shanghai gaoxiao wei shangshan xiaxiang qing-nian shiban hanshou jiaoyu de qingkuang" 上海高校为上山下乡青年试办函授教育的情况 (Report on Universities in Shanghai Offering Distance Education for Sent-Down Youth), *Jiaoyu geming jianbao* 教育革命简报, 83, June 25, 1974, SHMA. Also see Shanghai shi jiaoyuju hanshouzu 上海市教育局函授组, "Guangkuo tiandi xin daxue: Ji shangshan xiaxiang zhishi qingnian yeyu hanshou daxue" 广阔天地新大学：记上山下乡知识青年业余函授大学 (New Universities in the Vast Heaven and Earth: Report on the

Even if the courses were designed to address specific rural needs, they were clearly intended to benefit sent-down youth still there. Between 1974 and 1976, some 90,000 Shanghai sent-down youth enrolled in these classes. At a single commune in Anhui, 620 Shanghai youth participated.[39] As one 1974 report pointed out, "Many sent-down youth could not go to college and so they like the distance learning: it enables them to study in the countryside."[40] One woman recalled the intensity with which she and her classmates seized the opportunity to participate in classes offered by faculty from Shanghai. "The first day, the auditorium of the Party school was filled with sent-down youth, and many who arrived late sat in the open field outside ... We all worked so hard, taking notes, sharing notes. We treasured this opportunity and would never miss it." She explained that her course met only twice in a year, those enrolled studying on their own the rest of the time. To get to the class she had to sit on a tractor for more than ten *li*, during which she "vomited all the way" but still "went straight to class." With no chairs or desks, the students sat on the ground and took notes with paper on their knees.[41] A sent-down youth in Huaibei recalled a similar sense of excitement when he heard about the distance learning and had the opportunity to enroll. "Although in the past I liked to read, I never tried to analyze why the author wrote the book or its significance. But the course changed everything." He described his deep admiration for the professor from Shanghai whose simple outfit, old hat, long scarf, and glasses reminded him of a revolutionary leader of Yan'an days. "He instilled in us confidence and inspiration ... This was a turning point in my life." As a result of the course, he began to edit a newspaper, the *5/7 Bulletin*. From then on, he found that his position at the commune changed. "Because we were always busy writing and printing, the cadres at the commune began to look at us differently."[42]

More important than garnering the attention of local cadres, these courses dramatically increased the possibilities for Shanghai sent-down youth to assume nonagricultural jobs in the countryside. For example, a Shanghai sent-down youth in Jilin spent a year enrolled in a class on

Spare-Time Distance Learning for Sent-Down Youth), *Xuexi yu pipan* 学习与批判, 5, 1976, SHMA.

[39] Shanghai shi jiaoyuju hanshouzu.

[40] Guowuyuan kejiaozu, "Shanghai gaoxiao wei shangshan xiaxiang qingnian shiban hanshou jiaoyu de qingkuang," SHMA.

[41] Li Jianping, "Zhiqing shidai de 'chongdian'" (Getting a "Recharge" during the Era of Sent-Down Youth), http://shzq.net/jxpd/zqcd.html, accessed February 2, 2017.

[42] Fan Kangming, "Ma Lie jingdian zhuzuo hanshou duanxun ban" (Short-Term Distance-Learning Course on Selected Marxist and Leninist Works), in Fan Kangming, Yang Jidong, and Wu Hao, 89–100.

acupuncture and herbal medicine offered by the Shanghai Academy of
Traditional Medicine. He then visited every family in the county, providing treatment to 2,900 individuals.[43] Some Shanghai youth who completed a course on rural electronics were selected as electricians.[44] One
woman recalled that after completing a course on electronics offered by
Shanghai Normal University in Huma, she was put in charge of her
production brigade's electric mill and hydroelectric plant.[45] Even
a distance-learning course on sewing enabled a Shanghai youth in
Anhui to move from fieldwork to an indoor job as a seamstress at the
headquarters of a reservoir construction project. Eventually she garnered
a job at the county seat as a tailor.[46] Reports on long-distance courses
boasted more widespread achievements: "The 20,000 who completed
courses in politics have become leaders in political studies; the 10,000
who have completed courses in writing produce posters, engage in broadcast and other media work; the more than 10,000 who completed courses
on preventive medicine have become barefoot doctors and nurses."[47]

While these reports most likely aimed to affirm the ways in which urban
institutions were supporting the sent-down youth movement, they also
unwittingly convey the ways in which these programs provided educational advantages to urban youth. Perhaps to preclude such an interpreta-
tion, the reports emphasized that the graduates of these training courses
"were identical to ordinary laborers" and far different "from those elite
college graduates who have an attitude of superiority."[48] What emerges is
that distance-learning courses that might appear an innocuous effort to
mollify urban youth who, having been sent to the countryside, were
deprived of the educational opportunities they would ordinarily have
had, also reflect the determination of the Shanghai government to promote its youth to the most skilled occupations in local rural communities.
Moreover, instead of receiving education from peasants, urban youth
were learning from books published in Shanghai, and from teachers of
educational institutions in Shanghai.[49] These courses also contributed to
the determination of sent-down youth to maintain their status and

---

[43] Shanghai shi jiaoyuju hanshou zu, "Guangkuo tiandi da you zuowei."   [44] Ibid.
[45] Qiu Liyin, "Heilongjiang de huiyi" (Memories of Heilongjiang), in Liu Shijie, *Huma zhiqing fengyunlu*, 156.
[46] Interview with Xu Yi.   [47] Shanghai jiaoyuju hanshouzu.   [48] Ibid.
[49] Sent-down youth also had access to a vast range of publications that they could then take back to the countryside. In the early and mid-1970s, Chinese bookstores carried a plethora of technical books, including highly specialized books for senior engineers; translations of foreign books and articles; and books aimed at popularizing technology for workers, peasants, and educated youth. Books on scientific farming, fertilizer application, agricultural machinery and maintenance, animal husbandry, carpentry, and elementary medicine enabled sent-down youth to acquire technical information which they could then apply to the development of agriculture, industry, and medicine in the countryside.

identity as educated. It was, as one woman described it, a "recharge" for their education.[50]

An "Enterprise with Great Promise"

The training workshops and distance-learning courses offered by educational and industrial institutions in Shanghai intensified the gap between sent-down youth and locals, with the former gaining even more skills to qualify for jobs requiring literacy and technical training, the latter continuing to perform most of the field work. Meanwhile, a new means of separating sent-down youth from villagers emerged, one that involved physically distancing them from locals through the establishment of sent-down youth stations.

The impetus for the youth stations involved more than a simple desire to separate urban youth from rural residents. It reflected certain problems of the sustained presence of urban youth in villages. In many places, sent-down youth were unable to support themselves. In Xishuangbanna, for example, after four years in the countryside, many youth still depended on their parents in Shanghai for cooking oil and money to buy vegetables. The Shanghai *weiwentuan* reported that locals were unable to provide an acceptable standard of housing and food, and found it difficult to handle problems involving the urban youth. Responding to these complaints, the Xishuangbanna district government expressed its lack of confidence in the ability of local leaders to manage the Shanghai youth. Unable to support themselves in the countryside, a substantial number of youth stayed in Shanghai for long periods.[51] While local leaders had no means of preventing this, the presence of unemployed youth (many of whom were now in the their mid- to late twenties) in the city constituted a burden on both municipal government leaders and parents who most likely objected to their sons' and daughters' assignment to remote rural regions yet did not have the financial means to provide them long-term support in the city. The combination of open dissatisfaction by rural leaders and by urban residents made it imperative to consider alternative models for managing the sent-down youth whose official residence still belonged to production brigades.

As Shanghai government officials, as well as many other urban communities, sought alternative ways of conforming to Mao's directive to send youth to the countryside, the one that attracted widespread publicity

---

[50] Li Jianping, "Zhiqing shidai de 'chongdian'."
[51] XSBNDOSY, "Weiwentuan zhunbei baogao" 慰问团准备报告 (Report on Preparations of the *weiwentuan*), March 17, 1974, JHCA.

was initiated by Zhuzhou, an industrial city in Hunan. Beginning in 1972, urban factories and government bureaus created farms on nearby communes to which their children could be sent after graduating from high school. Cadres from the parents' work units led the youth on these farms, with a small number of local residents providing assistance. Zhuzhou government bureaus and factories provided materials and financial resources to build housing, dining services, and libraries for these youth farms. They also installed electricity, running water, and broadcast systems, and provided subscriptions to newspapers and magazines for the youth. When the "youth farms" needed materials such as fertilizer or equipment, as well as technical support and repair services, they could request these from the parents' work units. Some of these Zhuzhou bureaus organized employees to join their children working on the farms during planting and harvest seasons. Even commune leaders liked this model because it provided them unprecedented access to urban resources. For instance, when the Huanglong commune suffered an infestation of insects, the Zhuzhou Electric Power Plant (which had established a youth farm on the commune) dispatched technicians to install some 300 black lights to control the insect problem.[52]

Two years after it began, with some 276 of these farms for urban youth established in the surrounding countryside, the Zhuzhou model became widely publicized. The *Renmin ribao* described it as "an enterprise with great promise," one that "provided satisfaction to the youth, and their parents, as well as the peasants." Urban governments throughout China adopted the Zhuzhou model with great enthusiasm, and many urban work units established their own youth farms on communes not too far from the city.[53]

Like the Shanghai state farms, the Zhuzhou model reflects local efforts to create methods of sending youth to the countryside that insulated them from the harshness of life in remote rural regions. They were sent to the countryside and learned a modicum of agricultural work, but had almost no contact with villagers, let alone education by them. Publicity in the *Renmin ribao* suggests the government's endorsement of this diminished form of "peasant re-education" as well as acknowledgement that the sent-down youth movement might not be continued in its original form.

Recent scholarship highlights the Zhuzhou model as an effort to assert more strict control over youth in the countryside, as well as a major attempt by the central government to revive the flailing sent-down youth movement.[54] The model did utilize both urban and rural resources to support the movement, and the number of youth sent to the

---

[52] *Renmin ribao*, June 12, 1974.   [53] Ibid.   [54] Bonnin, 94.

countryside appeared to increase, so long as these suburban "farms" counted as "the countryside." It helped solve some problems that had emerged in the early years of the movement. Affiliation with state enterprises provided youth in the countryside a sense of security and insulated them from the harshness of rural life. However, the Zhuzhou model signified a departure from the original ideals of the movement, disavowing the honored role of peasants as educators and, if anything, representing an effort to limit contact between urban youth and their rural hosts. The farms established in communes near Zhuzhou were economically independent, supported by urban resources unavailable to their neighboring villages. Sending urban cadres to lead these farms subverted rural jurisdiction. In other words, as with the state farms, the urban youth could live in the countryside and perform agricultural tasks without having any direct contact with rural residents. As the Nenjiang vice secretary of the Party so succinctly put it, the stations made it possible to "go down to the countryside without leaving the city." Although this Nenjiang official praised the Zhuzhou model for making peasants and workers relatives, he pointed out that some commune and production brigade leaders used the pretext of establishing these stations to demand money and equipment from urban units whose youth they were now accommodating. This, he complained, was "almost like asking for tips in a capitalist society."[55]

Once the central government sanctioned the Zhuzhou model, Shanghai government bureaus initiated and supported the establishment of stations for sent-down youth still on production brigades. One youth station in Nancheng county, Jiangxi, for example, accommodated thirty sent-down youth from Shanghai who had originally been assigned to different villages. The station had two newly built houses (one for males, one for females). The only local at this station was from a nearby village and was assigned by the commune to cook for them and teach them how to grow their own vegetables. In order for the sent-down youth to become self-sufficient, the commune authorized them to grow crops such as watermelon for the market, and to acquire machines to manufacture boxes for shipping oranges.[56] These privileges were not shared by other nearby villages, as they were required to grow grain for the state.

To Shanghai youth who had been sent to some of the most poverty-stricken parts of China, the sent-down youth stations represented an oasis. One at the Guanji commune in Huaibei brought together the

---

[55] NJCOSY, "Zuohao zhishi qingnian shangshan xiaxiang dongyuan he anzhi gongzuo" 做好知识青年上山下乡动员和安置工作 (Doing Good Work Mobilizing and Settling Sent-Down Youth), September 9, 1974, NJCA.

[56] Interview with Wang Pei.

nine scattered Shanghai youth who remained in the countryside. One youth, Yang Jidong, recalled that youth sent from other regions were left in the village when he and his classmates from Shanghai moved to the privileged youth station where they were provided grain for the first year and allotted land and a tractor. The building for the youth "looked very grand!" he recalled. Built entirely of brick, it had a meeting room, a kitchen, a storage room for grain and tools, and dormitories. "The rooms were many times bigger than in the village, and the brick building was almost as nice as the county government guest house. It was like a mirage to us." Although, unlike the state farms, the station did not provide youth a stipend, Yang recalled that they had three meals a day, could live together, and engaged in a range of activities.

It was so much better than in the village . . . As for what we would grow on the 20 *mu* or how to increase productivity—these are questions we never even considered. Every day we sat under the sun; the female youth knitted sweaters; boys played chess and cards . . . To us, it was a pretty good time.[57]

A more widespread form of sent-down youth station centered on the establishment of small factory workshops in the countryside. Many of these were initially proposed by members of the *weiwentuan* from Shanghai. For instance, based on a recommendation by the *weiwentuan* in 1975, the Shanghai government sent a seventeen-member team to Ganzhou and Jingganshan in Jiangxi to develop a plan for seventy-five small industries in these two regions. They requested that the Shanghai government provide equipment for these factories and forty-five trucks for transportation.[58] The *weiwentuan* in three other Jiangxi districts also advocated that Shanghai donate equipment for additional factories. A year later, the Shanghai Office of Sent-Down Youth reported to the municipal government that the experiences in Jiangxi "demonstrate that small workshops can centralize scattered sent-down youth" and also solve their problem of self-sufficiency. The Shanghai government announced its intention to build some 500 workshops in Jiangxi, Yunnan, and Jilin.[59]

---

[57] Yang Jidong, "Zai zhidian de rizi li" (My Days in the Sent-Down Youth Station), in Fan Kangming, Yang Jidong, and Wu Hao, 287.

[58] SHMOSY, "Shanghai shi geweihui gongjiaozu" 上海市革委会公交组 (To Shanghai Municipal Public Transportation Group), July 17, 1975, SHMA. And Shanghai shi geweihui gongjiaozu 上海市革委会公交组, "Guanyu zhiyuan benshi zhishi qingnian shangshan xiaxiang diqu de jishu gengxin yong jichuang, dianji de tongzhi" 关于支援本市知识青年上山下乡地区的技术更新用机床、电机的通知 (An Announcement about Machines and Engines to Be Used to Support Regions of Our City's Sent-Down Youth and Technological Improvement), September 24, 1975, SHMA.

[59] SHMOSY, "Guanyu 1976 nian zhiyuan shangshan xiaxiang qingnian suozai diqu wuzi he ban xiaozuofang de baogao" 关于 1976 年支援上山下乡青年所在地区物资和办小作

Like the sent-down youth stations, the establishment of these work-shops aimed to address some of the problems of settling youth in the countryside. In some ways, they were even more desirable to sent-down youth: the work was completely severed from agricultural labor and they were provided housing. Although these workshops belonged to the commune collectives, workers could expect a salary that far exceeded the value of work points. At a 1976 meeting, *weiwentuan* leaders explained that these workshops aimed "to solve the problems of Shanghai sent-down youth, not to develop commune and production brigade enterprises in general." They hailed this model as "a new path" and "the right direction."[60] Although not explicitly articulated, this "new path," far more than any other configurations for sent-down youth in the countryside, was sponsored by the Shanghai government, which directed the provision of equipment and skilled technicians as needed. The sent-down youth were working in enterprises that were essentially satellites of Shanghai. The role of peasants was all but eliminated.

Conclusion

With the establishment of sent-down youth stations and workshops, the spirit and practice of the sent-down youth movement had clearly changed. "Going to the village" (*chadui*), particularly for Shanghai youth, now could mean assignment to a special youth brigade supported by a small number of urban cadres and very few locals, or to a factory workshop that completely removed urban youth from agricultural production. In either context, Shanghai youth could be protected from the commonplace hardships of rural life, making it even more clear that they were "Shanghai people," or *Shanghai ren*.

The separation of sent-down youth from rural residents represented by the stations and workshops might at first glance seem a precipitous change in the movement. However, from the beginning, even when sent-down youth lived and worked on production brigades, their identity and experiences were always distinct from those of villagers. Even if compromised by the Cultural Revolution, their education marked them as different, and positioned them to assume the most skilled jobs in rural communities where the majority of residents were either illiterate or had little education.

坊的报告 (Report Concerning the Provision of Materials for the Regions with Sent-Down Youth and Establishing Small Workshops in 1976), SHMA.

[60] SHMOSY, "Guanyu zhaokai xuexi weiwentuan he xuexi gongzuozu fuzeren huiyi" 关于召开学习慰问团和学习工作组负责人会议 (Regarding the Conference of the Heads of the *weiwentuan* and Work Group Discussion), July 21, 1976, SHMA.

This intellectual advantage was accentuated by programs instituted by the Shanghai government, including the training workshops for youth on home visits and distance-learning programs for youth in the countryside. These may not have represented the kind of higher education that urban youth would have most wanted, particularly their emphasis on technical knowledge suited for rural conditions. But at a time when opportunities to enroll in college were extremely limited, many youth took advantage of these programs. Particularly since these programs were brought to the countryside by the Shanghai government, to participate was itself a privilege. Although a large number of youth remained in the countryside for many more years, these training programs and the efforts to establish sent-down youth stations and workshops enabled them to live and work in ways distinct from villagers.

Although sent to the countryside to receive peasant re-education and to live in villages like peasants, many sent-down youth instead were able to live and work in jobs of a much higher status than agricultural labor. This status certainly reflected the fact that these youth had more education than the locals, but it was also the product of an intensified intervention of Shanghai institutions in the sent-down youth movement.

This clearly benefited sent-down youth, and mitigated the hardships of life in the countryside. At the same, however, it increased the dependency of Shanghai youth on urban resources. The equipment, housing, and educational resources that Shanghai government bureaus provided for youth in the countryside were clearly far beyond anything their rural communes and villages could have imagined, highlighting the gap between urban and rural China, making it even less likely that urban youth would want to "set their roots" in the countryside. And so, as we shall see in the next chapter, very few Shanghai youth hesitated when opportunities to return to the city became available.

6   Things Fall Apart

Toward the end of 1978, sent-down youth commanded national attention when those on state farms began to organize open protests demanding that the central government allow them to return to their urban homes. In Yunnan, where some of the most dramatic protests began, some 50,000 sent-down youth organized a movement that included petitions, strikes, and demonstrations. They took over administration buildings; seized broadcast systems; and staged work stoppages, a hunger strike, and an occupation of railroad tracks. Some boarded a train to Beijing, where they held a silent vigil with banners declaring their demand to return to the cities. By early 1979, sent-down youth in numerous cities and provinces were involved in organized protests, forcing the government to engage in a dialogue with their representatives.[1]

Many studies of sent-down youth treat these events as representing the beginning of widespread "returning to the city" by sent-down youth and the subsequent end of the movement.[2] The movement, however, did not end abruptly in the wake of the protests. Instead, by the time the 1978 protests broke out, the movement had already been undermined, modified, and nearly dismantled by widespread and long-term interventions involving sent-down youth themselves, their parents, and both urban and rural government officials. For those sent to production brigades, the unraveling of the movement and the large-scale efforts of youth to leave the countryside have a history that began long before the death of Mao Zedong, the fall of the Gang of Four, and the newsworthy state farm

---

[1] One of the most detailed and widely circulated accounts of the protests is by one of its leaders, Ding Huimin. See Ding Huimin, "Banna zhiqing zai xingdong" (Sent-Down Youth in Action in Xishuangbanna), in Liu Xiaomeng, ed., *Zhongguo zhiqing koushu shi*, 390–441.

[2] See Thomas Gold, "Back to the City: The Return of Shanghai's Educated Youth," *China Quarterly*, 84 (1980), 755–770; Anne McLaren, "The Educated Youth Return: The Poster Campaign in Shanghai from November 1978 to March 1979," *Australian Journal of Chinese Affairs*, 2 (1979), 1–20. Bin Yang, "'We Want to Go Home!' The Great Petition of the *Zhiqing*, Xishuangbanna, Yunnan, 1978–1979," *China Quarterly*, 198 (June 2009), 401–421.

protests of the late 1970s. By the time of the 1978 national conference that triggered the state farm protests, the overwhelming majority of Shanghai youth on production brigades had either already left rural areas or were in the process of securing permission to go back to their urban homes.

The collapse of the program to settle urban youth in remote villages was a gradual process that took place over the course of a decade. It began when youth found ways to leave the countryside and culminated in the mid-1970s when the demand to return to Shanghai intensified. During this period of gradual dissolution of the program, both urban and rural cadres became more outspoken in questioning the goals of the movement and the viability of accomplishing the tasks they had been assigned.

The Situation "Is Not Normal"

The unraveling of the movement began the moment opportunities were created for sent-down youth to leave village production teams. As discussed earlier, as soon as youth from large cities arrived in the countryside, local government offices, agencies, and bureaus, as well as schools, health clinics, and factories, began to recruit them for jobs for which their literacy and urban education were an asset. Those with special talents, skills, or family connections, or those who had been deemed model youth because of their hard work and ideological commitment, were the first to be picked. A smaller number were selected to join the military or enroll in the extremely limited college programs. Parents mustered whatever personal connections they had to help arrange for their sons and daughters to leave. In Yunnan, by 1971, of the 9,524 youth sent from Shanghai to village production brigades, close to two-thirds had been recruited.[3]

During these early years, the Shanghai government did not recruit youth on production teams for jobs in Shanghai itself in large part because of the very unemployment problems that had plagued the municipality at the time of Mao's 1968 directive. However, it made constant efforts to seize employment and educational opportunities for its youth who had been sent to villages. This was most blatantly manifested in its interventions in the recruitment of students for the "worker–peasant–soldier" college programs authorized by the central government in 1970.

---

[3] Yunnan sheng geming weiyuanhui, "Guanyu tuijian chengzhen xiaxiang zhishi qingnian canjia gongye caimao wenjiao deng gongzuo tongzhi," June 17, 1971. In Jingganshan (Jiangxi), 5,000 of the total 19,700 youth from Shanghai had left the villages for the same reasons. See Yu Yuxiang 虞玉祥, "Baogao" 报告 (Report), 1974, SHMA. Yu was the head of *weiwentuan* sent to Jiangxi's Jinggangshan district.

College admissions had been terminated at the beginning of the Cultural Revolution in 1966. When, in June 1970, the central government announced the opening of a limited number of college programs for workers, peasants, and soldiers, the Shanghai government strategized to use these programs to privilege its own sent-down youth. A minimum of three years of experience as a worker, peasant, or solder was required at first. In order to ensure that sent-down youth could qualify as peasants, the Shanghai government disputed the three-year eligibility requirement, arguing that "we would have very few sent-down youth who would qualify."[4] It also pointed out that the Beijing and Qinghua university models, on which the government's policy was based, included sent-down youth who had yet to accumulate three years of experience.[5]

The use of the worker–peasant–soldier college programs to bring some urban youth back to the city was explicit at Shanghai's prestigious Fudan University, which in fall 1970 announced the inauguration of twenty-two programs that would admit 1,025 students. As a national university, Fudan in the past had allocated quotas to ensure the enrollment of students from most provinces, but its new recruitment plan listed only provinces to which Shanghai youth had been sent.[6] For the 1972 enrollments, Fudan accepted 300 from Heilongjiang, all but nine of whom were Shanghai sent-down youth.[7] Other universities in Shanghai also gave preferential treatment to the city's sent-down youth, such as Jiaotong University, which specified that its students would come from the ranks of Shanghai youth settled in Jinghong (Yunnan), Shangrao (Jiangxi), and Suxian (Anhui).[8] The preferential treatment of sent-down youth was not confined to individual institutions, as indicated by the Shanghai Cultural and Educational Bureau's 1973 plan for college enrollment, which proposed that the city's sixteen universities would reserve 3,684 slots for residents of Shanghai itself and distribute the rest among the ten

---

[4] Shanghai shi geweihui wenjiao zu 上海市革委会文教组, "Guanyu Fudan, Tongji, Shida, Keji Daxue, sisuo daxue zhaosheng gongzuo zhong ruogan wenti de qingshi baogao" 关于复旦、同济、师大、科技大学四所大学招生工作中若干问题的请示报告 (Report Concerning Problems of Student Recruitment of Four Universities—Fudan, Tongji, Shida, and Keji), October 12, 1970, SHMA.

[5] Ibid.

[6] Lu Xianliang, "Shuoshuo wenge zhao sheng nahui shi" (My Recollections of College Admission during the Cultural Revolution), *Dang'an chun qiu*, 6 (2012), 48–52.

[7] Shanghai shi geweihui wenjia zu 上海市革委会文教组, "Shanghai shi 1972 nian chunji zhaoshou fu waisheng xiaxiang shangshan zhiqing tongjibiao" 上海市 1972 年春季招收赴外省下乡上山知青统计表 (Statistical Table of Spring 1972 Recruitment of Shanghai Youth Sent to Other Provinces), May 23, 1972, SHMA.

[8] Shanghai Jiaotong daxue xiaoshi bianzhuan weiyuanhui, *Shanghai Jiaotong daxue jishi: 1896–2005* (Chronology of Shanghai Jiaotong University: 1896–2005) (Shanghai: Shanghai Jiaotong daxue chubanshe, 2006), 653.

provinces with Shanghai sent-down youth. The proposal was specific about the numbers of sent-down youth to be enrolled: 110 from Heilongjiang, 170 from Anhui, 979 from Jiangxi, 250 from Yunnan, 100 from Jilin, 50 from Zhejiang, 50 from Jiangsu, 40 from Guizhou, 40 from Inner Mongolia, and 5 from Liaoning. Remote provinces that had not accommodated Shanghai youth were completely ignored.[9] Li Jiaquan, who worked as the cadre responsible for college recruitment in the Fuyang (Anhui) Office of Sent-Down Youth, recalled, "It was agreed upon that slots for Shanghai colleges would primarily be given to sent-down youth from Shanghai."[10]

In addition to advocating for slots for Shanghai youth in college programs, the Shanghai government also negotiated with rural governments to secure other employment opportunities for its sent-down youth. When some industrial enterprises were relocated from Shanghai to interior regions as part of the Third Front Industry policy, workers who agreed to move were permitted to have their sons and daughters who had been sent to the countryside relocate to be with them.[11] When the Shanghai government contracted to build a new air force base in Guizhou in 1971, creating 15,000 jobs, the Shanghai Labor Bureau and Office of Sent-Down Youth demanded that all 4,000 unskilled positions be assigned to Shanghai sent-down youth in Guizhou.[12]

While sent-down youth and their parents surely welcomed these efforts, this preferential treatment of Shanghai youth became a source of conflict, in at least one case triggering the wrath of provincial government officials. When the Shanghai Bureau of Higher Education sent a work team to Yunnan in 1975 to announce that Shanghai planned to fill all its enrollment slots with its own sent-down youth, the Yunnan provincial government objected. Invoking the principle of equal treatment, Lu Shihua, head of the provincial office of college admissions, told representatives from Shanghai, "In recruiting college students, everyone should be eligible—regardless of whether they are sent-down youth from Shanghai or from our own province. Which university they will attend should be decided by our local governments." Lu expressed his particular concern that Sichuan youth in Yunnan, as well as their families, had

---

[9] Shanghai shi geweihui wenjiaozu 上海市革委会文教组, "Guanyu benshi gaodeng xue-xiao 1973 nian zhaosheng gongzuo de qingshi baogao" 关于本市高等学校 1973 年招生工作的请示报告 (Proposed Report on the Work of Recruting Students in Our City's Universities in 1973), May 25, 1973, SHMA.

[10] Li Jiaquan, "Yingxiangli de lishi" (History in a Photo Album), *Jianghuai wenshi*, 4 (2013), 126–131.

[11] See Xu Youwei and Chen Donglin, *Xiao san xian jianshe yanjiu luncong* (Selected Essays on the Third Front Industry) (Shanghai: Shanghai daxue chubanshe, 2015).

[12] Jin Dalu and Lin Shengbao, 127.

become resentful and he worried that they might go to the provincial capital, Kunming, to protest. The Shanghai delegation responded by offering 5 percent of the slots to local youth or sent-down youth from other provinces, and summoned Zhu Kejia, a high-profile Shanghai sent-down youth who had become Party secretary of the Yunnan Youth League and a member of the National People's Congress, to argue on its behalf. The provincial government surrendered, in the end agreeing to allocate more slots to Shanghai sent-down youth on the condition that at least 30 percent return to Yunnan after graduation. Unwilling to make such a commitment, the Shanghai delegation replied, "We are afraid that not that many would return."[13] Likewise, when the Shanghai government wanted to allocate the 4,000 air force base jobs in Guizhou to its sent-down youth, the provincial government responded, "It will be hard to justify the recruitment of only Shanghai youth and that will make it even more difficult for us to work effectively at the local level." The Shanghai government, however, ignored these concerns, and Mayor Ma Tianshui spoke directly with the head of the air force to secure the positions for Shanghai youth.[14]

These efforts to privilege individual Shanghai sent-down youth not only created tensions with rural leaders, but also made it difficult to manage youth who remained in the countryside. A *weiwentuan* member called to help recruit Shanghai sent-down youth in Anhui for college admission was so troubled by the implications of this recruitment that he submitted a detailed letter to the Shanghai grievance office (*xinfang bangongshi*).[15] His complaint charged that the provincial-level leader of the Shanghai *weiwentuan* had instructed its members to do their "absolute best" to recruit as many of the Shanghai youth as possible. They were even to recruit model youth who had resolved to settle for life in the countryside. If all the model youth were recruited, the cadre reasoned, other sent-down youth might feel betrayed and conclude that those models had worked hard for the sole purpose of being able to leave. "If the locals want to recommend them, that's one thing," his letter continued, "but to have the *weiwentuan* demand that they be selected is wrong." The same issue was raised by the Guizhou government, which argued that the remaining

[13] SHMOSY, "Guanyu lianxi luoshi zai Yunnan sheng zhao Shanghai zhiqing wenti de huibao" 关于联系落实在云南省招上海知青问题的汇报 (A Report on the Issue of Negotiating the Recruitment of Shanghai Sent-Down Youth in Yunnan), 1976, SHMA.
[14] Jin Dalu and Lin Shengbao, 127–128.
[15] Shanghai shi geming weiyuanhui bangongshi xinfangzu 上海市革命委员会办公室信访组, "Lai xin zai bao" 来信摘报 (Summary of Grievance Letters), December 25, 1974. The original letter was dated December 23, 1974. SHMA.

5,000 sent-down youth not recruited for the air force base would "become unstable and difficult to manage."[16]

Some of these management problems resulted from the government's inability to promise jobs to all sent-down youth. The recruitment implied that hard work in the countryside would enable urban youth to leave the countryside. Yet, relative to the number of sent-down youth on production brigades, the slots for colleges or jobs in factories were few and far between. As model youth, student leaders, and individuals with skills or family connections began to leave, it became increasingly difficult for local cadres and members of *weiwentuan* to persuade those who remained to accept a future of permanent settlement in the countryside.

Disillusioned, many sent-down youth found ways to spend less time in the countryside and more at home in Shanghai. Permitted to return to the city for medical treatment and often for the winter slack season, many extended their stay in Shanghai, sometimes for an indeterminate number of months. According to reports from Heilongjiang province, beginning in 1972, an increasing number of the sent-down youth granted certificates approving their travel to Shanghai for health care never returned to the countryside.[17]

The phenomenon of sent-down youth extending their stays in Shanghai disturbed the municipal government, which in early 1972 convened 1,600 district, street, alley, factory, and school representatives to discuss the "ideological problems of sent-down youth who returned to Shanghai." The title of a *Jiefang ribao* editorial expressed the government's position: "Hoping that all the sent-down youth who have come to Shanghai for family visits will return to the countryside as soon as possible."[18] A year later, in April 1973, the Zhabei District Office of Sent-Down Youth reported that although the Spring Festival had long since ended and the busiest agricultural season begun, a sizeable number of sent-down youth remained in Shanghai. The problem was so overwhelming that the municipal government convened three meetings. Mayor Ma Tianshui declared that this situation "is not normal." "We must analyze the reason," he commanded. "We cannot let them stay in the city and must find ways to encourage them to go back."[19]

While many sent-down youth extended their home visits in Shanghai, some tried to obtain permission to return permanently on the basis of illness or family difficulties. A very small number of urban youth with serious health conditions such as epilepsy, heart disease, arthritis, or

---

[16] Jin Dalu and Lin Shengbao, 127.   [17] Lü Qiaofen and Xie Chunhe, 105.

[18] Jin Dalu and Lin Shengbao, 133, 135; *Jiefang ribao*, February 22, 1972.

[19] ZBDOSY, "Shi xiang ban huiyi qingkuang huibao" 市乡办会议情况汇报 (Report on the Conference of the City Sent-Down Youth Office), April 27, 1973, JADA.

mental illness were permitted to return to the city in the early years of the movement. In some cases, it was the local governments that requested Shanghai to take back the youth who were unable to do agricultural work. These youth regained their Shanghai *hukou* and received job assignments.[20] The numbers increased following the 1971 National Planning Conference: its stipulation that middle school graduates with illnesses or physical handicaps would not be required to go to the country-side prompted many already sent to the countryside to solicit medical examinations to determine their eligibility to return home. Suddenly, youth who had returned to Shanghai for a holiday visit and their parents lined up for inquiries at district offices of sent-down youth, hoping to obtain information on what sorts of illness qualified. The Zhabei district office registered some 100 visitors—and sometimes up to 300—each day. The staff complained that the visitors often vomited because the small appointment office was located in a storage facility for poisonous sub-stances. In late 1973, with a backlog of 600 youth waiting for medical examinations, the office complained as well about the insufficient number of doctors.[21]

Directives from the 1971 planning conference also permitted youth suffering from "family hardships" to return the city with official sanction. Although the Shanghai government initially hesitated, a number of pro-vinces hosting sent-down youth proceeded to issue directives that "if their parents are sick or have no one to take care of them, or if the parents are already dead and their siblings are young," they should be allowed to return to the city.[22] In one county in Heilongjiang, the number of sent-down youth invoking this stipulation to return to Shanghai became so large that county leaders had to hold special meetings labeled "sent-down youth returning to the cities." By 1973, such meetings were held several times a month to evaluate requests to leave. At one, officials approved twenty-five of the forty-seven requests to return to cities, including one who was an only child, one who was sick, one whose mother was sick, one with seven siblings whose mother had died, one whose father had been

[20] SHMOSY, "Guanyu you yanzhong jibing buneng canjia laodong er yi xiaxiang shang-shan de zhishi qingnian tuihui Shanghai de chuli yijian" 关于有严重疾病不能参加劳动而已下乡上山的知识青年退回上海的处理意见 (Proposed Ideas on the Returning to Shanghai of Sent-Down Youth Who Cannot Work Due to Serious Illness), June 16, 1969, SHMA.

[21] ZBDOSY, "Guanyu wo qu zhishi qingnian shangshan xiaxiang qingkuang huibao," 关于我区知识青年上山下乡情况汇报 (A Report on Sent-Down Youth from Our District), March 1974, JADA.

[22] Zhonggong Jiangxi shengwei 中共江西省委, "Guanyu zhishi qingnian shangshan xia-xiang ruo gan wenti de shixing guiding" 关于知识青年上山下乡若干问题的试行规定 (Experimental Regulations on Issues Concerning Sent-Down Youth), September 1973, SHMA.

injured at work, one whose father had died, one whose mother had psychological problems, one with a bone spur, one with arthritis, one with diabetes, and one who had a bed-wetting problem.[23]

That the Shanghai government did not initially endorse such practices is not entirely surprising, as the prospect of large numbers of youth returning to the city would present confounding problems. During the decade of the Cultural Revolution, industrial growth in Shanghai was extremely slow and housing construction minimal, and the municipal government struggled to control the city's swelling population.[24] In 1974 the Labor Bureau pointed out that jobs still had not been found for most of the 20,000 graduates who were eligible to remain in the city.[25] At the time, close to 7,000 sent-down youth whose return to Shanghai had been authorized were also waiting for jobs, and many more were in the process of getting residential registration.[26] When, in August 1974, the Shanghai Office of Sent-Down Youth proposed to the municipal government that it allow the return to Shanghai of sent-down youth whose families had "special difficulties," the government approved the principle but simultaneously specified that this decision not be publicized. Furthermore, it stipulated that such cases would be evaluated one at a time, and that cadres should continue to educate the individuals involved and advocate for them to remain in or return to the countryside.[27]

[23] NJCOSY, "Guanyu yanjiu fancheng wenti" 关于研究返城问题 (Consideration of Issues Concerning Returning to the City), August 20, 1971, NJCA; NJCOSY, "Yanjiu xiaxiang qingnian fancheng wenti" 研究下乡青年返城问题 (Consideration of Sent-Down Youth Returning to the City), September 4, 1971, NJCA; Nenjiang xianwei changweihui huiyi [jilu] 嫩江县常委会会议 [记录] (Minutes of the Executive Committee of the Nenjiang County Government), January 9, 1973, NJCA.

[24] Chen Kuan, Wang Hongchang, Zheng Yuxin, Gary H. Jefferson, and Thomas G. Rawski, "Productivity Change in Chinese Industry, 1953–1985," *Journal of Comparative Economics*, 12, 4 (1988), 584. Lynn Whyte III, "The Road to Urumchi: Approved Institutions in Search of Attainable Goals during Pre-1968 Rustication from Shanghai," *China Quarterly*, 79 (September 1979), 483–484. Farhad Atash and Xinhao Wang, "Satellite Town: Development in Shanghai, China. An Overview," *Journal of Architecture and Planning Research*, 7, 3 (1990), 245–257; Yuemin Ming and Zhongmin Yan, "The Changing Industrial and Spatial Structure in Shanghai," *Urban Geography*, 16, 7 (1995), 588–589.

[25] Shi laodong ju geming weiyuanhui 市劳动局革命委员会, "Guanyu bingxiu tekun zhishi qingnian anpai qingkuang he jinhou yijian de baogao" 关于病休特困知识青年安排情况和今后意见的报告 (A Report on Arrangements and Future Suggestions for Sent-Down Youth Who Have Health Problems or Special Difficulties), July 17, 1974, SHMA.

[26] Ibid. The memo notes that in 1974, more than 6,000 sent-down youth had returned to Shanghai for family difficulties and 5,000 due to personal illnesses.

[27] SHMOSY, "Guanyu zhishi qingnian xiaxiang hou jiating fasheng kunnan zhaogu huihu de qingkuang huibao" 关于知识青年下乡后家庭发生困难照顾回沪的情况汇报 (A Report on Allowing the Return to Shanghai of Educated Youth Whose Families Encountered Difficulties after They Went to the Countryside), August 8, 1974, SHMA.

But the change in policy made it even more difficult for cadres to mobilize those who had extended their home visits in Shanghai to return to the countryside. The cadres "have some doubts," according to one report. Some complained that this work with sent-down youth had become extremely difficult. Not knowing how to persuade those who were ill or who were only children to go back to the countryside, some cadres were unwilling to perform their assigned duty. The report pointed out that many cadres "don't want to deal with this work" because they believe that "it is too hard to make people go back to the countryside." "So, the difficulties increase and progress decreases," the report concluded.[28]

By the next year the problem had worsened. Faced with 25,000 youth back in Shanghai, cadres in the Zhabei district directed to persuade them to return to the countryside had become even more frustrated by their job. The district sent-down youth office reported that "they are intimidated by the difficulties of this job. They visit families and often have no result: the families keep changing their minds and sometimes the cadres have to confront cold faces. They do not have confidence in their work." Observing that only 50 percent of youth were persuaded to return to the countryside, the report acknowledged, "We do not have a clear understanding of their real problems. All we have done is to ask them to leave . . . We have not dealt with them at the individual level. We have not done an effective job."[29]

Throughout the next few years, the Shanghai government intensified its efforts to persuade youth to return to the countryside, its labor bureau in 1975 commanding all work units to enlist parents in the project.[30] The government provided financial assistance to the families for winter clothing and travel.[31] "This job needs to be continued," declared Ma

---

[28] ZBDOSY, "Shi xiang ban huiyi qingkuang huibao" 市乡办会议情况汇报 (Report on the Meeting at the Municipal Office of Sent-Down Youth), April 27, 1973, JADA.

[29] ZBDOSY, "Guanyu wo qu zhishi qingnian shangshan xiaxiang qingkuang huibao" 关于我区知识青年上山下乡情况汇报 (Report on the Condition of Sent-Down Youth in Our District), March 1974, JADA.

[30] SHMOSY, "Guanyu fangwen buzhu gongzuo de qingkuang huibao" 关于访问补助工作的情况汇报 (Report on the Work of [Family] Visiting and [Financial] Relief), February 1, 1975, SHMA.

[31] Ibid. Relief to sent-down youth families, especially to those who went to villages in remote regions, continued throughout the movement. In addition to the municipal government, district and neighborhood allies as well as work units of sent-down youth parents also provided funding. The money was to help families to pay medical expenses, repay debts, or purchase tickets for the youth to return to the countryside. The Jing'an District Sent-Down Youth Office appropriated part of its administrative budget as a monthly stipend to some sent-down youth. SHMOSY, "Jing'an qu zhiqingban jiji bangzhuzai Shanghai meiyou jiating zhiyuan de xiaxiang qingnian jiejue shiji kunnan, zhichi tamen jianchi xiangcun" 静安区知青办积极帮助在上海没有家庭支援的下乡青年

Tianshui.[32] Hongkou district alone mobilized some 13,000 cadres to visit 93,000 families; in Luwan and Huaihai districts, some 6,600 families were visited.[33] This massive effort resulted in the modest success of some 60 percent of the youth visiting home returning to the countryside. Regardless, most of those who returned to the countryside would likely go back to Shanghai the following winter. Ultimately, the project of persuading youth to go back to the countryside could not in and of itself solve the problem, one which was deeply related to the unaltered gap between conditions in urban and rural China.

By this point in the mid-1970s, the problem of persuading youth to return (or even go) to the countryside had become a nationwide problem, even when the rural areas to which youth would be sent were not far from the city. For example, Nenjiang county organized more than 50 cadres to help recruit potential sent-down youth. In the county seat they secured a small truck, decorated it with banners propagating Mao's directive on sent-down youth and attached loud speakers as well. The truck maneuvered through small streets in the city's neighborhoods. Cadres expressed grave disappointment at the results of their seemingly heroic effort: during meetings with parents of youth, many fled before it was even half over; their efforts to talk directly with the youth were thwarted by the difficulty of finding them. Their goal was to mobilize 300, but after a few months of hard work, only fifty had agreed to go, and in the end, a mere eight actually went. The cadres dispatched a car to pick up a young man whose parents had agreed to send him, only to find that the entire family had gone into hiding. "Doing things like this," the county vice head complained, "they've undermined the plans made by many of the brigades, where peasants had cleaned their dwellings, killed pigs, and steamed bread to greet them. They were waiting for the youth to arrive to hold a parade. They waited and waited, and no one arrived."[34] Meanwhile, a Nenjiang county leader complained that anyone assigned to work with sent-down youth would try to "pass the buck" to someone else, but no one wanted to take it. When

解决实际困难，支持他们坚持乡村 (The Jing'an District Office of Sent-Down Youth Proactively Helps Sent-Down Youth Who Have no Family Support in Shanghai Solve Practical Problems, Supporting Them to Stay in the Countryside), *Qingkuang huibao* 情况汇报, May 20, 1976; SHMOSY, "Guanyu dui xiaxiang qingnian jingxing kunnan buzhu de jidian yijian" 关于对下乡青年进行困难补助的几点意见 (A Few Ideas on Providing Relief for Sent-Down Youth), July 1, 1977, SHMA.
[32] Jin Dalu and Lin Shengbao, 216–217.
[33] SHMOSY, "Guanyu fangwen buzhu gongzuo de qingkuang huibao."
[34] "Nenjiang xian wei fushuji, Li Wenxiang tongzhi zai zhiqing gonzuoshang de jianghua," 1975, NJCA.

county-wide meetings were convened to discuss sent-down youth, many people found excuses to skip them.[35]

Mission Impossible

If in Shanghai the major effort to continue the sent-down youth movement was to recruit cadres to persuade youth to return to the villages, in the countryside the Shanghai government tried to support sent-down youth by increasing the ranks of the *weiwentuan*.

When, in September 1973, the Shanghai Office of Sent-Down Youth declared that an additional 1,200 cadres needed to go to the countryside for one to three years, the government convened a conference to recruit them to join.[36] Although city leaders Ma Tianshui and Xu Jinxian spoke to the 10,000 participants, not all cadres responded with enthusiasm to this call. Some were quoted as saying, "Hey! The point is to mobilize cadres in leadership positions, not us ordinary ones." Others said, "This is for those working in government offices, not us at the lowest levels."[37] Eventually the government was able to constitute new *weiwentuan*, which by early 1974 were sent to several provinces. One of the largest was a 684-member team sent to Heilongjiang.[38] However, problems recruiting for the *weiwentuan* continued. A report from summer 1975 cited complaints by cadres who openly expressed their unwillingness to participate. One cadre from the Jing'an district said, "I do not expect a promotion and I don't need more nurturing. Let those people who have great ambitions join the *weiwentuan*." Another reportedly said, "I'm not qualified for the *weiwentuan*: my ideological level is not high enough, and in the past big-character posters said I was guilty of affairs (*nannü guanxi*). Plus, I just had surgery. So why are you trying to mobilize me?" The report found that only those frustrated with their situation in Shanghai were likely to join the *weiwentuan*, with some imagining that "they'd get to do a little sight-seeing."[39]

Even more challenging than mobilizing cadres to join the *weiwentuan* was the increasing opposition of rural officials toward the presence of Shanghai cadres. Some local governments complained that accommodating these

---

[35] Ibid.   [36] Jin Dalu and Lin Shengbao, 169, 176–179.

[37] JADOSY, "Quwei fuze tongzhi zai qu geweihui jiguan dongyuan ganbu shangshan xiaxiang dahuishang de jianghua" 区委负责同志在区革委会机关动员干部上山下乡大会上的讲话 (A Speech by the Head of the District at the Administrative Bureau Rally to Mobilize Cadres to the Countryside), December 29, 1973, JADA.

[38] Jin Dalu and Lin Shengbao, 194–201.

[39] SHMOSY, "Guanyu dongyuan ganbu canjia xuexi weiwentuan de qingkuang" 关于动员干部参加学习慰问团的情况 (Report on the Conditions of Mobilizing Cadres to Join the *Weiwentuan*), *Qingkuang fanying*, 45, July 21, 1975, SHMA.

teams of urban cadres was too burdensome. In March 1974, alarmed by the news of the imminent arrival of a ninety-member *weiwentuan* from Shanghai, the Party head of Xishuangbanna, in a phone conversation with the head of the district office of sent-down youth, angrily refused to assume responsibility for their accommodation. "We don't have enough places ourselves, so how can we solve the housing and office problems for so many more people?" he said. "Tell the provincial government to appropriate money to build housing for them." Responding to this, the head of the Yunnan Provincial Office of Sent-Down Youth explained that most members of the *weiwentuan* would not stay at the district seat, but could instead be sent to counties and communes, where they would be subordinate to local government leadership.[40] County government officials were equally uninterested in accommodating the *weiwentuan*: Mengla county leaders, hearing that a *weiwentuan* would come, phoned the district office of sent-down youth to urge that the Shanghai representatives be sent to the army farm where most of the county's youth from Shanghai were located. Should the county have any issues, the Mengla officials added, "we can contact them there."[41]

These attitudes of local officials alarmed the Yunnan provincial government, as conflict with the *weiwentuan* could jeopardize its relationship with Shanghai, potentially costly both politically and economically, particularly in light of the material resources that Shanghai had been sending to villages hosting sent-down youth. At a meeting in March 1974, the head of the Yunnan Office of Sent-Down Youth reprimanded local leaders. "Ask the Xishuanbanna leaders to change their attitude," he admonished. "They deserve a good criticism." "I heard that in the past you did not provide them office space," he complained. "Do you think they could bring telephones or desks with them? What do you mean by not giving them an office?" He commanded local leaders to stage a "warm welcome" for the new *weiwentuan*, greeting them personally at the train station. The provincial head also instructed that the *weiwentuan* be "treated as our own unit," invited to all meetings, and considered the equals of local leadership. Moreover, he directed local leaders to report problems to the *weiwentuan* and solicit their suggestions. He concluded that if local officials did not handle this well, it would not be simply "wrong" but constitute an "extreme error."[42]

---

[40] XSBNAPOSY, "Dianhua jilu" 电话记录 (Transcript of a Phone Call), March 4, 1974, JHDA.

[41] XSBNAPOSY, "Mengla xian zhiqingban laidian jilu" 勐腊县知青办来电记录 (Transcript of Telephone Call from Mengla Office of Sent-Down Youth), March 15, 1974, JHDA.

[42] XSBNAPOSY, "Dong Chaoxing lai dian jilu" 董朝兴来电记录 (Transcript of Phone Call from Dong Chaoxing), March 15, 1974, JHDA.

This time, Xishuangbanna district leaders had to take the *weiwentuan* seriously. In anticipation of its arrival from Kunming, Jinghong officials conferred with a number of local units and proposed a detailed plan for the welcome. This included a six- to eight-course banquet to honor them on their first night, to be attended by fifty local officials as well as the ninety-eight members of the *weiwentuan*. They would be given accommodation in Jinghong for seven days, during which the government would provide meat, fish, cigarettes, tea, sugar, and soap. They would also be entertained by two performances and two movies (although the plan noted that providing electricity for the movies would involve special efforts).[43]

Apparently, the warm welcome did not preclude conflicts between the local district and the *weiwentuan*. In its own evaluation, the *weiwentuan* in Xishuangbanna acknowledged that some of its members believed their job was to investigate problems and direct the locals to "change and improve." Some had an attitude of superiority, introducing their speeches by saying, "Our *weiwentuan* came here under the instruction of the central government; we are representatives of the Shanghai government and ten million Shanghai people." Some cadres hastily blamed local officials for the problems faced by sent-down youth, sometimes "engaging in battles" with them by declaring, "If the local government does not want to solve the problems, we will report them to the provincial government; if the provincial government does not want to address the problems, we will report them to the central government." "This mindset of treating local officials as the opponent," the report concluded, "had led to the distrust and tension between the Shanghai *weiwentuan* and local government officials."[44]

A *weiwentuan* sent from Shanghai to Anhui reported similar conflicts with the local government. One member of the team, based in Suxian, wrote to the Shanghai government in late 1974 to complain about instructions from the Anhui government that the local office of sent-down youth should provide leadership and guidance for the Shanghai *weiwentuan*. The letter writer stated that his colleagues resented

---

[43] XSBNAPOSY, "Wei yingjie Shanghai shi shangshan xiaxiang weiwentuan you guan wenti de qingshi baogao" 为迎接上海市上山下乡慰问团有关问题的请示报告 (Proposed Report on Welcoming the Shanghai Sent-Down Youth *Weiwentuan*), March 20, 1974, JHDA.

[44] Shanghai weiwentuan Xishuangbanna fentuan, "Zai dang de yiyuanhua lingdao xia zhudong jiji fahui zhushou, canmou zuoyong, Xishuangbanna fentuan kaizhan xuexi weiwen gongzuo de tihui" 在党的一元化领导下主动积极发挥助手、参谋作用, 西双版纳分团开展学习慰问工作的体会 (Under Unilateral Supreme Party Leadership, Playing Proactive Roles as Assistants and Advisers, Lessons of the Xishuangbanna Branch *Weiwentuan*), undated (most likely 1975), JHDA.

subordination, believing they "should be on an equal footing" with the local office of sent-down youth. "We do not have power and we don't have money. The only thing we have is a mouth and two legs. How can we solve any problems?" he asked.[45]

Local officials had their own complaints. Those in Suxian noted that the *weiwentuan* only "pays attention to the dark side and exaggerates problems; their main interest is digging out sensational stories."[46] To local officials in Xishuangbanna the *weiwentuan* "was here to find fault with us and entrap local officials," which explained why the locals did not welcome them.[47] No matter where they were sent, the *weiwentuan* seemed to trigger resentment. In 1975, the Shanghai Office of Sent-Down Youth received a letter from an officer, Sun Yanping, at an army farm in Heilongjiang, complaining that the Shanghai *weiwentuan*, which had been there for two years, was "interfering in everything that has to do with Shanghai youth" and harboring "very serious regional bias." "They never listen to opinions of youth from other regions, but deal only with things involving Shanghai youth. They are very opinionated and in reality are causing regional divisions," he continued, adding, "They should not stay in the office but should go to the grass roots to work with all youth, not just Shanghai youth." Invoking the principle of unified Party leadership (*yiyuanhua*), Sun questioned the rationale of the Shanghai *weiwentuan*, arguing that since members of the army farm came from all parts of China, they should be managed by the central government, not a single city's *weiwentuan*.[48] In a letter drafted to Sun, the Shanghai Office of Sent-Down Youth confirmed that the *weiwentuan* was not charged to investigate or correct errors and was to be subordinate to the Heilongjiang provincial government. The vice head of the Shanghai government, however, decided it was best not to

---

[45] Shanghai shi geming weiyuanhui bangongshi xinfangzu 上海市革命委员会信访组, "Laixin zhaibao" 来信摘报 (Summery of Grievance Letters), December 25, 1974, SHMA. The original letter was dated December 23, 1974.

[46] SHMOSY, "Anhui Suxian weiwentuan chengyuan lai xin de baogao" 安徽宿县慰问团成员来信的报告 (Report on Letters from Members of the *Weiwentuan* in Suxian, Anhui), December 25, 1974, SHMA.

[47] Shanghai shi fu Yunnan sheng shangshan xiaxiang xuexi weiwentuan Xishuangbanna fentuan 上海市赴云南省上山下乡学习慰问团西双版纳分团, "Shanghai shi fu Yunnan sheng shangshan xixiang xuexi weiwentuan Xishuangbanna fentuan 1970 nian gongzuo zongjie" 上海市赴云南省上山下乡学习慰问团西双版纳分团 1970 年工作总结 (Summary of Work during 1970 of the Xishuangbanna Sub-team of the Shanghai Sent-Down Youth *Weiwentuan* in Yunnan), November 26, 1974, JHCA.

[48] SHMOSY, "Renmin laixin chulidan: Heilongjiang 38 bingtuan Sun Yanping zhi Zhang Chunqiao" 人民来信处理单：黑龙江 38 兵团孙炎平致张春桥 (Form on Handling Grievance Letter: Heilongjiang 38 Bingtuan Sun Yanping to Zhang Chunqiao), June 5, 1975, SHMA.

respond, and so the letter was never sent, effectively silencing Sun's grievance.[49]

If the Shanghai *weiwentuan* presented challenges to local leadership, sent-down youth were themselves becoming increasingly resistant to rural authorities. By 1973, reports citing the obstreperous actions of urban youth began to surface. For example, at production brigades in Xunke county, some youth were openly refusing to co-operate with the directions issued by village leaders. At the Bianjiang commune, a number of youth did not go to work. When confronted by the village head, they yelled at him, "Why are you asking us to work, you rotten egg?!" At the nearby Donglu commune, sent-down youth cursed local cadres, "Those cadres—their mouths are worse than prostitute pee. Who cares what they say!" At yet another commune, when a village cadre tried to "educate" a youth who routinely went to collect wood ears in the mountains instead of working, he retorted, "You still think you can treat us sent-down youth like this?" and threatened, "You'd better be careful!"[50] Some village cadres, for their part, began to believe that training urban youth was a waste of time, and curtailed their efforts to encourage them to work.[51]

Not only did *weiwentuan* reports on conditions of sent-down youth become desperately pessimistic, but they also both implicitly and explicitly questioned the principles of the movement. Some began to declare that as long as urban youth could not support themselves on production teams, the movement could not succeed. One from Anhui reported that not being able to obtain enough food, a large number of youth spent three to four months each year in Shanghai depending on their parents, who in turn were finding this burden difficult to sustain.[52] Another about youth in Yunnan reported that some youth, unable to support themselves, had become "emotionally unstable" and "want to return to Shanghai or find other alternatives."[53] Yet another highlighted that 97 percent of Shanghai youth in Guizhou could not support

---

[49] Ibid.

[50] XKCOSY, "Diaochazu baogao"调查组报告 (Investigative team report)1973. XKCA.

[51] XKCOSY, "Zhishi qingnian shangshan xiaxiang daibiao dahui cailiao" 知识青年上山下乡代表大会材料 (Materials for Conference of Sent-Down Youth Representatives), September 11, 1973, XKCA.

[52] Geng Changlan 耿昌兰, "Guanyu Anhui Chuxian diqu fengyang xian dui xiaxiang qingnian anzhi jiaoyu gongzuo zhong de yixie wenti" 关于安徽滁县地区凤阳县对下乡青年安置教育工作的一些问题 (Some Problems on Arranging and Educating Sent-Down Youth in Fengyang County of Chuxian District in Anhui), April 25, 1974, SHMA.

[53] MHCOSY and Shanghai weiwentuan, "Menghai xian Shanghai xiaxiang chadui qing-nian de qingkuang diaocha" 勐海县上海下乡插队青年的情况调查 (Investigative Report of Shanghai Youth Sent to Production Brigades of Menghai County), June 5, 1976. Also see Jin Dalu and Lin Shengbao, 265.

themselves.[54] At a *weiwentuan* conference convened in Shanghai in 1976, representatives warned that if the problem of self-sufficiency could not be solved, "it is not possible for sent-down youth to stay in the countryside."[55] This was tantamount to admitting that in spite of all the efforts made, the proposition of settling urban youth in village production teams was in jeopardy.

Under all of these circumstances—the erosion of local authority, the pessimism of the *weiwentuan*, and the persisting impoverishment of the countryside—it is not difficult to understand why so many youth wanted to return to Shanghai and why local authorities would not prevent them from doing so. In other words, by the mid-1970s, well before the death of Mao and fall of the Gang of Four, disillusionment with the sent-down movement not only was expressed by sent-down youth themselves and their parents, but was shared by local government officials and members of the *weiwentuan*. For the Shanghai youth who remained on production teams, finding ways to return to Shanghai became the new norm.

The End of an Era

Political events in the second half of the 1970s intensified dissatisfaction with the movement. The Lin Biao Incident of 1971 had created widespread questioning of the Cultural Revolution, but it was not until the death of Zhou Enlai in January 1976 that this questioning became a political movement. Mourning for Zhou Enlai culminated in the Tian'anmen Incident of April 5, when thousands of citizens used the occasion of the Qingming festival for the commemoration of the dead to express their growing doubts about China's leadership. Many posted poems, slogans, and messages that attacked the Cultural Revolution and some indicted Mao himself.[56]

These events created a political opening that recalled the outbreak of the Cultural Revolution, when a previous generation of urban youth who had been sent to settle in villages staged public demonstrations to demand their right to return to cities, issuing slogans such as "We want *hukou*," or

---

[54] SHMOSY, "Guanyu Guizhou sheng jiejue Shanghai chadui zhiqing shenghuo zigei wenti de qingkuang huibao" 关于贵州省解决上海插队知青生活自给问题的情况汇报 (Report on Guizhou Province Solving Self-Sufficiency Problems for Shanghai Youth Sent to Production Brigades), July 22, 1976, SHMA; also see Jin Dalu and Lin Shengbao, 272.

[55] July 12, 1976, in Jin Dalu and Lin Shengbao, 271.

[56] Frederick C. Teiwes and Warren Sun, "The First Tiananmen Incident Revisited: Elite Politics and Crisis Management at the End of the Maoist Era," *Pacific Affairs*, 77, 2 (Summer 2004), 211–235.

"It's right to rebel for *hukou*."[57] Likewise, shortly after the 1976 Tian'anmen demonstration, the Shanghai Office of Sent-Down Youth reported the "intense emotions and strong anger" expressed by sent-down youth and their parents, who were demanding that sent-down youth be brought back to the city and threatening to "make trouble." One group of sent-down youth authored a letter titled "The Bleak Fate," stating that sending the graduates of 1968 and 1969 to the countryside was the result of an "erroneous direction" that is "driving us to a dead end." It charged that they had been given no choice but to join rural production brigades, and unlike factory workers whose apprenticeship would end after three years of training, their assignment to villages had no termination. "This kind of unreasonable policy," the letter proclaimed, "is a lethal stimulus for us." A second letter pointed out that the Shanghai sent-down youth on his brigade were no longer being recruited as workers, students, or soldiers and that the only remedy was for Shanghai to allow them back in the city. The most effective way to do this, the writer of this letter argued, would be for sent-down youth to take their parents' jobs when they retire, as demonstrated by a number of cities in other provinces. The letter questioned why Shanghai had not implemented a similar *dingti* (children inherit their parents' jobs after they retire) policy. Many more letters reiterated the demand that sent-down youth be allowed to return to the city, one threatening to "do anything to fight on."[58]

When, four months later, in September 1976, Mao died and almost immediately the Gang of Four were arrested, many people assumed the sent-down youth movement would be ended, and anxiously awaited an announcement that all youth sent away would be brought back to the city. However, Mao's successor Hua Guofeng not only failed to repudiate the policy but instead upheld it in principle, nowhere making it clear whether the movement would be continued in its original form, how long sent-down youth should stay in the countryside, and whether those who had been in the countryside for many years would be allowed to return to the city. Hua may have had ideological as well as practical reasons to refrain from addressing these questions or repudiating the

---

[57] Yiching Wu, 166–67.
[58] SHMOSY, "Zhishi qingniang shangshan xiaxiang qingkuang fanying" 知识青年上山下乡情况反映 (Reflections on the Condition of sent-Down Youth in the Countryside), April 15, 1976, SHMA. Another letter by "seven sent-down youth from Shanghai" complained that, as graduates of 1968 and 1969 required to go to the countryside, "we, the pioneering sent-down youth, are looked down upon, forgotten, and deceived." A final complaint concerned the predicament of sent-down youth who had returned to Shanghai on the pretext of health problems, and were then assigned to jobs in neighborhood collectives instead of state enterprises, which at least one writer considered an "inhumane measure" and "torture."

entire movement. Having been appointed by Mao to be his successor, Hua could not reject Mao altogether, and he was also most likely concerned that there were not enough jobs in the city to employ youth who would return from the countryside.

As the government did not immediately issue a new policy, members of the Shanghai *weiwentuan*, who had long considered themselves victims of political struggle in Shanghai, pressed for their assignment to be terminated. Many of them, particularly those commanded to go to the countryside in 1969 or 1970, were eager to return to Shanghai to claim status as victims of the Gang of Four, three members of whom (Zhang Chunqiao, Wang Hongwen, and Yao Wenyuan) had been powerful leaders in Shanghai. It is not surprising that members of the *weiwentuan* sent to Heilongjiang were among the first to declare themselves victims of the Gang of Four, as it was Zhang Chunqiao who had originally sent them there. In late October 1976, returning from a meeting in Shanghai, the two heads of the provincial-level Shanghai *weiwentuan* in Heilongjiang found forty representatives of county teams waiting for them at the Harbin train station. Hearing no new instructions from their leaders, they demanded to return to Shanghai immediately to participate in the exposure of crimes committed by the Gang of Four. They argued it would be impossible to continue their work, as local officials in Nenjiang and Heihe counties had already told Shanghai cadres that they were no longer welcome in the countryside and that it was "time for you to go back to Shanghai." The two heads proposed seeking permission from the Shanghai Office of Sent-Down Youth for a small group of representatives to return, but this was not satisfactory to those gathered at the train station, who then rushed back to their communes and production brigades to inform other *weiwentuan* members that "everyone is going back immediately." The two heads alerted the Shanghai office, which in turn phoned the Shanghai municipal government. "What should we do?" they asked. "Please figure this out as soon as possible and provide us instructions!"[59] A few days later, the Shanghai Office of Sent-Down Youth called the municipal government again to discuss the potential return of the *weiwentuan* to Shanghai. The head of the municipal government stated that the *weiwentuan* could not return, but should instead consider the broader situation and work under local Party leadership, criticize the Gang of Four, and do "good work" with sent-down youth. Those who had returned should be persuaded to go back.[60] Still not

---

[59] SHMOSY, "Dianhua jilu" 电话记录 (Record of Telephone Conversation), October 30, 1976, SHMA.
[60] Jin Dalu and Lin Shengbao, 177.

satisfied by the government's response, the next month the Shanghai Office of Sent-Down Youth sent a report to the municipal government, concluding with questions about the necessity and political rationale for the *weiwentuan*.[61]

By mid-March of the following year, the Shanghai Office of Sent-Down Youth reached its own conclusion that the *weiwentuan*, and the office of sent-down youth itself, had been a project of the Gang of Four and most clearly represented a political error. In a report to the municipal government, the office acknowledged that its leaders had "mistakenly trusted" Gang of Four followers—Ma Tianshui, Xu Jingxian, Wang Xiuzhen, and Zhu Yongjia. "We did whatever they asked and made many mistakes." The chronicle of "mistakes" included overemphasizing an investigation of problems involving local leaders and interfering in the work of provincial leaders, disregarding the opinions of locals, establishing too many sent-down youth stations and small factory workshops, and exaggerating their successes. Gang of Four followers also allegedly emphasized improving the material conditions for sent-down youth, overlooking their political education, and failing to encourage them to set roots in the countryside. The report blamed Gang of Four policies for preventing peasants from educating youth and teaching them to engage in hard labor. And the result of adhering to the instructions of Gang of Four followers in Shanghai—Ma, Xu, and Wang—was that relationships with locals had been severed. Therefore, the report concluded that it would be impossible for the *weiwentuan* to continue its job.[62] Apparently, the Office of Sent-Down Youth was ready to attribute all efforts to support sent-down youth through the *weiwentuan* to the Gang of Four, perhaps hoping that this would shift attention away from its own potentially tarnished reputation.

The municipal government finally relented, as a week later it issued instructions to the Office of Sent-Down Youth to dismantle the teams. The office recalled all 111 members of the Jilin *weiwentuan*, for example, reassigning them jobs as cadres in Shanghai, most often at the institutions where they had previously worked, including four to Fudan University, four to Jiaotong University, fifteen to a publishing house, and eight to the Municipal Health Bureau. The Shanghai office reported that it would dispatch two cadres to Jilin to "end the *weiwentuan* work."[63]

[61] SHMOSY, "Guanyu fu waisheng qu shangshan xiaxiang xuexi weiwentuan de qingkuang baogao" 关于赴外省区上山下乡学习慰问团的情况汇报 (Report on the Conditions of the *Weiwentuan* Sent to Remote Districts), December 24, 1976, SHMA.

[62] SHMOSY, "Dui xuexi weiwentuan gongzuo de jiben kanfa yaodian" 对学习慰问团工作的几点看法和要点 (Some Opinions and Points about the Work of the *Weiwentuan*), March 12, 1977, SHMA.

[63] SHMOSY, "Guanyu Jilin weiwentuan shiyi huibao" 关于吉林慰问团事宜报告 (Report on Matters Concerning the Jilin *Weiwentuan*), March 20, 1977, SHMA.

It was not that complicated to declare the *weiwentuan* a product of the Gang of Four and recall its members to Shanghai. As their numbers were relatively small and most remained employees of urban institutions, accommodating them in the city would not constitute a major burden. But to explicitly link the entire sent-down youth movement to the Gang of Four would have resulted in bringing all the sent-down youth back to the city. The predicament for the Office of Sent-Down Youth was that terminating the movement would dramatically intensify the urban unemployment problem, yet it still concluded it was impossible to continue its task of keeping youth in the countryside.

The Office of Sent-Down Youth appeared frustrated that the central government was not providing a clear policy. In a lengthy report to the central government in October 1977, it described its own office staff as "confused," not knowing what they should be doing. During the Cultural Revolution, the report explained, the media had pronounced that the sent-down youth movement was the only way to train revolutionary successors. But now that the Gang of Four had been denounced, cadres in the office were perplexed that the media was not condemning the entire sent-down youth movement as a Gang of Four project. Some people in the office reportedly called newspapers to inquire, only to be informed that no one knew. "Now that it is the one-year anniversary of Mao's death," the authors of the report wrote, "nothing is said about sent-down youth and this is confusing."[64]

Although framed as questions, the report suggests that the leaders of the Shanghai Office of Sent-Down Youth were already convinced that the movement was in fact a product of the Gang of Four. Perhaps to support this conclusion, the report cited letters from the public that called for the movement to be deemed a misguided plan of the Gang of Four that should be ended. One from a sent-down youth declared, "The three former leaders of Shanghai turn out to be part of the Gang of Four, and have now been exposed. We should now be liberated!"[65] "I want the Party to give me an answer," the author of another letter declared. "I insist that I have the right to have an answer!" Public demands are "urgent," and "everyone wants a solution," the report continued. "All the sent-down youth are waiting for us; their parents are waiting for us. But we do not know how to solve this problem." The report complained that whatever efforts it made to implement the government's existing policy seemed to be subverted by public resentment.[66]

---

[64] SHMOSY, "Zhishi qingniang shangshan xiaxiang qingkuang fanying" 知识青年上山下乡情况反映, October 10, 1977.
[65] Ibid.   [66] Ibid.

The report concluded with a clear statement about the unwillingness of the office to continue mobilizing for the sent-down youth movement and an implicit recommendation that youth be allowed to return to the city by implementing the *dingti* policy, which allowed youth to replace parents who retired from their jobs. It advised that without such a policy in place, a worrisome number of parents were refusing to retire unless their jobs were given to their children in the countryside. The report noted that almost half of the individuals who reached retirement age in 1977 had not retired, resulting in some 100,000 people who held on to their jobs.[67] Following the example of Beijing and Tianjin, the office proposed adoption of a *dingti* policy that would enable returning youth to have urban jobs.[68]

In spite of escalating protests against the movement—now not only by sent-down youth and their parents, but also by the municipal sent-down youth office itself—the central government wavered, perhaps because state leaders themselves were desperately trying to determine how to resolve the problems caused by the sent-down youth movement. The State Council's All China Sent-Down Youth Office summoned a meeting of leaders of provincial, municipal, and district sent-down youth offices in December 1977. Again, participants questioned how the movement itself should be evaluated in light of the fall of the Gang of Four. "Should the movement be continued?" they asked. "How long should 're-education' last?" Their intense confusion is reflected in the admission of Chen Yonggui, a vice premier of the state council, that evaluating the sent-down youth movement had given all the state council leaders headaches. Chen, as well as other vice premiers, caught between the inadequate number of jobs to absorb urban youth and widespread dissatisfaction with the movement, avoided clear and direct responses to the questions. They half-heartedly expressed that Mao's movement would continue, urging provincial and municipal offices of sent-down youth to do the best job they could.[69]

In the absence of instructions from the central government, officials at local, provincial, and municipal government levels took initiatives to facilitate a far greater number of youth to leave the countryside and return to their urban homes. For example, in spring 1977, the Yunnan Office of Sent-Down Youth dispatched a group of thirty-six cadres to Shanghai from fifteen of its county offices, although by then only 251 Shanghai sent-down youth remained on production brigades in these counties. During their fifty-eight days in Shanghai, they visited the families of the sent-down youth, and then negotiated with the Shanghai government to

---

[67] Ibid.   [68] Ibid.   [69] Jin Dalu and Lin Shengbao, 282–283, 290, 295–296.

accept eighty-seven, of whom eighty were approved by Shanghai. The delegation, in an effort to "carry out government policy," also undertook efforts to persuade some fifty-odd youth who were in Shanghai to return to the countryside. They conveyed to the Shanghai Office of Sent-Down Youth that in spite of their efforts, these youth adamantly insisted on remaining in the city. Before returning to Yunnan, they expressed their intention to "stay in touch with the Shanghai government" to enable more sent-down youth with county documentation for illness to return to their urban homes.[70] Yunnan province was not unique, as over the course of the next year, a number of provinces also sent cadres to Shanghai to negotiate the return of youth with illnesses.[71]

Responding to complaints by rural residents, some provinces determined that accommodating sent-down youth constituted an unsustainable burden. "From this moment on," instructed the Yunnan Provincial Office of Sent-Down Youth, "we need to educate the sent-down youth to advance self-sufficiency and embrace the spirit of hard labor." The instructions also specified that locals should calculate how much they had paid to support the sent-down youth and be reimbursed by the provincial government.[72]

At a local level, officials devised their own strategies to reduce the burden of hosting sent-down youth. This is illustrated by the experience of Li Jiaquan, a cadre who, since 1970, had worked in the Fuyang (Anhui) county office of sent-down youth. Responsible for 20,000 sent-down youth, including more than 7,000 from Shanghai, Li recalled that in 1977, the head of his office instructed the staff to help solve the problems faced by the sent-down youth in order to "prevent them from causing trouble." Li suggested that the office give sent-down youth an excuse to return. When he proposed using health issues as a pretext, the office head initially hesitated because the Shanghai government had already rejected some of the youth his own office had approved. Furthermore, there was no directive from above that sanctioned this practice. When the office leader eventually decided to proceed, Li went to the county hospital to

[70] YNPOSY, "Guanyu fu hu jiafang gongzuo qingkuang he jixu zuohao Shanghai chadui zhiqing gongzuo de yijian" 关于赴沪家访工作情况和继续做好上海插队知青工作的意见 (Ideas on the Work of Visiting Families and Continuing to Do Good Work with Shanghai Youth Sent to Production Brigades), July 12, 1977, JHDA.

[71] SHMOSY, "Zai waidi chadui de zhishi qingnian yaoqiu 'bingtui' de renshu jizeng" 在外地插队的知识青年要求病退的人数急增 (Rapid Increase in the Number of Sent-Down Youth on Production Brigades Requesting to Return Home because of Illness), *Zhishi qingnian qingkuang fanying*, 12, June 21, 1978, SHMA.

[72] YNPOSY, "Guanyu guanche luoshi zhongyang [1978] 37 hao wenjian de tongzhi" 关于贯彻落实中央 [1978] 37 号文件的通知 (Notice on Implementing the Central Committee [1978] Directive No. 37), August 2, 1978, JHDA.

consult doctors about what would be an undisputable diagnosis. Claims of lower back pain, the physicians advised, would be hard to challenge. Using the county hospital letterhead, Li then issued certificates to every Shanghai youth still there. "I worked sixteen hours a day for two weeks," he boasted. The office head then dispatched two cadres to carry all the personnel files with the medical certificates to Shanghai. By then, the Shanghai government had apparently become more lenient, approving every certificate without requiring a health check.[73] In Nenjiang, medical doctors issued certificates of health problems on a daily basis, recording diagnoses such as: "Long-term illness; cannot work." Health conditions they certified as precluding work in the countryside included athlete's foot, broken bones, infected mosquito bites, nearsightedness, mental illness, and being "a little dumb and slow." Scores of clinic certificates featured a stamped image of a lung, on which the clinician used a pencil to indicate a dark or shady patch, demonstrating infections that would justify a return to the city.[74] In Jiangxi, too, county sent-down youth offices reported that most of the youth in the villages suddenly had "this or that kind of illness."[75] It appears that local government officials were willing to issue almost any kind of document that would enable youth to obtain permission to return to cities.[76] When doctors or officials did not readily issue permission, sent-down youth pressured and threatened them. In Huma, some youth proclaimed, "If a doctor refuses to issue a certificate of ill health, we'll crack his head!" In several cases, sent-down youth "caused big trouble," beating commune cadres.[77]

By early 1978, the Shanghai Office of Sent-Down Youth formalized its lenient treatment of youth still in villages who claimed medical reasons as an excuse to return to the city. Up until then, only doctors at municipal and district hospitals in Shanghai could provide final approval of the

---

[73] Li Jiaquan.

[74] NJCOSY, "Fancheng shenpi huiyi jilu" 返城审批会议记录 (Minutes of Screening Meeting for Returning to the City), December 1975, NJDA. In April and May 1975, numerous certificates were issued by the county clinics and hospitals verifying diagnoses of lung problems. See, for example, Nenjiang xian renmin yiyuan 嫩江省人民医院, "X xian toushi qingqiu baogao dan" X 线透视请求报告单 (Application form for X-Rays), April 21, 1975; Nenjiang guanli ju di yi zhigong yiyuan 嫩江管理局第一职工医院, "Menzhen bingzhi" 门诊病志 (Clinic Record), April 23, 1975, NJDA.

[75] SHMOSY, "Zai waidi chadui de zhishi qingnian yaoqiu 'bingtui' de renshu jizeng."

[76] Later on, such certificates were not only about health conditions, but also about divorce and death (sometimes false), so that sent-down youth who were married could be eligible to return to Shanghai. Huang Jianzhong, "Liangzhang jiehunzheng yu yizhang lihunzheng" (Two Marriage Certificates and One Divorce Certificate), in Wang Lili, Xingguang mantian de qingchun 星光满天的青春, vol. 2 (Shanghai: Shanghai renmin chubanshe, 2012), 421–424; and Han Meiying, "Wo de kule rensheng" (My Bittersweet Life), in Wang Lili, 482–486.

[77] HMCOSY, "Jianbao" 简报, July 24, 1978, HMCA.

county-issued medical certificates. The office now declared this was too strict, instructing cadres to just "use their eyes" to diagnose the apparent illness. All those who fit the category "should be treated leniently," the instructions explained. "So long as their medical history is clearly documented, or if the illness is obvious, then a hospital's confirmation is unnecessary." The office also decided that approval could be issued at "neighborhood clinics." Following this, the Huangpu district sent-down youth office organized twenty cadres, none of whom had medical training, to visit 171 sent-down youth and their families in one of its neighborhoods. These cadres visually diagnosed and approved the return of all but eighteen, whose illness they deemed "relatively mild."[78]

The ease with which health problems could now be used to return to Shanghai is illustrated by the experience of Fan Kanming, a Shanghai youth in Huaibei. In early 1978, still unable to secure official employment, Fan heard that he would be allowed to return to Shanghai if he could document a health issue. Although he had never had any problems and considered himself fairly strong, he went to see a doctor at the county hospital. When he reported that he had a weak lower back, the doctor ordered an X-ray and concluded that he might have "undetectable bone fractures" that would be aggravated by working in the fields. The doctor wrote this on hospital letterhead and stamped it with an official seal. "Doctors at that time," Fan wrote, "probably issued many of these certificates for Shanghai youth."[79]

In many of the counties that hosted sent-down youth, the sight of them packing their belongings to return to the city became commonplace in late 1978. One report observed that as soon as youth obtained a certificate of ill health, they sold clothes and furniture that they did not want to take home, ate everything in their vegetable patches, and if they had animals such as pigs, killed them to eat as well.[80]

Once Shanghai had a "wide-open door" for youth on production brigades with health problems, the rate of returning youth accelerated.

---

[78] SHMOSY, "Dangqian zhiqing bingtui gongzuo zhong cunzai de yixie wenti" 当前知青病退工作中存在的问题 (Existing Problems of the Current Work of Sick-Return to the City of Sent-Down Youth), March 18, 1978, SHMA.

[79] Fan Kangming, "Zai zhiqing da fancheng de rizi li" (During the Days of the Great Returning to the City by Sent-Down Youth), in Fan Kangming, Yang Jidong, and Wu Hao, 132–135. Many other memoirs by sent-down youth recall the schemes they worked out to make it seem they had health issues. For example, Gao Wuyi, "Zai fancheng de dachao zhong" (In the Great Wave of Returning to the City), in Wang Lili, 415–420. The numbers of youth applying for permission to leave increased dramatically: by April 1978, an average of thirty Shanghai youth in Huma each month requested certificates of ill health to return to Shanghai. In May and June, more than 200 submitted requests each month. HMCOSY, "Jianbao," July 24, 1978, HMCA.

[80] HMCOSY, "Jianbao," July 24, 1978.

In the first six months of 1978, 17,226 sent-down youth returned to Shanghai. During the same half-year, some 3,158 filed applications in the single district of Zhabei, while 3,596 applied in Huangpu district. As this lenient policy applied only to youth who remained in village production brigades, many on state farms began to transfer to the villages in order to become eligible to return. So too did youth who had been recruited by local factories and government agencies.[81] This concerned the Shanghai Office of Sent-Down Youth, which, in mid-June, convened a meeting with the heads of the city's district sent-down youth offices and warned that these practices would not be tolerated, asserting that "we need to control the policy."[82] By the end of 1978, the vast majority of youth on production brigades had left or were in the process of leaving. Even those who had been promoted to positions of commune leadership and had in the past rejected opportunities to leave the countryside now filed papers to sick-return to Shanghai.[83] In Yunnan, district and county offices of sent-down youth found that a very small number of Shanghai youth still had their legal residence in the countryside and had not made any requests. Since these individuals had been absent from the villages for years, the Yunnan officials requested that Shanghai help locate them and transfer their *hukou* back to the city.[84]

Protests Revisited

The sent-down youth movement, however, did not end when urban governments allowed youth on production brigades to return to the city. Rather, the movement came to a halt only when the central government finally extended this privilege to those on state farms in the wake of

---

[81] SHMOSY, "Zai waidi chadui de zhishi qingnian yaoqiu 'bingtui' de renshu jizeng." For transfer from state farms to production brigades, also see YNPOSY, "Fu Dongfeng nongchang zhishi qingnian gongzuo xuexi diaochazu baogao" 赴东风农场知识青年工作学习调查组报告 (Report on the Work by the Sent-Down Youth Study and Investigative Working Team to the Dongfeng Farm), June 1976, JHDA. HMCOSY, "Guanyu banli bingtui de buchong tongzhi" 关于办理病退的补充通知 (Supplementary Notice of Processing Sick-Return Applications), July 12, 1978, HMCA.

[82] Of those who had returned in the first half of 1978, two-thirds were from villages as opposed to state farms. The Shanghai Office of Sent-Down Youth proposed a quota of 40,000 for 1978. SHMOSY, "Zai waidi chadui de zhishi qingnian yaoqiu 'bingtui' de renshu jizeng."

[83] HMCOSY, "Jianbao," July 24, 1978.

[84] The Xishuangbanna Office of Sent-Down Youth, for example, issued letters to several district offices of sent-down youth in early 1979. Apparently, there were only a few Shanghai youth who still had their *hukou* in the countryside by then. These letters stated that "after consulting with the communes and production brigades, we found it very difficult for them to work in the field or for us to make other arrangements locally." JHDA.

protests, demonstrations, and work and hunger strikes. The details of these protests have been described extensively in a number of scholarly accounts and need not be repeated here. However, treating sent-down youth as an undifferentiated category, most of these accounts obscure the fact that only youth on state farms participated in the protests.[85]

The dramatic protests did not involve youth on production brigades because, as we have seen, most of them had left. At this time, it seemed that the government had no intention of extending leniency to youth on state farms, where self-sufficiency was not an issue. While rural leaders had actually facilitated the departure of youth on production brigades, the departure of state farm youth would have been extremely detrimental, depleting the labor force and seriously jeopardizing the sustainability of these enterprises that had received substantial investments during their early years. There was also the problem of urban employment: municipal governments throughout China had struggled to accommodate youth returning from production brigades as well as more recent secondary school graduates, and would be hard-pressed to create jobs for those on state farms.

It appears that Shanghai confronted a far more serious employment problem than that of other major cities, which more readily allowed state farm youth to return. Watching their coworkers from other cities leave, Shanghai youth became increasingly agitated. Some of them wrote complaints to the Shanghai Office of Sent-Down Youth, one signed by fifty-three youth from Shanghai on state farms in Inner Mongolia. The letter pointed out that Beijing had allowed all of its youth there to use illness as a pretext to return to the city; and that the Tianjin government had sent representatives to Inner Mongolia to assist in processing youth returning from state farms, including those who had married. Youth from Zhejiang, the letter pointed out, had been allowed to take their parents' jobs through *dingti*. "They all cheerfully packed their luggage and returned home, taking jobs in factories and other enterprises." Noting that in the past youth on state farms were from all parts of China, the letter bemoaned that "now only our lone army of Shanghai sent-down youth are still here."[86] In the end, the Shanghai Office of Sent-Down Youth, responding both to state farm leaders and to the youth who had signed the

[85] See Gold, McLaren, and Bin Yang.

[86] SHMOSY, "Neimeng nongchang de Shanghai qingnian lianming lai xin yaoqiu bingtui huihu" 内蒙农场的上海青年联名来信要求病退回沪 (Shanghai Youth on the Inner Mongolia State Farm Signed a Petition Demanding Sick-Return to Shanghai), September 16, 1978, SHMA. In Yunnan, at the time protests began, 70 percent of the 8,372 youth from Beijing on state farms had returned home, while only 22.4 percent from Shanghai had returned. Zhonggong Yunnan shengwei dangshi yanjiushi, "Yunnan shengchan jianshe bingtuan (nongken) zhiqing gaikuang," 160–161.

letter, indicated that it would determine what to do after receiving instructions from the anticipated national sent-down youth conference.[87]

Youth on state farms were also waiting for the national conference. According to a Shanghai youth in Xishuangbanna, Lu Rong, many were "hoping that the new policy will meet our expectations. Everyone was talking about how to get back to the city."[88] It was in this context that 1,000 sent-down youth in Yunnan signed a petition to central government leaders, hoping to influence the national sent-down youth conference, about to begin in October 1978. Convened by the central government's national council, this conference spent more than a month considering the future of the movement. In the middle of this conference, an editorial in *China Youth News* (*Zhongguo qingnian bao*), blaming Lin Biao and the Gang of Four for the sent-down youth movement, urged all government bureaus to help solve the problem by creating jobs and increasing college enrollment.[89] This ignited popular hope that the conference would both end the sent-down youth movement and allow all youth to return.

The conference summary, issued and broadcast as Document 74 in mid-December 1978, came as a deep disappointment to youth on state farms. Carefully avoiding an explicit denunciation of the movement, it stated that "[the] movement has been successful." In contrast to *China Youth*, which had categorized the movement as a conspiracy launched by Lin Biao and the Gang of Four, Document 74 only blamed them for having undermined the movement. Nonetheless, it specified that the movement would continue, and that hopefully, with the Four Modernizations and changes in the structure of employment, the number of sent-down youth will be reduced "until we do not have to pursue the current form of the sent-down youth movement." It called upon all bureaus to create jobs and to expand opportunities in higher education. "Cities that have the ability to assign jobs to graduates," Document 74 stated, "may curtail the mobilization of youth to go to the countryside."[90]

Document 74 reinforced the distinction between youth on production brigades and those on state farms, stipulating that the former would be eligible to return to the city, while the latter would not. If those "sent to villages outside their home province indeed have difficulties performing agricultural labor, and therefore need special care, the mobilizing and allocating regions should work together to make arrangements for them. When necessary, the state labor bureau will provide support." As for

---

[87] SHMOSY, "Neimeng nongchang de Shanghai qingnian lianming lai xin yaoqiu bingtui huihu," September 16, 1978, SHMA.
[88] Lu Rong, 431.   [89] *Zhongguo qingnianbao*, November 23, 1978.   [90] Yang Xinqi, 446.

youth on state farms, in contrast, Document 74 instructed that "we should encourage and support them to settle and contribute to the development of the farms." More specifically, it declared that future sick-return or hardship-return requests would not be approved for state farm youth, and that they would no longer be permitted to transfer to village production brigades. Sent-down youth, the document stated, would receive the same benefits as other state farm workers, the only exception being that those who were married would be granted three additional paid visits to their parents in the city.[91] In other words, the single document that officially specified that all youth remaining on production brigades could return to the cities rejected the same privilege for youth on state farms.

News of the central government's policy not only enraged state farm youth, but escalated actions they had already initiated to demand a return to the cities. While the conference was taking place in Beijing, sent-down youth on some seventy state farms in Xishuangbanna had, since their first petition, continued to organize. When the government ignored their petitions, 50,000 of them staged a strike during which they took over the broadcast station and administrative offices of some state farms. They also mobilized a delegation to go to Beijing to ensure that their demands be heard. The promulgation of Document 74 made it clear that their opinions had been dismissed, provoking anger, described by Ding Huimin as "one hundred times more intense than a stirred-up hornet's nest." In Xishuangbanna, when Document 74 was announced, some youth grabbed the document and tore it up, shouting, "We don't want to listen to empty words! We do not want to be cheated!" When cadres arrived, sent-down youth ambushed them and seized their car.[92]

In the following weeks, sent-down youth, blocked by public security officers from boarding a train from Kunming to Beijing, staged a sit-in on the tracks. A group that reached Beijing held demonstrations near Tian'anmen Square, carrying banners with slogans such as "We want to appeal!" "We demand to see Chairman Hua and Vice Chairman Deng!" Demonstrations also took place in major cities including Shanghai (where some 10,000 people gathered in front of the municipal government buildings), Chengdu, and Kunming.[93]

---

[91] Zhonggong zhongyang bangongshi, "Zhonggong zhongyang tongzhi" (Announcement of the CCP Central Committee), December 12, 1978, in Zhonggong Yunnan shengwei dangshi yanjiushi, *Yunnan zhishiqingnian shangshan xiaxiang yundong*, 368–379.

[92] Yang Xinqi, 187.

[93] In Shanghai demonstrators were said not only to have attacked government buildings and blocked traffic, but also to have assaulted women, robbed stores, and beaten the police. For an account of the protests in Shanghai, see Gold; Bonnin, 149–154; McLaren; and Yang Xinqi, 438.

It was the protests on the Mengding State Farm (in Xishuangbanna) in January 1979 that compelled the central government to shift its position. After being ignored for weeks, 1,500 marched to the Mengding headquarters, occupied the administrative offices, and announced by phone to the central government that some 200 were beginning a hunger strike. Zhao Fan, head of the state agricultural bureau that oversaw state farms, was summoned to Mengding to meet the protestors. In order to bring the hunger strike to an end, he promised the participants that their "reasonable demands" would be met.[94] This was the first indication that the government might concede to the strikers' demands.

By early February, the State Council reversed the provisions in Document 74. It contacted the Yunnan provincial government, expressing its hope that some state farm youth would stay to promote "stability and the Four Modernizations." However, now any urban youth wanting to transfer back to the city could use sickness-return, difficulty-return, or *dingti*. A day later, on February 6, the State Council's revised document was officially circulated. Almost immediately, state farms began to negotiate with urban representatives for the return of their youth. The Yunnan provincial government, by offering them a salary increase, promised to "let those unwilling to stay on the farms leave."[95] At this point in time, government appeals about contributing to the nation, socialism, and modernization by staying on the state farms rang hollow. By May 1979, some 94 percent of state farm sent-down youth in Yunnan had left.[96] During that same year, close to 4 million sent-down youth throughout China returned to their urban homes.[97]

An Ambivalent State

It might be tempting to regard these events as a story of a protest movement that successfully achieved its goal of changing government policy, and, likewise, that the changed policy was a result of the protests. To a certain extent, it was. These demonstrations and strikes by state farm youth would have been unimaginable before the fall of the Gang of Four,

---

[94] Yang Xinqi, 443.
[95] Yunnan sheng geming weiyuanhui, "Guanyu Guanche zhixing zhongyang (1978) 74 hao wenjian tongchou jiejue wosheng guoying nongchang zhiqing ji youguan wenti de tongzhi" (Announcement Concerning the Implementation of the Central Committee 1978 Directive 74 and Systematically Solving Problems of Sent-Down Youth on State Farms in Our Province), February 6, 1978, in Zhonggong Yunnan shengwei dangshi yanjiushi, *Yunnan zhishi qingnian xiaxiang shangshan yundong*, 380–381.
[96] Yang Xinqi, "Yunnan nongchang zhiqing dafancheng," 189.
[97] Gu Hongzhang, 162.

and more particularly its sanctioning of public assemblies in November 1978. It is not coincidental that the protests expanded and intensified at precisely this time and intersected with the nascent democracy movement that was also emerging.

However, a closer look at what transpired during the protest movement reveals that this was more than a story of discontent and angry state farm youth whose protests compelled the government to surrender to their demands. Were it not for the large-scale exodus of youth on production brigades who had been returning to the city throughout the previous years, it is unlikely that the state farm protests would have erupted. Furthermore, the leadership structure of the state farms was wavering, although for reasons very different from what happened on the production teams. Leaders did not openly support the protests, but, more importantly, they did not invoke their authority to stop them. This absence of intervention on their part—as well as that of government officials—reflects a resignation to the demise of the farms.

The passivity of state farm leadership faced with thousands of protesting youth is particularly striking in the recollection by Ding Huimin, one of the principal leaders of the protests in Yunnan. He was surprised that cadres appeared to avert their eyes and pretend not to see the gatherings of protesting youth. Rather than commanding Ding to bring the gatherings of protestors to an end, state farm officials suggested that they avoid intruding on busy central government leaders and offered to convey their grievances to the government. Almost two months later, when the protestors decided to go to Beijing, they went first to report to the district government in Jinghong and to alert officials of their intended send-off gathering of 10,000 people. During the thirty hours they spent at the government building, it seemed that the officials had all deserted their offices and refused to be seen. Perhaps perplexed that leaders made no effort to "educate" or persuade, let alone threaten, them to stop their protests, Ding recalled that instead, "they were determined to avoid us."[98]

When the protestors staged a strike, the provincial government sent a work team to Jinghong to dissuade them from going to Beijing. The work team made no effort to stop the strike, but instead repeatedly tried to assure them that they would do everything within their power to meet the "reasonable demands of sent-down youth." At the following meeting, the work team conveyed that the state farm and district government should refrain from interfering with the strike. When striking youth at the Mengpeng State Farm seized control of the broadcast station and

[98] Ding Huimin, 390–441.

declared independence, heads of the state farm dared not return to the farm, fearing confrontation with the protesting youth. This avoidance of the protests was implicitly sanctioned by the district government, which had instructed the fearful cadres to simply "educate them in a positive way."[99] The message that the strikers would not be punished was repeated a month later, in January, when the strikers demanded to be paid for the time they had stopped work. The government's investigative team agreed to do so once they returned to work. In addition, the team recommended that those who continued to strike be issued a portion of their salary to cover food.[100]

This is not to say there was a complete absence of government efforts to suppress the movement. For example, when the state farm youth sat in on the tracks at the Kunming train station, the central government issued three orders to disband, threatening to punish anyone who in future beat up police or railroad workers and commanding the youth to return to the state farm. When these measures failed, the government sent police to disperse the sit-in. But more striking is how little farm officials did to restrict the movement: they allowed the protests, tolerated a month-long strike, and made a barely minimal effort to stop occupations of state farm administrative offices or seizures of broadcast systems. Possibly they were overwhelmed by the tens of thousands of state farm youth who joined the protests. More likely, they did not want to intervene without explicit instructions from the central government. At the same time, they repeatedly informed the central government that they had "lost control," that the state farms were "paralyzed," and that they were waiting for the central government to act.[101] Whatever the reason, it is clear that administrative officials who would normally ensure stability and control took no action. Perhaps they believed that the only solution was to allow the youth to leave, a measure that would have required authorization by the central government.

Another complexity in the story of the state farm protests concerns the role of district and provincial governments in the central government's ultimate decision to end the sent-down youth movement. This is particularly evident in the government's decision to reverse the policy about state farms in Document 74. From Zhao Fan's account of his meeting with the hunger strikers, we learn that the Sichuan provincial government, recognizing the participation of Sichuan youth in the state farm protests, had already proposed to transfer home all youth sent to Yunnan before 1972, a proposal that Zhao Fan supported. "I will report this to the central government," he told the hunger strikers. "Comrades, your demand has hope. But we need to give Chairman Hua and the central government a little time."[102] Meanwhile, co-ordinated by the national office of sent-down youth, governments of all the provinces and cities involved in either sending or receiving youth crafted a six-point proposal, the most important of which was to allow state farm youth to use the same pretexts as production brigade youth to return home.[103] Within several weeks, the Yunnan provincial government, having secured approval from the Shanghai and Beijing municipal governments, transmitted a similar proposal to the central government. Not receiving a response, it sent two more telegrams, declaring, "We are waiting for your approval." When, on February 5, the State Council contacted the Yunnan government, its initial statement was simply, "We approve!" This suggests that the new directive was essentially an endorsement of policy crafted by municipal and provincial leaders.

There is one additional complexity to the story of the policy finally permitting all youth to return to the cities, and that concerns the role of major cities, particularly Shanghai. If a major, albeit unspoken, impetus to mobilize youth to go to the countryside in the late 1960s was to resolve serious employment problems in urban centers, then allowing them to return would produce an equally serious problem. As those on production brigades had already been leaving villages and returning to the city, quite possibly the only way to avoid an employment crisis would be to draw a distinction between the urban youth sent to villages and those sent to state farms. Undoubtedly government leaders who convened in late 1978 harbored conflicting views of the relationship between the sent-down youth movement, Mao, the Cultural Revolution, and the Gang of Four, reflected in the confusing language of Document 74 that both upheld and denounced the movement. Yet these disagreements were most likely eclipsed by recognition of the impossibility for Shanghai to provide jobs for the huge number of state farm youth who would suddenly be back in the cities. The particular problems for Shanghai were more explicitly acknowledged in January 1979: when the head of the Yunnan provincial government reported to the state agricultural bureau that although Yunnan agreed with the proposed revision of Document 74 permitting state farm youth to return to the city, he urged Shanghai youth to consider staying on the farms, as their return would "create the most problems for Shanghai."[104] It is not possible to determine what caused the Shanghai government to finally agree to accept all the sent-down

---

[102] Yang Xinqi, "Yunnan sheng zhishi qingnian shangshan xixiang yundong dashiji," 443.
[103] Gu Hongzhang, 152.   [104] Ding Huimin, 437.

youth. But it is clear not only that Shanghai government representatives participated in the deliberations that produced the revision of Document 74, but also that the revision specifically addressed the resettlement of Shanghai youth.

Conclusion

Unlike the launching of the sent-down youth movement, announced by newspaper headlines, banners, and loudspeakers on city streets, there was no analogous fanfare marking the movement's termination. And in contrast to the massive sending-off gatherings when youth departed for the countryside, no public ceremonies greeted them upon their return. As we have seen, beginning in the mid-1970s, youth on production brigades, often assisted by members of the *weiwentuan*, by cadres in both local and Shanghai sent-down youth offices, and by health care providers, found excuses or policy loopholes to return to the city. Document 74 simply acknowledged and sanctioned practices that had been taking place for a number of years. The revised version of Document 74, although not declaring a definitive end to the movement, provided a final solution by allowing state farm youth as well as youth on production brigades to return to the city. Subsequent Shanghai government documents that addressed sent-down youth issues focused not on whether or not they could return, nor on whether or not the movement had ended, but rather on the practical means by which they could be housed and employed in the city. Meanwhile, and perhaps imperceptibly, the administrative apparatus of the sent-down youth movement dismantled, as both urban and rural sent-down youth offices merged into labor bureaus, the national one folding into the labor bureau in late 1981. The return of the majority of sent-down youth to the cities and the closure of sent-down youth offices may have represented the final message: that the gulf between the city and countryside could not be bridged.

7 Epilogue

In May 2013, visiting the area near Heihe, Heilongjiang, we encountered a group of young men working in the cornfield. Directing them to use a new high-powered sowing and planting machine was a tall sixty-year-old man, Yang Xiaohu, a former sent-down youth from Shanghai who had lived in this area from 1970 to 1976. After his return to Shanghai, Yang attended college, worked for an oil company, and spent several years in Africa engaged in a business venture. After retiring he decided to settle in the same village to which he had been sent three decades ago. Having been a production brigade leader during the time he was a sent-down youth, villagers eagerly turned to him to help solve problems that resulted from three decades of privatization of agriculture, especially the dismantling of irrigation systems, the difficulty of acquiring large farming machines, and the lack of support for families with no male offspring. To help confront some of these problems, he lobbied for government grants to help organize an agricultural co-operative in 2013, which also received substantial support from former sent-down youth.

Yang Xiaohu was not the only former sent-down youth who returned to live in northern Heilongjiang. Two others, both women, had gone back to nearby Shanhe village in Xunke county. Perhaps expecting that thirty years of economic reform would have made the village more prosperous, Jia Aichun found it desolate and dreary, as most young people had left to seek jobs in urban areas and village houses were now older, worn down, and dilapidated. Jia's first project was to raise money from former sent-down youth to build a clubhouse, restoring a space for public gathering that had been dismantled in conjunction with the end of the collective production system.[1] When some villagers asked her to help establish a co-operative, she turned to Xu Juju, a friend from her time in the village,

---

[1] Yu Zhejie and Pan Gaofen, "Zuodian neng gaibian xianzhuang de shi: Xiri Shanghai zhiqing Xu Juju chongfan di'er guxiang Heilongjiang dailing baixin zhifu de gushi" (Do Something That Could Change the Current Situation: A Story about the Former Shanghai Sent-Down Youth Xu Juju Returning to Her Second Native Place in

Photo 7.1 Former sent-down youth Yang Xiaohu at Heihe, Heilongjiang,
helping villagers organize a co-op.
Photo by Emily Honig.

who, after returning to Shanghai in 1979, had established a successful
accounting career.[2] Xu and Jia proved to be effective lobbyists, known
to sit for days at the door of stubborn local officials. After securing
"new village" funding from the government, they persuaded most of

Heilongjiang to Lead Ordinary People to Become Prosperous), *Xinmin wanbao*,
September 29, 2012.
[2] Ibid.

the villagers to pool their land and establish an agricultural co-operative in 2012, hoping that additional grants would enable the village to purchase its own machinery.[3]

When Yang, Xu, and Jia returned to Heilongjiang, decades had passed since the end of the sent-down youth movement. Ideals of fostering prosperity in the remote villages in which they had lived during the Cultural Revolution would have been inconceivable during the years immediately following their return to the city in the late 1970s. At that time, most sent-down youth, grateful to have returned to their urban homes, sought to put behind them the years spent in the impoverished countryside. As widespread denunciation of Mao and the Cultural Revolution erupted, their identity as sent-down youth was not embraced or celebrated. If anything, their experience in the countryside disadvantaged them, and many, already approaching their thirties, had to accept low-level jobs in the city. These were the people that literature and the media referred to as the "lost generation."

The return to the countryside by individuals such as Yang, Jia, and Xu took place in a profoundly different context. By the early twenty-first century, former sent-down youth had spent two decades living and working in Shanghai. Although most struggled financially and socially, some were able to take advantage of opportunities that became available with the economic reforms of the 1980s and 1990s. Former sent-down youth who became prominent government leaders, business entrepreneurs, scholars, acclaimed writers, or artists invariably attributed these achievements to their experience living in the countryside. Even the world-famous go player, Nie Weiping, explained his winning strategies as a product of the wide-ranging perspective he developed during his years navigating life in the "vast land of Heilongjiang."[4]

Approaching (or having reached) retirement, a large number of former sent-down youth began to reconnect with the villages in which they had lived in the late 1960s and the 1970s. Some, through membership in a rapidly growing network of sent-down youth associations, traveled to their former villages to visit peasant friends, or to bring their own children to see the places where they had lived as adolescents. Some gave donations to village schools, while others invested in local economic development projects. The villagers welcomed their old acquaintances from the city. "When you return to the countryside," Jia Aichun explained, "you

---

[3] Ibid.

[4] Zhou Han, "Nie Weiping: Beidahuang zouchu de qisheng" (The Go Master Who Came Out from the Great Northern Wilderness), October 10, 2010, www.people.com.cn/GB/198221/198819/204159/12909939.html, accessed February 1, 2017.

Photo 7.2 The coauthor reunited with old friends in the village thirty years later.
Photo by Emily Honig.

are considered a treasure ... Coming to Shanhe, so many people care about you and need you."[5]

Initiated by former sent-down youth, this reconnection with villages was soon utilized by rural leaders, who, because of the impact of economic reform on the countryside, began reaching out to urban youth, encouraging them to re-engage with and contribute to their "second hometowntown" (di'er guxiang). To many villages in remote regions, the former sent-down youth, residents of China's most prosperous city, could provide resources and expertise to which they otherwise did not have access. Although these contemporary reconnections between former

---

[5] Yu Zhejie, "Beijing Shanghai nü zhiqing lianshou tuixiu er ci 'chadui' bangzhu nongmin zhifu"; Gong Minmin and Zhou Xuefen, "Taiyan meitian xianhuo, chongfan nongcun dailing xiangqin gongtong zhifu de lao zhiqing Jia Aichun fangtan" (The Sun Is Sparkling Every Day: An Interview with Former Sent-Down Youth Jia Aichun Who Returned to the Countryside to Lead the Peasants to Get Rich), www.myoldtime.com/a/shidai/guandian/2015/1106/2416.html, accessed July 16, 2017.

sent-down youth and the villages are beyond the scope of this study, a cursory consideration suggests legacies of the movement both for individuals and more importantly for urban–rural connections, ones established during the movement which did not dissolve when the movement ended.

At first glance, the reconnection between former sent-down youth and rural villages might appear to have erupted quite suddenly in the 1990s, but in fact such relationships had never been completely severed. In the years following the end of the sent-down youth movement, although few former sent-down youth went back to visit their villages, rural residents sometimes traveled to the city, and whenever they did so, they invariably contacted youth whom they knew. Most of the returned youth did not yet have stable jobs, but they offered their rural friends temporary housing, food, and company. Almost anything that the returned youth could provide was critical to visitors who had little money and no experience in large cities. When Liu Fachun from Huma brought his gravely ill father to Shanghai in the late 1970s, former sent-down youth with whom he had worked in the village not only met him at the train station but arranged for a car and housing for them and negotiated the father's admission to the prominent Huashan Hospital.[6] At that point in time, these former sent-down youth seemed to share a sense of responsibility for the villagers who had once hosted them and who had otherwise no access to privileges that urban residents took for granted.

In the 1990s, contact between returned youth and their former rural hosts expanded. The relaxation of policies restricting migration enabled far more rural residents to seek education and urban work, particularly as menial laborers in construction and domestic service. Connections with returned youth also became important in the efforts of rural counties to develop their local economy. As the central government implemented new policies on prices and taxes, relaxed restrictions on trade, and privatized state enterprises, marketing regional products and seeking investment for local enterprises became priorities for local governments.[7] Large cities with established enterprises could easily take advantage of the reforms and consolidate their dominance of the domestic market, while at the same time expanding into international trade. The situation was very different for remote and isolated regions with little industrial base. For them, connections with Shanghai and Beijing, where money, skill, technology, and consumers were concentrated, became crucial.

---

[6] Liu Fachun, "Cuotuo suiyue zhu zhenqing" (Deep Feelings Developed in Those Unremarkable Years), in Liu Shijie, *Huma zhiqing fengyunlu xuji*, 272–274.

[7] Graeme Smith, "The Hollow State: Rural Governance in China," *China Quarterly*, 203 (2010), 601–618.

The role of former sent-down youth in enabling rural leaders to compete in the market economy is illustrated by the efforts of Huma county leaders to market local products in Shanghai. In 1995, former sent-down youth now working in Shanghai not only negotiated a prominent downtown location for a trade fair, but also arranged a press release about the event.[8] At the trade fair they helped promote the products of Huma, such as blueberry juice and wine.[9] Three years later, when the Huma county head Xu Shoule went to Shanghai as part of a delegation to seek business and attract investments (*zhaoshang yinzi*), 300 former sent-down youth gathered to welcome him.[10]

Throughout this time, some returned youth also initiated efforts to promote the educational and economic development of their former villages. One, having become a professor in Shanghai, established a program to provide intensive training courses for 1,000 middle school English teachers in a county in Jiangxi where she had lived.[11] Another who had become an entrepreneur donated money to help peasants in Shangrao (Jiangxi) repair their homes, build a school, and establish a scholarship. He also helped bring village children to Shanghai to see doctors.[12] Meanwhile, Shanghai sent-down youth who had been sent to Inner Mongolia raised funds to finance schooling for children of poor families, develop a sent-down youth forest, establish a medical laboratory, and engineer running water in peasants' homes.[13] Similar stories of "giving back to their second hometown" include investments in local enterprises by former sent-down youth such as a textile mill in Guizhou and a clothing factory in Jiangxi.[14] And two others contributed funds for a soy

---

[8] Wang Yuchen, "Zhandou cun jie shuoguo" (Zhandou Village Bears Big Fruits), in Liu Shijie, *Huma zhiqing fengyunlu*, 35–36.

[9] Xu Shoule, "Wo de Shanghai zhiqing yuan" (My Destined Connection with Sent-Down Youth), in Liu Shijie, *Huma zhiqing fengyunlu*, 42.

[10] Ibid.

[11] Chen Guoliang and Luo Haoping, "Qing xi hong tudi: Shanghai zhiqing zai gannan" (Feelings Tied to the Red Soil: Shanghai Sent-Down Youth in Southern Jiangxi), May 21, 2009, www.mr699.cn/new/html/tndb/2009–05-21/205043.htm, accessed July 28, 2017.

[12] "Qing wujia, wangshi kan huishou" (Priceless Sentiments: The Past Is Remembered), *Jiangxi huabao*, September 2001, http://shzq.net/jxpd/wskhs.html, accessed June 26, 2014.

[13] Wang Jiarong, "Shanghai zhiqing zai Neimengu" (Shanghai Sent-Down Youth in Inner Mongolia), *Zhiqing* (Sent-Down Youth), 3 (2015), http://shzqyjh.cn/archives/view-178 5–1.html, accessed July 12, 2017.

[14] Zhang Mingyong, "Qinggan zhaoshang po changgui: Ji Guizhou zhiqing Yang Yanshu" (Breaking Customs to Attract Business through Sentimentality: A Story of Guizhou Sent-Down Youth Yang Yanshu), May 6, 2012, http://zhiqingwang.shzq.org/guizhouD es.aspx?ID=5446, accessed June 26, 2014. Also see Xiao Ge, "Dongri de nuanliu" (A Warm Feeling on Winter Days), August 27, 2010, http://zhiqingwang.shzq.org/jiangxA rtD.aspx?ID=2290, accessed June 26, 2014.

bean paste factory in Huma to upgrade its equipment and acquire automatic bottling machines, turning the "Happy Huma" (Huyue) bean paste into a prize-winning product.[15]

Not all former sent-down youth became financially successful (most did not), but even those with far more limited means made small contributions to their former villages, now commonly referred to as their "second hometown." While some of these contributions represented their own initiative, often they were also part of a growing establishment of associations of former sent-down youth. In the mid-1990s, almost all major cities witnessed the emergence of sent-down youth associations. In Shanghai, separate associations for each province (and sometimes each county) to which youth had been sent all affiliated with the umbrella Shanghai Sent-Down Youth Association. These associations organized reunions, sponsored trips to the countryside, and invited former sent-down youth to gather when local officials visited Shanghai. The Shanghai-wide association published magazines and newsletters and sponsored research projects.

With the growing availability of the internet in the late 1990s, these associations created websites which enabled far more extensive exchanges among former sent-down youth, including the posting of anecdotes, memories, and photographs, as well as discussion forums.[16] The websites also made possible more intensive connections between returned youth and villagers, some of whom used them to post messages to former sent-down youth, hoping to reconnect with them. A small number of younger rural residents used the Web even to search for the sent-down youth whom they had been told were their birth parents, such as one young man, now the father of an eight-year-old son, who tried to locate his birth mother, whom he had never met. All he knew was that his adopted mother first met the sent-down youth at a marketplace when the latter was pregnant.[17]

The websites also proved useful to local officials hoping to obtain support for economic development projects. Some used the Shanghai website's "long bridge of loving hearts" link to post information about local projects, to honor individual entrepreneurs who had already donated or invested, to announce visits of local officials to Shanghai,

[15] Huma xian zhengfu, "Jinian xiaxiang zhiqing sishi zhou nian jianghua gao" (Outline of a Speech on the 40th Anniversary of Sent-Down Youth), June 24, 2010, www.reader8.cn /data/20100624/511163.html, accessed July 12, 2017.

[16] It was originally named Lao zhiqing yizhan ("old sent-down youth hostel"), created by Zi Yan. Its name changed to Shanghai zhiqing wang in 2000. See Xiao Ge, "Shanghai zhiqingwang shinian."

[17] Message of August 7, 2013, http://zhiqingwang.shzq.org/message.aspx?type=6&page=2, accessed June 14, 2014.

and to invite former sent-down youth to meetings that would take place during such visits.[18]

The cultivation of connections with former sent-down youth was part of a broader effort by rural counties to compete in the market economy that accompanied the economic reforms. Rural leaders throughout China scrambled to identify potential sources of investment, in many cases establishing "investment working groups" that have produced glossy guides to opportunities and provided lavish banquets for prospective investors.[19] In the parts of China with a history of overseas emigration (particularly Guangdong and Fujian), local leaders have worked to cultivate connections with overseas Chinese, sometimes holding conventions to attract financial contributions and investments.[20] Not having overseas connections, remote counties perceived former sent-down youth, now urban residents, as a potential source of economic investment.

Remote counties in Heilongjiang, which hosted some of the largest numbers of Shanghai youth, have been particularly active in utilizing connections with former sent-down youth in Shanghai. Liu Shichang, district vice Party secretary of Huma whose family had formed close friendships with many sent-down youth, praised them for having broken down "the isolation of a remote frontier region." He went on to describe their relationship as "a knot that could never be untied."[21] Extending this to the recent past, county head Xu Shoule explained that

these Shanghai sent-down youth are the treasure of Huma . . . They are a unique human resource that we are so fortunate to have. Cultivating this resource will enable us to access ideas and concepts, new technology, and financial investment from Shanghai . . . We have natural resources and we need to combine those with the intellectual resources of Shanghai.

He labeled this effort "calling the phoenix back to its nest" (*yinfeng huanchao*).[22]

Through connections with a former sent-down youth who had been elected vice head of the Shanghai suburb Fengxian, Xu Shoule established a "sister county" relationship between Huma and Fengxian. When Xu went to Shanghai for the ceremony, he seized the opportunity to

---

[18] Xiao Ge, "Shanghai zhiqingwang shinian" (10 Years of the Shanghai Sent-Down Youth Website), September 21, 2011, http://blog.sina.com.cn/s/blog_3f7ebf3c0100umlk.html, accessed June 12, 2014.

[19] Graeme Smith, 601–618.

[20] Hong Liu, "Old Linkages, New Networks: The Globalization of Overseas Chinese Voluntary Associations and Its Implications," *China Quarterly*, 155 (1998), 588–609.

[21] Liu Shichang, "Huifang, huiyi, sikao" (Going Back, Remembering, and Contemplating), in Liu Shijie, *Huma zhiqing fengyunlu xuji*, 567.

[22] Xu Shoule, 43.

gather several hundred former sent-down youth and organized panel discussions for them to share their memories. The participating former youth included leaders of Shanghai industrial bureaus, banks, and districts, who volunteered their ideas for the economic development of Huma. Excited by this, Xu planned to establish a Huma office in Shanghai, and an affiliated restaurant that would feature northeastern cuisine and provide a gathering place for former sent-down youth. Summarizing his project, Xu wrote that "our effort was to refresh old memories of sent-down youth and to stimulate their strong sentimental attachment to Huma. This is to build a bridge connecting the hearts of people in Shanghai and the remote Huma county."[23]

Huma's neighboring city, Heihe, likewise engaged in efforts to "call the phoenix back to its nest." In October 2003, its mayor and Party secretary held a meeting with sent-down youth entrepreneurs in Shanghai, humbly addressing them as "respected Shanghai sent-down youth friends":

Thirty five years ago, following Chairman Mao's call, you came to Heihe … With a heroic spirit of bitter struggle you not only made a huge contribution to the development of your second native place, but also left the treasure of high civilization, creativity, and selfless devotion. After your return to Shanghai you fully developed your talent and wisdom, relying on the strong will that had been tested on the frontier … The villages of your second native place are proud of you and because of you, are proud of themselves, especially that you have not forgotten the development of your second native place, contributing ideas, plans, money, and energy … Heihe will not forget you and deeply thanks you.

Lamenting that his district lacked resources, he expressed its need to collaborate with places like Shanghai, "the center of China and the world." He concluded by highlighting the "precious business opportunities" that would await Shanghai entrepreneurs in this northeastern frontier.[24]

Although northern Heilongjiang counties such as Heihe and Huma stand out for their proactive efforts to recruit former sent-down youth, they are by no means unique. In March 2014, four major leaders from Suiyang in Guizhou, having traveled to Shanghai to explore investment possibilities, participated in a celebration of the 45th anniversary of sent-down youth. At the Shanghai celebration, they showed a film, *Impressions of Suiyang*, to more than 300 former sent-down youth. The county head expressed his delight in seeing these former sent-down youth and having the opportunity to share with them recent local developments:

[23] Ibid., 45.
[24] Yu Xiaodong, "Zai Shanghai Heihe zhiqing ji minying qiyejia kentanhui shang de jianghua" (A Talk to Former Heihe Sent-Down Youth and Private Entrepreneurs in Shanghai), October 30, 2003, http://shzq.net/hljpd/yxdjh.html, accessed June 22, 2014.

You left a sparkling trace in Suiyang ... We miss you and thank you. Now Suiyang, influenced by your spirit, is changing. Our guiding principle is to treat our guest businessmen as family and to hold entrepreneurs high above our heads. I sincerely hope that you will often come to visit your second hometown in Suiyang ... At the same time, we especially welcome you, your friends, and family to explore investment opportunities. Let's work together to make our homeland achieve even greater prosperity!

According to the news report, the Shanghai former sent-down youth all expressed their willingness to build a bridge between Shanghai and Suiyang to facilitate the county's efforts to attract business investment.[25]

In addition to efforts to attract business investment, some rural counties used sent-down youth connections to promote tourism. In 2008, Yunnan tourist agencies organized the first China Sent-Down Youth Travel Festival to commemorate the fortieth anniversary of Mao's 1968 call for urban youth to go to the countryside. The idea was to invite former sent-down youth from throughout China to travel in Yunnan. The next year, in 2009, Xishuangbanna held a second sent-down youth culture travel festival featuring performances by former urban youth to advance the tourist industry of Yunnan and Xishuangbanna.[26]

Tourist bureaus in other provinces made similar efforts to expand their business using sent-down youth as a travel theme. In 2012, the Jiangxi government sponsored the Third All-China Sent-Down Youth Culture–Tourist–Art Festival, called Lushan bei ("the Mount Lu cup"). More than a thousand former sent-down youth from all over the country, accompanied by families and friends, congregated in Lushan, where several model sent-down youth, such as Xing Yanzi and Hou Jun were among the invited speakers. The participants then visited Jinggangshan and Nanchang.[27] A county in Guizhou decided to create a China Sent-Down Youth Culture Park that would feature models of old sent-down youth dwellings. In conjunction with Guizhou's tea and Miao ethnic

---

[25] Zhao Zhenlin, "Xian lingdao kanwang weiwen Guizhou Suiyang Shanghai zhiqing xuanchuan tuijie Suiyang" (The County Leaders Came to Visit and Introduce Suiyang to the Former Sent-Down Youth), March 27, 2014, http://zhiqingwang.shzq.org/gui zhouDes.aspx?ID=8170, accessed June 13, 2014.

[26] Peng Xi, "Xishuangbanna zhiqing wenhua lüyoujie jiang yu 12 yue zai Jinghong juxing" (The Sent-Down Youth Tourist Culture Festival of Xishuangbanna Will Be Held in December in Jinghong), November 18, 2009, http://news.ifeng.com/history/zhiqing/huo dong/200911/1118_6853_1441863.shtml, accessed April 6, 2014.

[27] Lushan lüyou fazhan gufen youxian gongsi, "Lushan bei disanjie Zhongguo zhiqing lüyou wenhuajie zai Lushan kaimu" (The Third Lushan Cup Opens at the Chinese Sent-Down Youth Travel Culture Festival at Lushan), June 11, 2012, www.prnasia.com/sto ry/63063-1.shtml, accessed July 12, 2017.

culture, the government imagined this reserve would become a nationally known lucrative tourist site.[28]

Of course, the effort to harness local history and culture to the promotion of tourism is not confined to places with former sent-down youth. Throughout China, small remote towns and cities have searched for historical events that might earn them a place on tourist maps. This is most obvious in the emergence of "red tourism," which has brought both foreign and domestic visitors to places significant in the history of the CCP revolution, such as Jinggangshan, Yan'an, and otherwise desolate locations along the path of the legendary Long March. Almost any obscure historical event could become the focus of a museum or monument that would potentially lure tourists to places with little else to offer. For example, Aihui had established a museum to commemorate the 1858 "Sino-Russian Treaty of Aihui," described in textbooks as one of the many unequal treaties to which China was subjected. Located on the banks of the river separating China and Russia, Aihui also tried advertising itself as a "cradle" for a blended "Chinese–Russian culture." It turned out that the nearby museum focused on the experiences of sent-down youth drew far more tourists than the one commemorating a nineteenth-century treaty or allegedly unique cultural form. The city now boasts a sprawling, bright red modernistic building. Like other sent-down youth museums throughout China, it displays photos of sent-down youth working, playing musical instruments, performing plays or dances, and serving as barefoot doctors, as well as "artifacts" of that time, such as old tractors, spades, eating utensils, and ragged clothes.

Some counties also solicited and published memoirs, a project often welcomed by former sent-down youth. When a Huma county official, Liu Shijie, went to Shanghai in 2001 to solicit memoirs, hundreds of former sent-down youth greeted her, with dozens visiting her hotel every evening. They continually expressed to her their gratitude for recording this challenging part of their lives and "turning it into history." According to her account, they thanked the local government and people for remembering and praising their contributions and the price they paid.[29]

These renewed connections suggest two parallel agendas: those of former sent-down youth wanting to "give back to their second hometown" and the aspirations of rural leaders to invoke connections with these individuals to promote economic development. These agendas are not mutually exclusive. It may well be that the former sent-down youth

[28] Zheng'an xian Banzhu xiang renmin zhengfu, "Zhongguo zhiqing buluo shengtai wenhua lüyou qu" (China Sent-Down Youth Ecological and Cultural Tourist Site), April 2, 2013, www.gztoptour.com/html/2015/zy_0126/1367.html, accessed July 12, 2017.

[29] Liu Shijie, "Zhuanshu ji shenqing," 678–679.

Photo 7.3 Aihui Sent-Down Youth Museum.
Photo by Emily Honig.

Photo 7.4 Sent-down youth remembrance wall in Huma, Heilongjiang.
Photo by Emily Honig.

did not scoff or summarily dismiss documents explicitly "calling the phoenix back to its nest" because these initiatives evoked their emotional attachment to the countryside and intersected with their own desires to commemorate that part of their lives or to make their years of retirement significant by contributing to rural economic development.

The publication of memoirs, the organization of sent-down youth reunions, group trips to revisit villages, and jubilant expressions of attachment to their "second hometown" surprised, confused, and even disturbed some social commentators. One attributed it to nostalgia and argued that this reconnection with villages purported to express resistance to the economic reforms of the 1990s.[30] Reflecting the extent to which almost anything associated with the Cultural Revolution remains deeply political, some accused these former sent-down youth of being "victims" who "love the past."[31] And when an exhibit about the sent-down youth movement at the Olympic Stadium in Beijing attracted crowds of visitors, an outspoken Peking University professor described it as "turning evil into a grand enterprise."[32] Responding more directly to former sent-down youth reconnecting with their former villages, some mockingly asked, "Why don't you send your own sons and daughters, or grandsons and granddaughters, to the harshest and most impoverished countryside in the northwest and let them stay there for eight years?"[33]

Not everyone shared these critical characterizations of former sent-down youth reconnecting with rural communities, one magazine editor retorting that "chickens cannot possibly understand eagles."[34] Some former sent-down youth proclaimed that theirs was "an unregrettable youth."[35] Furthermore, the plethora of memoirs and accounts they wrote could hardly be described as romanticizing or glorifying the years of the sent-down youth movement or suggesting that it should be repeated. At most, some implied that experience in the countryside instilled in them a perspective on social and economic issues distinct from that of people who had never left the city.

[30] GuobinYang, "China's zhiqing generation: Nostalgia, Identity, and Cultural Resistance in the 1990s," *Modern China*, 29 3 (2016), 267.
[31] Dai Yugang, "Zhiqing wenxue de zouxiang" (The Direction of Sent-Down Youth Literature), *Changzhi ribao*, September 9, 2012, http://blog.tianya.cn/post-4877164-57356968-1.shtml, accessed July 28, 2017.
[32] Xu Zhigao, 213.   [33] Ibid.   [34] Ibid.
[35] Xu Xiao, "Gai zenme pingjia zhiqing shangshan xiaxiang: 'qingchun wuhui' nandao cuole me?" (How Should the Sent-Down Youth Be Evaluated: Is the "Unregrettable Youth" Possibly Wrong?) December 22, 2014, www.thepaper.cn/newsDetail_forward_1287904, accessed July 12, 2017. In fact, some conferences of former sent-down youth invoked the theme "an unregretful youth."

The renewed connections between former sent-down youth and their "second hometowns," and more particularly the roles they have assumed in promoting the development of the villages in which they lived, do not represent a linear story of old relationships being reconfigured in a new historical moment. Nor can they be reduced to a remnant of Maoist politics (urban youth receiving peasant re-education) that has proved useful to local officials having to navigate a new set of economic policies. All of this is taking place in a social landscape—both rural and urban—that has undergone a dramatic transformation. From the 1990s, when former sent-down youth began to visit and make new commitments to their "second hometowns," these villages, not frozen in time, had instead experienced profound change. Some may have been almost unrecognizable as a result of vast improvements in material conditions; others may have more resembled the one Jia Aichun described: a dilapidated ghost town. Like so many villages throughout China, most young and middle-aged adults had left these villages, migrating to cities to work and secure education for their children. As a vast number of small cities emerged throughout what had once been rural China, these villages became shells of what they had once been.[36]

Urbanization has not diminished the significance of urban–rural conflict in contemporary China. The sent-down youth movement, unique in generating a migration of urban residents to the countryside, did little to narrow the urban–rural divide. The post-Mao economic reforms triggered a reversion to the far more familiar pattern of peasants migrating to urban areas. With the relaxation of the household registration system, the boundary between cities and the countryside blurred. By the early twenty-first century, urban–rural conflict was no longer confined to the crossing of a geographic divide between countryside and city, but has also been forged and fought about within cities, where the division between urban residents and rural migrants is among the most salient social issues.

When urban youth first went to the countryside, they were fully aware that the world of the city and that of the countryside were entirely different. As adolescents at the time, few could perceive this urban–rural divide as a product of Maoist policies that impoverished the countryside by extracting its resources to promote urban industrial development. Like the sent-down youth who could observe rural poverty but not understand its contribution to urban wealth, contemporary urban residents complain about the backwardness of rural migrants but for the most part do not recognize the necessity of migrant labor for urban

---

[36] Xiang Biao, "How Far Are the Left-Behind Left Behind?", *Population Space and Place*, 13, 3 (2007), 179–191.

development and prosperity. All of this highlights the stubborn persistence of beliefs that urban society is advanced, modern, and futuristic, while rural society represents an impoverished past to which no one should look back. During the Cultural Revolution, these beliefs helped to thwart the sent-down youth movement, and the movement itself also perpetuated such beliefs.

Over the nearly five decades since the movement's end, stories of sent-down youth have been widely consumed by a fascinated urban public. Whether in the form of anecdotes, memoirs, fiction, paintings, photographs, films, or even academic articles, these stories are almost without exception produced by urbanites for an exclusively urban audience. The heroes and heroines, as well as the victims, in these stories are most often sent-down youth. Rural villagers, some of whom may well have been victimized by the movement, appear as malevolent abusers to be despised, or as benevolent, if backward, hosts to be pitied, the majority simply an invisible backdrop to the experiences of urban youth sent to live with them. In this context, not only did the sent-down youth movement itself reflect and perpetuate the urban–rural divide, but also the very telling and retelling of stories about sent-down youth unwittingly continues to fuel the conviction that city residents, sophisticated and civilized, are superior to rural villagers, and that China's urban–rural divide is indeed impossible to cross.

Bibliography

Abbreviations

OSY (Office of Sent-Down Youth)

AHCOSY: [Heilongjiang] Aihui County Office of Sent-Down Youth (Aihui xian zhishi qingnian shangshan xiaxiang bangongshi 爱辉县知识青年上山下乡办公室)

AHPOSY: Anhui Provincial Office of Sent-Down Youth (Anhui sheng zhishi qingnian shangshan xiaxiang bangongshi 安徽省知识青年上山下乡办公室)

BJMOSY: Beijing Municipal Office of Sent-Down Youth (Beijing shi zhishi qingnian shangshan xiaxiang bangongshi 北京市知识青年上山下乡办公室)

GZPOSY: Guizhou Provincial Office of Sent-Down Youth (Guizhou sheng zhishi qingnian shangshan xiaxiang bangongshi 贵州省知识青年上山下乡办公室)

HJCOSY: [Heilongjiang] Hanjiang★ County Office of Sent-Down Youth (Hanjiang xian zhishi qingnian bangongshi 寒江县知识青年上山下乡办公室)

HLJPOSY: Heilongjiang Provincial Office of Sent-Down Youth (Heilongjiang sheng zhishi qingnian shangshan xiaxiang bangongshi 黑龙江省知识青年上山下乡办公室)

HMCOSY: [Heilongjiang] Huma County Office of Sent-Down Youth (Huma xian zhishi qingnian shangshan xiaxiang bangongshi 呼玛县知识青年上山下乡办公室)

JADOSY: [Shanghai] Jing'an District Office of Sent-Down Youth (Jing'an qu zhishi qingnian shangshan xiaxiang bangongshi 静安区知识青年上山下乡办公室)

JLPOSY: Jilin Provincial Office of Sent-Down Youth (Jilin sheng zhishi qingnian shangshan xiaxiang bangongshi 吉林省知识青年上山下乡办公室)

★ Hanjiang is the fictitious name for a county in Heilongjiang, used in Chapter 4 to protect the anonymity of individuals involved in criminal investigations.

JXPOSY: Jiangxi Provincial Office of Sent-Down Youth (Jiangxi sheng zhishi qingnian shangshan xiaxiang bangongshi 江西省知识青年上山下乡办公室)

JYCOSY: [Heilongjiang] Jiayin County Office of Sent-Down Youth (Jiayin xian zhishi qingnian shangshan xiaxiang bangongshi 嘉荫县知识青年上山下乡办公室)

MCCOSY: [Jiangxi] Micang* County Office of Sent-Down Youth (Micang xian zhishi qingnian shangshan xiaxiang bangongshi 米仓县知识青年上山下乡办公室)

MHCOSY: [Yunnan] Menghai County Office of Sent-Down Youth (Menghai xian zhishi qingnian shangshan xiaxiang bangongshi 勐海县知识青年上山下乡办公室)

NJCOSY: [Heilongjiang] Nenjiang County Office of Sent-Down Youth (Nenjiang xian zhishi qingnian shangshan xiaxiang bangongshi 嫩江县知识青年上山下乡办公室)

NMGAROSY: Inner Mongolia Autonomous Region Office of Sent-Down Youth (Neimenggu zizhiqu zhishi qingnian shangshan xiaxiang bangongshi 内蒙古自治区知识青年上山下乡办公室)

PTDOSY: [Shanghai] Putuo District Office of Sent-Down Youth (Putuo qu zhishi qingnian shangshan xiaxiang bangongshi 普陀区知识青年上山下乡办公室)

SHMOSY: Shanghai Municipal Office of Sent-Down Youth (Shanghai shi zhishi qingnian shangshan xiaxiang bangongshi 上海市知识青年上山下乡办公室)

XKCOSY: [Heilongjiang] Xunke County Office of Sent-Down Youth (Xunke xian zhishi qingnian shangshan xiaxiang bangongshi 逊克县知识青年上山下乡办公室)

XSBNAPOSY: [Yunnan] Xishuangbanna Autonomous Prefecture Office of Sent-Down Youth (Xishuangbanna zizhizhou zhishi qingnian shangshan xiaxiang bangongshi 西双版纳自治州知识青年上山下乡办公室)

YNPOSY: Yunnan Provincial Office of Sent-Down Youth (Yunnan sheng zhishi qingnian shangshan xiaxiang bangongshi 云南省知识青年上山下乡办公室)

ZBDOSY: [Shanghai] Zhabei District Office of Sent-Down Youth (Zhabei qu zhishi qingnian shangshan xiaxiang bangongshi 闸北区知识青年上山下乡办公室)

Archives

AHCA: [Heilongjiang] Aihui County Archives (Aihui xian dang'an guan 爱辉县档案馆)

BJMA: Beijing Municipal Archives (Beijing shi dang'an guan 北京市档案馆)

---

* Micang is the fictitious name of a county in Jiangxi, used in Chapter 4 to protect the anonymity of individuals involved in criminal investigations.

HJCA: [Heilongjiang] Hanjiang* County Archives (Hanjiang xian dang'an guan 寒江县档案馆)

HMCA: [Heilongjiang] Huma County Archives (Huma xian dang'an guan 呼玛县档案馆)

JADA: [Shanghai] Jing'an District Archives (Jing'an qu dang'an guan 静安区档案馆)

JHDA: [Yunnan] Jinghong District Archives (Jinghong diqu dang'an guan 景洪地区档案馆)

JYCA: [Heilongjiang] Jiayin County Archives (Jiayin xian dang'an guan 嘉荫县档案馆)

MCCA:[Jiangxi] Micang* County Archives (Micang xian dang'an guan 米仓县档案馆)

NJCA: [Heilongjiang] Nenjiang County Archives (Nenjiang xian dang'an guan 嫩江县档案馆）

PTDA: [Shanghai] Putuo District Archives (Putuo qu dang'an guan 普陀区档案馆)

SHMA: Shanghai Municipal Archives (Shanghai shi dang'an guan 上海市档案馆)

XKCA: [Heilongjiang] Xunke County Archives (Xunke xian dang'an guan 逊克县档案馆)

ZBDA: [Shanghai] Zhabei District Archives (Zhabei qu dang'an guan 闸北区档案馆)

Special Collection

CCRD: Chinese Cultural Revolution Database (Zhongguo wenhua da geming wen ku 中国文化大革命文库), 2010. CD Rom compiled by Song Yongyi 宋永毅. Hong Kong: Chinese University of Hong Kong.

Books and Articles

Atash, Farhad and Xinhao Wang. 1990. "Satellite Town Development in Shanghai, China: An Overview." *Journal of Architecture and Planning Research* 7(3): 245–257.

Ba Shan 巴山. 1992. "Bei pohai de qingchun: Dalu shangshan xiaxiang nü zhiqing canzao roulin lu" 被迫害的青春： 大陆上山下乡女知青惨遭蹂躏录 (A Record of the Tragic Oppression of Female Sent-Down Youth). *Zhongguo zhichun* 108 (May): 58–64.

Beijing shi difangzhi bianzhuan weiyuanhui 北京市地方志编撰委员会, ed. 2007. *Beijingzhi zonghejuan: Renmin shenghuozhi* 北京志综合卷:人民生活志 (The Beijing Comprehensive Volume: People's Livelihood Gazetteer). Beijing: Beijing chubanshe.

---

* For Hangjian and Micang, see above note.

Bernstein, Thomas P. 1977. *Up to the Mountains and Down to the Villages: The Transfer of Youth from Urban to Rural China.* New Haven: Yale University Press.

Bonnin, Michel. 2013. *The Lost Generation: The Rustication of China's Educated Youth (1968–1980)* (trans. Krystyna Horko). Hong Kong: The Chinese University Press.

Brown, Jeremy. 2012. *City versus Countryside in Mao's China: Negotiating the Divide.* Cambridge: Cambridge University Press.

Brown, Jeremy. 2014. "Spatial Profiling: Seeing Rural and Urban in Mao's China," in James Cook, Joshua Goldstein, Matthew D. Johnson, and Sigrid Schmalzer, eds., *Visualizing Modern China: Image, History, and Memory, 1750–Present.* London: Lexington Books, 203–218.

Brown, Jeremy and Matthew D. Johnson. 2015. *Maoism at the Grassroots: Everyday Life in China's Era of High Socialism.* Cambridge, MA: Harvard University Press.

Cao Wensheng 曹文胜. 2004. "Shanghai ganbu zai Huma" 上海干部在呼玛 (Shanghai Cadres in Huma), in Liu Shijie, *Huma zhiqing fengyunlu xuji,* 610–614.

"Chadui luohu shi Lichuan wengongtuan zhiqing de naxieshi" 插队落户时黎川文工团知青的那些事 (Lichuan Performing Troupe during the Time of the Sent-Down Youth). www.redgx.com/hongselicheng/wenge/13553.html. Accessed July 16, 2017.

Changning qu zhi bianzhuan weiyuanhui 长宁区志编撰委员会. 1999. *Changning qu zhi* 长宁区志 (Changning District Gazetteer). Shanghai: Shanghai shehui kexueyuan chubanshe.

Chen Guoliang 陈国梁 and Luo Haoping 罗浩平. 2009. "Qing xi hong tudi, Shanghai zhiqing zai gannan" 情系红土地：上海知青在赣南 (Feelings Tied to the Red Soil: Shanghai Sent-Down Youth in Southern Jiangxi), May 21. www.mr699.cn/new/html/tndb/2009–05-21/205043.htm. Accessed July 28, 2017.

Chen, Janet Y. 2012. *Guilty of Indigence: The Urban Poor in China, 1900–1953.* Princeton: Princeton University Press.

Chen Jian 陈健. 2013. "Zhiqing yiyi" 知青意义 (The Significance of Sent-Down Youth), January 25. http://zhiqingwang.shzq.org/guizhouDes.aspx?ID=6793. Accessed September 8, 2013.

Chen Jiang 陈绛. 2015. *Chen Jiang koushu lishi* 陈绛口述历史 (An Oral History of Chen Jiang). Shanghai: Shanghai shudian chubanshe.

Chen Jianhua 陈建华. 2002. "Zhiqing shengya zaji" 知青生涯杂记 (Life as a Sent-Down Youth), in Liu Shijie, *Huma zhiqing fengyunlu,* 321–325.

Chen, Joan, dir. 1998. *Xiu Xiu: The Sent-Down Girl.* Good Machine Production.

Chen, Kuan, Wang Hongchang, Zheng Yuxin, Gary H. Jefferson, and Thomas G. Rawski. 1988. "Productivity Change in Chinese Industry, 1953–1985," *Journal of Comparative Economics* 12(4): 570–591.

Chen Liming 陈黎明. 2002. "Niu yuan" 牛缘 (My Destiny: Cows), in Liu Shijie, *Huma zhiqing fengyunlu,* 179–181.

Chen Ping 陈平. 2011. "Yuxi shi zhishi qingnian shangshan xiaxiang yundong zongshu" 玉溪市知识青年上山下乡运动综述 (Overview of Sent-Down

Youth Movement in the City of Yuxi), in Zhonggong Yunnan shengwei dangshi yanjiu shi, *Yunnan zhishi qingnian shangshan xiaxiang yundong*, 64–73.

Chen Xiaofang 陈晓方. 1998. (Untitled), in Pei Yulin, Huang Hongji, Jin Dalu, and Tian Dawei, *Lao zhiqing xiezhen*, 12.

Chen Yingfang 陈映芳. 2006. *Penghu qu: Jiyi zhong de shenghuoshi* 棚户区：记忆 中的生活史 (Shantytown: Life History through Memory). Shanghai: Shanghai guji chubanshe.

Cheng Yunting 陈云亭. 2002. "Buyu lixianji" 捕鱼历险记 (Fishing Adventures), in Liu Shijie, *Huma zhiqing fengyunlu*, 174–176.

Dai Yugang 戴玉刚. 2012. "Zhiqing wenxue de zouxiang" 知青文学的走向 (The Direction of Sent-Down Youth Literature), *Changzhi ribao* 长治日报, September 9. http://blog.tianya.cn/post-4877164-57356968-1.shtml. Accessed July 28, 2017.

Davis, Angela. 1981. *Women, Race and Class*. New York: Vintage Books.

Deng Xian 邓贤. 1996. *Zhongguo zhiqing meng* 中国知青梦 (The Dream of China's Sent-Down Youth). Beijing: Wenhua shehui chubanshe.

Diamant, Neil J. 2000. *Revolutionizing the Family: Politics, Love, and Divorce in Urban and Rural China, 1949–1968*. Berkeley: University of California Press.

Diao Xiaoming 刁晓明. 2012. "Yunnan Dongfeng nongchang daibiao chuxi shoujie Zhongguo zhiqing bowuguan yantaohui" 云南东风农场代表出席首 届中国知青博物馆研讨会 (Representatives of the Yunnan Dongfeng State Farm Participating in the First All-China Conference on Sent-Down Youth Museums), September 10. http://zhiqingwang.shzq.org/yunnanDes.aspx?I D=6080. Accessed April 6, 2014.

Ding Huimin 丁惠民. 2004. "Banna zhiqing zai xingdong" 版纳知青在行动 (Sent-Down Youth in Action in Xishuangbanna), in Liu Xiaomeng, ed., *Zhongguo zhiqing koushu shi*, 390–441.

Ding Yizhuang 定宜庄. 1998. *Zhongguo zhiqingshi: Chulan 1953–1968* 中国知青 史：初澜 1953–1968 (History of the Early Sent-Down Youth in China, 1953–1968). Beijing: Zhongguo shehui kexue chubanshe.

Eyferth, Jacob. 2009. *Eating Rice from Bamboo Roots: The Social History of a Community of Handicraft Papermakers in Rural Sichuan, 1920–2000*. Cambridge, MA: Harvard University Press.

Esherick, Joseph W., Paul G. Pickowicz, and Andrew G. Walder. 2006. *The Chinese Cultural Revolution as History*. Stanford: Stanford University Press.

Fan Kangming. 2008. "Diyici chugong" 第一次出工 (The First Time I Went to Work), in Fan Kangming, Yang Jidong, and Wu Hao, *Guntang de nitu*, 30–32.

Fan Kangming. 2008. "Jieshou zai jiaoyu" 接受再教育 (Receiving Re-education), in Fan Kangming, Yang Jidong, and Wu Hao, *Guntang de nitu*, 43–48.

Fan Kangming. 2008. "Ma Lie jingdian zhuzuo hanshou duanxun ban" 马列经典 著作函授短训班 (Short-Term Distance-Learning Course on Selected Marxist and Leninist Works), in Fan Kangming, Yang Jidong, and Wu Hao, *Guntang de nitu*, 89–101.

Fan Kangming. 2008. "Nanwang de rizi" 难忘的日子 (Days That Are Difficult to Forget), in Fan Kangming, Yang Jidong, and Wu Hao, *Guntang de nitu*, 12–17.

Fan Kangming. 2008. "Shanghai manzi" 上海蛮子 (Shanghai Barbarian), in Fan Kangming, Yang Jidong, and Wu Hao, *Guntang de nitu*, 49–53.

Fan Kangming. 2008. "Wo de zhiqing rensheng" 我的知青人生 (My Life as a Sent-Down Youth), in Fan Kangming, Yang Jidong, and Wu Hao, *Guntang de nitu*, 21.

Fan Kangming. 2008. "Zai zhiqing da fancheng de rizi li" 在知青大返城的日子里 (During the Days of the Great Returning to the City by Sent-Down Youth), in Fan Kangming, Yang Jidong, and Wu Hao, *Guntang de nitu*, 132–135.

Fan Kangming 范康明, Yang Jidong 杨继东 and Wu Hao 吴浩. 2008. *Guntang de nitu: Sange Shanghai zhiqing de wangshi* 滚烫的泥土:三个上海知青的往事 (Boiling Hot Soil: Stories of Three Shanghai Sent-Down Youth). Hangzhou: Zhejiang daxue chubanshe.

Fan Zi 凡子. 2011. "Yi wenge zhuming yuan'an: 'qiangjian nü zhiqing an' shimo" 忆文革著名冤案:"强奸女知青案"始末 (The Full Story of Remembering the Famous Case Of "the Rape of a Female Sent-Down Youth"), *Fenghuang wang lishi* 凤凰网历史, 10, 13.

Feng Xiaoping 冯小平. 2004. "Nanwang de 84 muqi chang" 难忘的 84 木器厂 (The Unforgettable No. 84 Woodwork Factory), in Liu Shijie, *Huma zhiqing fengyunlu xuji*, 182–183.

Fiskesjö, Magnus. 2016. "Bury Me with My Comrades: Memorializing Mao's Sent-Down Youth." *Asia-Pacific Journal: Japan Focus* 16(14) (April): 1–25.

Friedman, Edward, Paul G. Pickowicz, and Mark Selden. 1991. *Chinese Village, Socialist State*. New Haven: Yale University Press.

Gao Wuyi 高五一. 2012. "Zai fancheng de dachao zhong" 在返城的大潮中 (In the Great Wave of Returning to the City), in Wang Lili, *Xingguang mantian de qingchun*, vol. 2, 415–420.

Gardner, John. 1971. "Educated Youth and Rural–Urban Inequalities, 1958–1966," in John W. Lewis (ed.), *The City in Communist China*. Stanford: Stanford University Press, 268–276.

Gold, Thomas B. 1980. "Back to the City: The Return of Shanghai's Educated Youth." *China Quarterly* 84: 755–770.

Gong Minmin 龚敏敏 and Zhou Xuefen 周雪芬. 2015. Taiyang meitian xianhuo, chong fan nongcun dailing xiangqin gongtong zhifu de lao zhiqing Jia Aichun fangtan 太阳每天鲜活—重返农村带领乡亲共同致富的老知青贾爱春访谈 (The Sun Is Sparkling Everyday: An Interview with Former Sent-Down Youth Jia Aichun Who Returned to the Countryside to Lead the Peasants to Get Rich). www.myoldtime.com/a/shidai/guandian/2015/1106/2416.html. Accessed July 16, 2017.

Gross, Miriam. 2016. *Farewell to the God of Plague: Chairman Mao's Campaign to Deworm China*. Berkeley: University of California Press.

Gu Hongzhang 顾洪章. 2008. *Zhongguo zhishi qingnian shangshan xiaxiang dashiji* 中国知识青年上山下乡大事记 (Chronology of China's Sent-Down Youth). Beijing: Renmin ribao chubanshe.

Guowuyuan zhongyang junwei 国务院中央军委. 1973. "Guanyu Huang Yantian and Li Yaodong jianwu pohai nü zhishi qingnian anjian de tongbao" 关于黄砚田、李耀东奸污迫害女知识青年案件的通报 (Circular of the State Council and the Central Military Commission on the Case of Huang Tiantian and Li Yaodong Raping and Harming Female Sent-Down Youth), August 11, in Song Yongyi, ed., *The Chinese Cultural Revolution Database CD-ROM*. Hong Kong: The Chinese University Press, 2002.

Han, Dongping. 2008. *The Unknown Cultural Revolution: Life and Change in a Chinese Village*. New York: Monthly Review Press.

Han Meiying 韩梅英. 2012 "Wode kule rensheng" 我的苦乐人生 (My Bittersweet Life), in Wang Lili, *Xingguang mantian de qingchun*, vol. 2, 482–486.

He Jian 贺建. 1998. "Lanjiao monan" 烂脚磨难 (The Torture of an Infected Foot), in Pei Yulin, Huang Hongji, Jin Dalu, and Tian Dawei, *Lao zhiqing xiezhen*, 210–211.

Hodes, Martha.1993. "The Sexualization of Recontruction Politics: White Women and Black Men in the South after the Civil War." *Journal of the History of Sexuality* 3(3) (January): 402–417.

Honig, Emily. 1992. *Creating Chinese Ethnicity: Subei People in Shanghai, 1850–1980*. New Haven: Yale University Press.

Honig, Emily. 2000. "Iron Girls Revisited: Gender and the Politics of Work in the Cultural Revolution," in Barbara Entwisle and Gail E. Henderson, eds., *Redrawing Boundaries: Work, Households, and Gender in China*. Berkeley: University of California Press, 97–110.

Hua Zefei 花泽飞. 2010. "Zhiqing shenghuo shi wo de rensheng jishi" 知青生活是我的人生基石 (Being a Sent-Down Youth Is the Cornerstone of My Life), in Zhonggong Yunnan shengwei dangshi yanjiushi, *Yunnan zhishi qingnian shangshan xiaxiang yundong*, 199–203.

Huang Jianzhong 黄建忠. 2012. "Liangzhang jiehunzheng yu yizhang lihunzheng" 两张结婚证与一张离婚证 (Two Marriage Certificates and One Divorce Certificate), in Wang Lili, *Xingguang mantian de qingchun*, vol. 2, 421–424.

Huichun xian geming weiyuanhui wuqi bangongshi 珲春县革命委员会五七办公室. 2016. "Huichun xian xiaxiang zhishi qingnian gongzuo diaocha baogao" 珲春县下乡知识青年工作调查报告 (Report on Work with Sent-Down Youth in Huichun County), June 1, 1973, in Xu Zhigao, *Wenge shigao: Wuchan jieji wenhua da geming*, 263–280.

Huma xian zhengfu 呼玛县政府. 2010. "Jinian xiaxiang zhiqing sishi zhounian jianghua gao" 纪念下乡知青四十周年讲话稿 (Outline of a Speech on the 40th Anniversary of Sent-Down Youth), June 24. www.reader8.cn/data/20 100624/511163.html. Accessed July 12, 2017.

Huo Mu 火木. 1990. *Guangrong yu mengxiang: Zhongguo zhiqing ershiwu nian shi* 光荣与梦想：中国知青二十五年史 (Glory and Dream: The Twenty-Five-Year History of China's Sent-Down Youth). Chengdu: Chengdu chubanshe.

Jiang Danping 蒋旦萍. 2014. "Nongnong de qingsi: Huiyi Anhui sheng shangshan xiaxiang gongzuo" 浓浓的情思：回忆安徽省上山下乡工作 (Thick

Affections: Recalling "Up to the Mountains and Down to the Countryside" Work in Anhui Province), in Zhonggong Anhui shengwei dangshi yanjiushi, *Anhui zhiqing koushu shilu*, vol. 1, 37–54.

Jiangxi sheng difangzhi bangongshi 江西省法院志办公室. 1996. *Jiangxi sheng fayuanzhi* (Jiangxi Province Court Gazetteer). Jiangxi: Fangzhi chubanshe.

Jiefang ribao 解放日报 (*Liberation Daily*). Shanghai.

Jin Dalu 金大陆 and Jin Guangyao 金光耀, eds. 2014. *Zhongguo xin difangzhi: Zhishi qingnian shangshan xiaxiang shiliao jilu* 中国新地方志：知识青年上山下乡史料辑录 (China's New Gazetteers: Historical Materials on the Sent-Down Youth Movement), 6 vols. Shanghai: Shanghai renmin chubanshe and Shanghai shudian chubanshe.

Jin Dalu 金大陆 and Jin Guangyao 金光耀, eds. 2009. *Zhongguo zhishi qingnian shangshan xiaxiang yanjiu wenji* 中国知识青年上山下乡研究文集, 1–3 (Collected Research Essays on Sent-Down Youth in China), 3 vols. Shanghai: Shanghai shehui kexueyuan chubanshe.

Jin Dalu 金大陆 and Lin Shengbao 林升宝. 2014. *Shanghai zhishi qingnian shangshan xiaxiang yundong jishilu* 上海知识青年上山下乡运动纪事录 (Chronicle of Shanghai Sent-Down Youth). Shanghai: Shanghai shudian chubanshe.

Johnson, Kay Ann. 1983. *Women, the Family and Peasant Revolution in China*. Chicago: University of Chicago Press.

Li Jianping 李建萍. 2007. "Zhiqing shidai de 'chongdian'" 知青时代的"充电" (Getting a "Recharge" during the Era of Sent-Down Youth). http://shzq.net/jxpd/zqcd.html. Accessed February 2, 2017.

Li Jiaquan 李家全. 2013. "Yingxiangli de lishi" 影相里的历史 (History in a Photo Album) *Jianghuai wenshi* 江淮文史 4: 126–131.

Li Weiliang 李维良. 2004. "Nanwang Huma guan aiqing" 难忘呼玛关爱情 (The Love and Care of Huma Is Unforgettable), in Liu Shijie, *Huma zhiqing fengyunlu xuji*, 251–252.

Li Xinquan 李新泉. 2004. "Beiguo daoxiang: Huiyi Shanghai zhishi qingnian zai gaohan diqu shizhong shuidao chenggong de gushi" 北国稻香：回忆上海知识青年在高寒地区试种水稻成功的故事 (A Story of Recalling the Shanghai Sent-Down Youth Who Succeeded in an Experiment with Rice Cultivation in a High-Altitude and Cold Region), in Liu Shijie, *Huma zhiqing fengyunlu xuji*, 680–685.

"Lishi de tiankong: Zhiqing shangshan xiaxiang dashiji" 历史的天空：知识青年上山下乡大事记 (The Sky of History: A Chronology of Sent-Down Youth), May 18, 2007. www.chsi.com.cn/jyzd/jygz/19200705/20070518/908609.html. Accessed April 18, 2017.

Litwack, Leon. 2017. "Hell Hounds," in James Allen, Hilton Als, John Lewis, and Leon F. Litwack, eds., *Without Sanctuary: Lynching Photography in America*. Santa Fe: Twin Palms Publishers, 8–37.

Liu Fachun 刘发春. 2004. "Cuotuo suiyue zhu zhenqing" 蹉跎岁月铸真情 (Deep Feelings Developed in Those Unremarkable Years), in Liu Shijie, *Huma zhiqing fengyunlu xuji*, 272–274.

Liu, Hong. 1998. "Old Linkages, New Networks: The Globalization of Overseas Chinese Voluntary Associations and Its Implications." *China Quarterly* 155: 588–609.

Liu Lianying 刘连英. 2013. "Wo qu Shanghai jie zhiqing" 我去上海接知青 (I Went to Shanghai to Pick Up Sent-Down Youth). *Zhiqing* 知青 (Sent-Down Youth) 2: 42–43.

Liu Shichang 刘世常. 2004. "Huifang, huiyi, sikao" 回访、回忆、思考 (Going Back, Remembering, and Contemplating), in Liu Shijie, *Huma zhiqing fengyunlu xuji*, 567–569.

Liu Shijie 刘世杰, ed. 2002. *Huma zhiqing fengyunlu* 呼玛知青风云录 (The Story of Sent-Down Youth in Huma). Shanghai: Shangwu lianxi chubanshe.

Liu Shijie 刘世杰, ed. 2004. *Huma zhiqing fengyunlu xuji* 呼玛知青风云录续集 (The Story of Huma Sent-Down Youth, vol. 2). Shanghai: Shangwu lianxi chubanshe.

Liu Shijie 刘世杰. 2004. "Zuanshu ji shenqing" 纂书寄深情 (Compiling a Book to Express Deep Sentiment), in Liu Shijie, *Huma zhiqing fengyunlu xuji*, 673–679.

Liu Xiaohang 刘晓航. 2008. *Women yao huijia: 1979 Yunnan zhiqing da fancheng zhenxiang jiemi* 我们要回家:云南知青大返城真相揭密 (We Want to Return Home: Revealing the Secret about the Great Return to the City of Yunnan Sent-Down Youth). Hong Kong: China Culture Art Publishing House.

Liu Xiaomeng 刘小萌. 2008. *Zhongguo zhiqingshi: Dachao (1968–1980)* 中国知青史：大潮 (1968–1980) (History of China's Sent-Down Youth, 1968–1980). Beijing: Dangdai zhongguo chubanshe (originally published by Zhongguo shehui kexue chubanshe, 1998).

Liu Xiaomeng, ed. 2004. *Zhongguo zhiqing koushu shi* 中国知青口述史 (Oral Histories of China's Sent-Down Youth). Beijing: Zhongguo kexue chubanshe.

Liu Xiaomeng. 1995. *Zhongguo zhiqing shidian* 中国知青事典 (Major Events and Documents of China's Sent-Down Youth). Chengdu: Sichuan renmin chubanshe.

Lu, Hanchao. 1995. "Creating Urban Outcasts: Shantytowns in Shanghai, 1920–1950." *Journal of Urban History* 21(5): 563–596.

Lu, Hanchao. 1999. *Beyond the Neon Lights: Everyday Shanghai in the Early Twentieth Century*. Berkeley: University of California Press.

Lü Qiaofen 吕巧凤 and Xie Chunhe 谢春河, eds. 2013. *Heilongjiang sheng zhishi qingnian shangshan xiaxiang dashiji* 黑龙江省知识青年上山下乡大事记 (Chronology of Sent-Down Youth in Heilongjiang). Harbin: Heilongjiang jiaoyu chubanshe.

Lu Rong 陆融. 2009. *Yige Shanghai zhiqing de 223 feng jiashu* 一个上海知青的223 封家书 (A Shanghai Sent-Down Youth's 223 Letters Home). Shanghai: Shanghai shehui kexueyuan chubanshe.

Lu Xianliang 陆宪良. 2012. "Shuoshuo wenge zhaosheng na hui shi" 说说文革招生那回事 (My Recollections of College Admission during the Cultural Revolution). *Dang'an chun qiu* 档案春秋 6: 48–52.

Lushan lüyou fazhan gufen youxian gongsi 庐山旅游发展股份有限公司. 2012. "Lushan bei: Disanjie Zhongguo zhiqing lüyou wenhua jie zai Lushan kaimu" 庐山杯：第三届中国知青旅游文化节在庐山开幕 (The Third Lushan Cup Opens at the Chinese Sent-Down Youth Travel Culture

Festival at Lushan), June 11. www.prnasia.com/story/63063–1.shtml. Accessed July 12, 2017.

McLaren, Anne. 1979. "The Educated Youth Return: The Poster Campaign in Shanghai from November 1978 to March 1979." *Australian Journal of Chinese Affairs* 2: 1–20.

Mann, Susan. 1984. "Urbanization and Historical Change in China." *Modern China* 10(1): 79–113.

Merkel-Hess, Kate. 2016. *The Rural Modern: Reconstructing the Self and State in Republican China*. Chicago: University of Chicago Press.

Ming, Yuemin and Zhongmin Yan. 1995. "The Changing Industrial and Spatial Structure in Shanghai." *Urban Geography* 16(7): 577–594.

Pan Ying 潘影. 2011. "Likai muqin de natian" 离开母亲的那天 (The Day I Left My Mother), in Zhu Mingyuan, *Nanwang Makuli*, 166.

Pan Zhigen 潘志根. 2004. "Wo wei dianchang zuo gongxian" 我为电厂做贡献 (I Contributed to the Electric Power Plant), in Liu Shijie, *Huma zhiqing fengyunlu xuji*, 50–52.

Pei Yulin 裴雨林, Huang Hongji 黄洪基, Jin Dalu 金大陆, and Tian Dawei 田大卫, eds. 1998. *Lao zhiqing xiezhen* 老知青写真 (Sketches of Former Sent-Down Youth). Shanghai: Shanghai wenhua chubanshe.

Peng Xi 彭锡. 2009. "Xishuangbanna zhiqing wenhua lüyoujie jiang yu 12 yue zai Jinghong juxing" 西双版纳知青文化旅游节将于12月在景洪举行 (The Sent-Down Youth Tourist Culture Festival of Xishuangbanna Will Be Held in December in Jinghong), November 18. http://news.ifeng.com/history/zhiqing/huodong/200911/1118_6853_1441863.shtml. Accessed April 6, 2014.

Perkins, Dwight. 1977. *Rural Small-Scale Industry in the People's Republic of China*. Berkeley: University of California Press.

Perry, Elizabeth J. 1994. "Trends in the Study of Chinese Politics: State–Society Relations." *China Quarterly* 139 (September): 704–713.

Perry, Elizabeth and Li Xun. 1997. *Proletarian Power: Shanghai in the Cultural Revolution*. Boulder, CO: Westview Press.

Qian, Zhenchao and Randy Hodson. 2011. "'Sent down' in China: Stratification Challenged but Not Denied," *Research in Social Stratification and Mobility* 29 (2): 205–219.

Qin Tingkai 秦廷楷. 2013. "Dangnian Anhui zhiqing weiwentuan Jiang Yue de jingli" 当年知青慰问团江月的经过 (The Experience of Jiang Yue as a Member of the Sent-Down Youth *Weiwentuan* to Anhui), July 24–August 11. http://shzq.net/pjq/thread.asp?tid=12442. Accessed July 28, 2017.

"Qing wujia, wangshi kan huishou" 情无价，往事堪回首 (Priceless Sentiments: The Past Is Remembered). *Jiangxi huabao* 江西画报, September 2001. http://shzq.net/jxpd/wskhs.html. Accessed June 26, 2014.

Qiu Liyin 邱丽瑛. 2002. "Heilongjiang de huiyi" 黑龙江的回忆 (Memories of Heilongjiang), in Liu Shijie, *Huma zhiqing fengyunlu*, 152–157.

Rene, Helena K. 2013. *China's Sent-Down Generation: Public Administration and the Legacies of Mao's Rustication Program*. Washington, DC: Georgetown University Press.

Renmin ribao 人民日报 (People's Daily). Beijing.

Riskin, Carl. 1978. "China's Rural Industries: Self-Reliant Systems or Independent Kingdoms?," *China Quarterly* 73: 77–98.

Rosen, Stanley. 1981. *The Role of Sent-Down Youth in the Chinese Cultural Revolution: The Case of Guangzhou.* Berkeley: University of California, Berkeley Center for Chinese Studies.

Rumney, Philip N.S. 2006. "False Allegations of Rape." *Cambridge Law Journal* 65(1) (March): 128–158.

Schmalzer, Sigrid. 2015. "Youth and the 'Great Revolutionary Movement' of Scientific Experiment in 1960s–1970s Rural China," in Brown and Johnson, *Maoism at the Grassroots*, 154–178.

Schmalzer, Sigrid. 2016. *Red Revolution, Green Revolution: Scientific Farming in Socialist China.* Chicago: University of Chicago Press.

Shanghai Jiaotong daxue xiaoshi bian zhuan weiyuanhui 上海市交通大学校史编撰委员会. 2006. *Shanghai Jiaotong daxue jishi: 1896–2005* 上海交通大学纪实 1896–2005 (Chronology of Shanghai Jiaotong University, 1896–2005). Shanghai: Shanghai Jiaotong daxue chubanshe.

Shanghai laodongzhi bianzhuan weiyuanhui 上海劳动志编撰委员会. 1998. *Shanghai laodongzhi* 上海劳动志 (Shanghai Labor Gazetteer). Shanghai: Shanghai shehui kexueyuan chubanshe.

Shanghai nongkenzhi bianzhuan weiyuanhui 上海农垦志编撰委员会. 2004. *Shanghai nongkenzhi* 上海农垦志 (Shanghai Agriculture Gazetteer). Shanghai: Shanghai shehui kexueyuan chubanshe.

Shanghai qingnianzhi bianzhuan weiyuanhui 上海青年志编撰委员会. 2002. *Shanghai qingnianzhi* 上海青年志 (Shanghai Youth Gazetteer). Shanghai: Shanghai shehui kexueyuan chubanshe.

Shanghai shenpan zhi bianzhuang weiyuanhui 上海审判志编撰委员会. 2003. *Shanghai shenpanzhi* 上海审判志 (Shanghai Trial and Sentencing Gazetteer). Shanghai: Shanghai shehui kexueyuan chubanshe.

Shanghai shi difangzhi bangongshi 上海市地方志办公室. 2013. "Pohuai shangshan xiaxiang yundong anjian" 破坏上山下乡运动案件 (The Cases of Damaging the Sent-Down Movement), in *Shanghai shenpanzhi* 上海审判志 (Shanghai Trial and Sentencing Gazetteer), vol. 3. www.shtong.gov.cn/node2/node2245/node81324/node81331/node81383/node81394/userobjec t1ai101321.html. Accessed June 16, 2015.

Shanghai shi difangzhi bangongshi 上海市地方志办公室. 2014. "Shanghai chengshi guihuazhi" (Gazetteer of Shanghai City Planning). www.shtong.gov.cn/node2/node2245/node64620/index.html. Accessed March 2, 2014.

Shanghai shi difangzhi bangongshi 上海市地方志办公室. 2013. "Yaoshuilong" 药水弄 (Medicine Water Lane). www.shtong.gov.cn/node2/node2245/node64620/node64634/node64735/node64739/userobject1ai58579.html. Accessed February 25, 2017.

Shen Guoming 沈国明, ed. 2014. *Zhiqing hui mou Yinlonghe* 知青回眸引龙河 (Sent-Down Youth Looking Back at Yinlonghe). Shanghai: Shanghai renmin chubanshe.

Shen Longgen 沈龙根. 2004. "Zai Huma de yixie wangshi" 在呼玛的一些往事 (Some Memories about Huma), in Liu Shijie, *Huma zhiqing fengyunlu xuji*, 78–82.

Shi Ruping 施如平. 2004. "Qing yuan" 情缘 (Sentimental Connection), in Liu Shijie, *Huma zhiqing fengyunlu xuji*, 44–49.

Shue, Vivienne. 1988. *The Reach of the State: Sketches of the Chinese Body Politic*. Stanford: Stanford University Press.

Singer, Martin M. 1971. *Educated Youth and the Cultural Revolution in China*. Ann Arbor: University of Michigan Press.

Skinner, G. William. 1985. "Rural Marketing in China: Repression and Revival." *China Quarterly* 102: 393–413.

Smith, Graeme. 2010. "The Hollow State: Rural Governance in China." *China Quarterly* 203: 601–618.

Song Fulin 宋富林. "Heitudi de qinqing" 黑土地的亲情 (Feeling of Family in the Black Soil), in Liu Shjie, *Huma zhiqing fengyunlu xuji*, 215–245.

Tan Guoxing 谈国兴. 2002. "Huma chadui de qianqian houhou" 呼玛插队的前 前后后 (Some Recollections of Being Sent Down to a Huma Village), in Liu Shijie, *Huma zhiqing fengyunlu xuji*, 137–139.

Teiwes, Frederick C. and Warren Sun. 2004. "The First Tiananmen Incident Revisited: Elite Politics and Crisis Management at the End of the Maoist Era." *Pacific Affairs* 77(2) (Summer): 211–235.

Tianjin shi difang zhi bianzhuan weiyuanhui 天津地方志编撰委员会. 1999. *Tianjin tongzhi: Renshi zhi* 天津通志: 人事志 (Tianjin Gazetteer: People and Events). Tianjin: Shehui kexue chubanshe.

Unger, Jonathan. 1979. "China's Troubled Down-to-the-Countryside Campaign." *Contemporary China* 3(2): 79–92.

Wan Xia 晚霞. 2012. "Nanwang yu women tonggan gongku de Shanghai chadui ganbu" 难忘与我们同甘共苦的上海插队干部 (The Unforgettable Sweetness and Woes That We Shared with the Shanghai Cadres), January 6. http://dn.wanxia.com/fenxiang/show/1/645.html. Accessed April 22, 2017.

Wang Jian 王健. 2004. "Mobudiao de jiyi" 抹不掉的记忆 (The Memory That Could Not Be Wiped Out), in Liu Shijie, *Huma zhiqing fengyunlu xuji*, 130–136.

Wang Jiarong 王家荣. 2015. "Shanghai zhiqing zai Neimengu" 上海知青在内蒙古 (Shanghai Sent-Down Youth in Inner Mongolia). *Zhiqing* 知青 (Sent-Down Youth) 3. http://shzqyjh.cn/archives/view-1785-1.html. Accessed July 12, 2017.

Wang Lili 王丽丽. 2012. *Xingguang mantian de qingchun* 星光满天的青春 (Youth under the Starlit Sky), vol. 2. Shanghai: Shanghai renmin chubanshe.

Wang, Shaoguang. 1995. *The Failure of Charisma: The Cultural Revolution in Wuhan*. Oxford: Oxford University Press.

Wang Shicheng 王世成. 2002. "Sanhe cun de zhiqingmen" 三合村的知青们 (The Sent-Down Youth in Sanhe Village), in Liu Shijie, *Huma zhiqing fengyunlu*, 203–219.

Wang Yuchen 王雨晨. 2002. "Zhandou cun jie shuoguo" 战斗村接硕果 (Zhandou Village Bears Big Fruits), in Liu Shijie, *Huma zhiqing fengyunlu*, 35–36.

Wang Zelin 王泽林. 2004. "Nanwang de di'er guxiang Shijiuzhan" 难忘的第二故 乡十九站 (Remembering My Second Home Village in Shijiuzhan), in Liu Shijie, *Huma zhiqing fengyunlu xuji*, 83–87.

Wenhui bao 文汇报 (Wenhui Daily). Shanghai.

White, D. Gordon. 1974. "The Politics of Hsia-hsiang Youth." *China Quarterly* 59 (July–September): 491–517.

Whyte, Lynn, III 1979. "The Road to Urumchi: Approved Institution in Search of Attainable Goals during Pre-1968 Rustication from Shanghai." *China Quarterly* 79 (September 1979): 481–510.

Whyte, Martin King. 2010. "The Paradoxes of Rural–Urban Inequality in Contemporary China," in Martin King Whyte, ed., *One Country, Two Societies: Rural–Urban Inequality in Contemporary China*. Cambridge, MA: Harvard University Press, 1–25.

Wong, Christine P.W. 1991. "The Maoist 'Model' Reconsidered: Local Self-Reliance and the Financing of Rural Industrialization," in William Joseph, Christine P.W. Wong, and David Zweig, eds., *New Perspectives on the Cultural Revolution*. Cambridge, MA: Harvard University Press, 183–196.

Wu Hao 吴浩. 2008. "Zai Huaibei shenghuo de rizi" 在淮北生活的日子 (Days Living in Huaibei), in Fan Kangming, Yang Jidong, and Wu Hao, *Guntang de nitu*, 368–370.

Wu, Xiaogang and Donald J. Treiman 2004. "The Household Registration System and Social Stratification in China: 1955–1996." *Demography* 41(2) (May), 363–84.

Wu, Yiching. 2014. *The Cultural Revolution at the Margins: Chinese Socialism in Crisis*. Cambridge, MA: Harvard University Press.

Xiang, Biao. 2007. "How Far Are the Left-Behind Left Behind?" *Population Space and Place* 13(3): 179–191.

Xiao Ge 晓歌. 2010. "Dongri de nuanliu" 冬日的暖流 (A Warm Feeling in Winter Days). August 27. http://zhiqingwang.shzq.org/jiangxArtD.aspx? ID=2290. Accessed June 26, 2014.

Xiao Ge. 2011. "Shanghai zhiqingwang shinian" 上海知青网十年 (10 Years of the Shanghai Sent-Down Youth Website), September 21. http://blog .sina.com.cn/s/blog_3f7ebf3c0100umlk.html. Accessed June 12, 2014.

Xie, Yu, Yang Jiang, and Emily Greenman. 2008. "Did Sent-Down Experience Benefit Youth? A Re-evaluation of the Social Consequences of Forced Urban–Rural Migration during China's Cultural Revolution." *Social Science Research* 37(2): 686–700.

Xu Feng 徐峰. 2004. "Zongshu" 综述 (Comprehensive Accounts), in Liu Shijie, *Huma zhiqing fengyunlu xuji*, 1–12.

Xu Shoule 徐守乐. 2002. "Wo de Shanghai zhiqing yuan" 我的上海知青缘 (My Destined Connection with Sent-Down Youth), in Liu Shijie, *Huma zhiqing fengyunlu*, 40–45.

Xu Xiao 徐萧. 2014. "Gai zenme pingjia zhiqing shangshan xiaxiang, 'qingchun wuhui' nandao cuole me?" 该怎么评价知青上山下乡 "青春无悔" 难道错了吗？ (How Should the Sent-Down Youth Be Evaluated: Is The "Unregrettable Youth" Possibly Wrong?) December 22. www.thepaper.cn/ newsDetail_forward_1287904. Accessed July 12, 2017.

Xu Yimin 徐逸敏. 2014. "Fu Beidahuang sishiwu zhounian ji" 赴北大荒四十五周年祭 (45th Anniversary of Going to the Great Northern Wilderness), in Shen Guoming, *Zhiqing hui mou Yinlonghe*, 518–520.

Xu Youwei 徐有威 and Chen Donglin 陈东林. 2015. *Xiao sanxian jianshe yanjiu luncong* 小三线建设研究论丛 (Selected Essays on the Third Front Industry). Shanghai: Shanghai daxue chubanshe.

Xu Zhigao 徐志高, ed. 2016. *Wenge shi gao: Wuchan jieji wenhua da geming* 文革史稿:无产阶级文化大革命 (Historical Documents of the Cultural Revolution: The Great Proletarian Cultural Revolution). Beijing: Shijie huayu chubanshe.

Yan Qianzi 严茜子. 2005. "Kegu minxin de kuayue" 刻骨铭心的跨越 (The Unforgettable Cross), in Zhongguo renmin zhengzhi xieshang huiyi Heilongjiang sheng weiyuanhui wenshi he xuexi weiyuanhui, *Zhishi qingnian zai Heilongjiang*, 238–244.

Yan Shaojun 燕邵俊. 2004. "Huixiang dang nian de Shibazhan" 回想当年的十八站 (My Recollections of That Year in Shibazhan), in Liu Shijie, *Huma zhiqing fengyunlu xuji*, 124–29.

Yan, Yuxiang. 2003. *Private Life under Socialism: Love, Intimacy, and Family Change in a Chinese Village, 1949–1999*. Stanford: Stanford University Press.

Yang, Bin. 2009. "'We Want to Go Home!' The Great Petition of the *Zhiqing*, Xishuangbanna, Yunnan, 1978–1979." *China Quarterly* 198 (June): 401–421.

Yang, Bin and Cao Shuji. 2016. "Cadres, Grain, and Sexual Abuse in Wuwei County, Mao's China." *Journal of Women's History* 28(2) (Summer): 33–57.

Yang, Dali. 1996. *Calamity and Reform in China: State, Rural Society and Institutional Change since the Great Leap Forward*. Stanford: Stanford University Press.

Yang, Guobin. 2003. "China's Zhiqing Generation: Nostalgia, Identity, and Cultural Resistance in the 1990s." *Modern China* 29(3): 267–296.

Yang, Guobin. 2016. *The Red Guard Generation and Political Activism in China*. New York: Columbia University Press.

Yang Jidong 杨继东. 2008."Xiaozapu" 小杂铺 (A Little Convenience Store), in Fan Kangming, Yan Jidong, and Wu Hao, *Guntang de nitu*, 305–308.

Yang Jidong. 2008. "Zai zhidian de rizi li" 在知青点的日子里 (My Days in the Sent-Down Youth Station), in Fan Kangming, Yang Jidong, and Wu Hao, *Guntang de nitu*, 286–193.

Yang Jidong. 2008. "Zui manchang de yige dongtian" 最漫长的一个冬天 (The Longest Winter), in Fan Kangming, Yan Jidong, and Wu Hao, *Guntang de nitu*, 319–322.

Yang Miaoxiang 杨庙祥. 2002. "Rensheng daolu shang de liangshi" 人生道路上的良师 (A Good Teacher on the Path of Life), in Liu Shijie, *Huma zhiqing fengyunlu*, 404–05.

Yang Shixiong 杨世雄. 2012. "Diandeng zhaoliang yantian cun" 电灯照亮炎田村 (Lights Illuminate Yantian Village), March 5. http://zhiqingwang.shzq.org/jiangxArtD.aspx?ID=4913. Accessed May 8, 2014.

Yang Shixiong. 2012. "Shouyinji li de gushi" 收音机里的故事 (Story from the Radio), February 12. http://zhiqingwang.shzq.org/jiangxArtD.aspx?ID=4773. Accessed April 10, 2014.

Yang Xinqi 杨新旗. 2011. "Yunnan nongchang zhiqing da fancheng" 云南农场知青大返城 (The Great Return to the City by State Farm Sent-Down Youth in

Yunnan), in Zhonggong Yunnan shengwei dangshi yanjiushi, *Yunnan zhishi qingnian shangshan xiaxiang yundong*, 170–189.

Yang Xinqi. 2010. "Yunnan sheng zhishi qingnian shangshan xiaxiang yundong da shiji" 云南省知识青年上山下乡运动大事记 (Chronology of the Sent-Down Youth Movement in Yunnan), in Zhonggong Yunnan shengwei dangshi yanjiushi, *Yunnan zhishi qingnian shangshan xiaxiang yundong*, 393–449.

Yang Xinqi. 2010. "Yunnan sheng zhishi qingnian shangshan xiaxiang yundong zongshu" 云南省知识青年上山下乡运动综述 (Comprehensive Accounts of the Sent-Down Youth Movement in Yunnan), in Zhonggong Yunnan shengwei dangshi yanjiushi, *Yunnan zhishi qingnian shangshan xiaxiang yundong*, 3–26.

Yu Xiaodong 于晓东. 2003. "Zai Shanghai Heihe zhiqing ji minying qiyejia kentanhui shang de jianghua" 在上海黑河知青暨民营企业家恳谈会上的讲话 (A Talk to Former Heihe Sent-Down Youth and Private Entrepreneurs in Shanghai), October 30. http://shzq.net/hljpd/yxdjh.html. Accessed June 22, 2014.

Yu Zhejie 虞哲杰. 2012. "Beijing Shanghai nü zhiqing lianshou tuixiu er ci 'chadui' bangzhu nongmin zhifu" 北京上海女知青联手退休二次"插队"帮助农民致富 (Female Sent-Down Youth from Beijing and Shanghai Jointly Retired and Return to the village a Second Time to Help the Peasants Get Rich). *Xinmin wanbao* 新民晚报, October 12.

Yu Zhejie 虞哲杰 and Pan Gaofen 潘高峰. 2012. "Zuodian neng gaibian xianzhuang de shi: Xiri Shanghai zhiqing Xu Juju chongfan di'er guxiang Heilongjiang dailing baixin zhifu de gushi" 做点能改变现状的事:昔日知青徐桔桔重返地二故乡黑龙江带领百姓致富的故事 (Do Something That Could Change the Current Situation: A Story about the Former Shanghai Sent-Down Youth Xu Juju Returning to Her Second Native Place in Heilongjiang to Lead Ordinary People to Become Prosperous). *Xinmin wanbao* 新民晚报, September 29.

Yunnan sheng geming weiyuanhui 云南省革命委员会. 1971. "Guanyu tuijian chengzhen xiaxiang zhishi qingnian canjia gongye caimao wenjiao deng gongzuo tongzhi" 关于推荐城镇下乡知识青年参加工业财贸文教等工作通知 (Notice on Recommending City and Township Sent-Down Youth for Work in Factories, Finance, and Education), June 17, in Zhonggong Yunnan shengwei dangshi yanjiushi, *Yunnan zhishi qingnian xiaxiang shangshan yundong*, 315–316.

Yunnan sheng geming weiyuanhui. 1979. "Guanyu guanche zhixing zhongyang (1978) 74 hao wenjian tongchou jiejue wosheng guoying nongchang zhiqing ji youguan wenti de tongzhi" 关于贯彻执行中央1978（74）号文件统筹解决我省国营农场知青及有关问题的通知 (Announcement Concerning the Implementation of the Central Committee 1978 Directive 74 and Systematically Solving Problems of Sent-Down Youth on State Farms in Our Province), February 6, in Zhonggong Yunnan shengwei dangshi yanjiushi, *Yunnan zhishi qingnian xiaxiang shangshan yundong*, 380–381.

Zhang Baoguo 张保国. 2005. "Xiaogou dadui huiyi" 小沟大队回忆 (Memories of the Xiaogou Village Production Brigade), in Zhongguo renmin zhengzhi xieshang huiyi Heilongjiang sheng weiyuanhui wenshi he xuexi weiyuanhui, *Zhishi qingnian zai Heilongjiang*, 744.

Zhang, Elva J. 2006. "To Be Somebody: Li Qinglin, Run-of-the-Mill Cultural Revolution Showstopper," in Esherick, Pickowicz, and Walder, *The Chinese Cultural Revolution as History*, 211–239.

Zhang Jie 张杰. 2002. "Beiji mohe yu xin ren" 北极漠河育新人 (Nurturing the Young in the Far Northern Mohe), in Liu Shijie, *Huma zhiqing fengyunlu*, 77–80.

Zhang Liang 张亮. 2011. *Cong hei tudi zoulai* 从黑土地走来 (Coming from the Black Soil). Shanghai: Xuelin chubanshe.

Zhang Mingyong 张明勇. 2012. "Qinggan zhaoshang po changgui: Ji Guizhou zhiqing Yang Yanshu" 情感招商破常规－记贵州知青杨言树 (Breaking Customs to Attract Business through Sentimentality: A Story of Guizhou Sent-Down Youth Yang Yanshu), May 6. http://zhiqingwang.shzq.org/guizhouDes.aspx?ID=5446. Accessed June 26, 2014.

Zhang Ren 张韧. 2008. "Wo zhege ren xihuan xinxian" 我这个人喜欢新鲜 (I Like to Try New Things), in Liu Xiaomeng, ed., *Zhongguo zhiqing koushu shi*, 22–55.

Zhang, Yingjin. 1996. *The City in Modern Chinese Literature and Film: Configurations of Space, Time, and Gender*. Stanford: Stanford University Press.

Zhao Zhenlin 赵亟麟. 2014. "Xian lingdao kanwang weiwen Guizhou Suiyang Shanghai zhiqing xuanchuan tuijie Suiyang" 县领导看望慰问贵州绥阳上海知青宣传推介绥阳 (The County Leaders Came to Visit and Introduce Suiyang to the Former Sent-Down Youth), March 27. http://zhiqingwang .shzq.org/guizhouDes.aspx?ID=8170. Accessed June 13, 2014.

Zheng'an xian ban zhu renmin zhengfu 正安县班竹乡人民政府. 2013. "Zhongguo zhiqing buluo shengtai wenhua luyou qu" 中国知青部落生态文化旅游区 (China Sent-Down Youth Ecological and Cultural Tourist Site), April 2. www .gztoptour.com/html/2015/zy_0126/1367.html. Accessed July 12, 2017.

Zheng Qian 郑谦. "Wenhua da gemming zhong zhishi qingnian shangshan xiaxiang yundong wuti" 文化大革命中知识青年上山下乡运动五题 (Five Issues Concerning the Sent-Down Youth Movement during the Cultural Revolution). http://history.sina.com.cn/bk/zqs/2014–02–18/153782759_2 .shtml. Accessed February 1, 2017.

Zheng, Xiaowei. 2014. "Images, Memories, and Lives of Sent-Down Youth in Yunnan," in James Cook, Joshua Goldstein, Matthew D. Johnson, and Sigrid Schmalzer, *Visualizing Modern China: Image, History, and Memory, 1750–Present*. London: Lexington Books, 241–258.

Zheng Yahong 郑亚鸿. 2014. "Zhiqing yi: Shangshan xiaxiang shi kan yizhuo chayi qufen zhiqing yu nongmin" 知青忆:上山下乡时看衣着差异区分知青与农民 (Reflections of a Sent-Down Youth: Differentiating Sent-Down Youth and Peasants by Their Clothing), April 24. http://history.sohu.com/201404 24/n398746630.shtml. Accessed July 20, 2016.

Zhonggong Anhui shengwei dangshi yanjiu shi 中共安徽省委党史研究室. 2014. *Anhui zhiqing koushu shilu* 安徽知青口述史 (Oral History of Anhui Sent-Down Youth), vol. 1. Anhui: Zhonggong dangshi chubanshe.

Zhonggong Huma xian weiyuanhui 中共呼玛县委员会. 1980. *Huma xianzhi* 呼玛县志 (Huma County Gazetteer). Heilongjiang: Huma xianwei.

Zhonggong Yunnan shengwei 中共云南省委. 1973. "Pifa 'Yunnan sheng zhishi qingnian shangshan xiaxiang gongzuo huiyi jiyao'" 批发《云南省知识青年上山下乡工作会议纪要》(Circulating "Summary of the Yunnan Province Conference on Work of Sent-Down Youth"), September 2, in Zhonggong Yunnan shengwei dangshi yanjiushi, *Yunnan zhishi qingnian shangshan xiaxiang yundong*, 332–337.

Zhonggong Yunnan shengwei dangshi yanjiushi 中共云南省委党史研究室. 2011. "Yunnan shengchan jianshe bingtuan (nongken) zhiqing gaikuang" 云南生产建设兵团（农垦）知青概况 (The General Condition of the Sent-Down Youth on Military and State Farms in Yunnan), in Zhonggong Yunnan shengwei dangshi yanjiushi, *Yunnan zhishi qingnian shangshan xiaxiang yundong*, 157–162.

Zhonggong Yunnan shengwei dangshi yanjiushi 中共云南省委党史研究室编, ed. 2011. *Yunnan zhishi qingnian shangshan xiaxiang yundong* 云南知识青年上山下乡运动 (The Sent-Down Youth Movement in Yunnan). Kunming: Yunnan daxue chubanshe.

Zhonggong zhongyang bangongshi 中共中央办公室. 1970. "Zhuanfa guojia jiwei jun daibiao guanyu jinyibu zuohao zhishi qingnian xiaxiang gongzuo de baogao" 转发国家计委军代表关于进一步做好知识青年下乡工作的报告 (Recirculating the Report by Military Representative of the State Planning Committee on the Improvement of Sent-Down Youth Work), May 12, in Zhonggong Yunnan shengwei dangshi yanjiushi, *Yunnan zhishi qingnian shangshan xiaxiang yundong*, 302–304.

Zhonggong zhongyang bangongshi, 1973. "Zhonggong zhongyang tongzhi" 中共中央通知 (Announcement of the CCP Central Committee), June 10, in Zhonggong Yunnan shengwei dangshi yanjiushi, *Yunnan zhishi qingnian shangshan xiaxiang yundong*, 319–321.

Zhonggong zhongyang bangongshi. 1978. "Zhonggong zhongyang tongzhi" 中共中央通知 (Announcement of the CCP Central Committee), December 12, in Zhonggong Yunnan shengwei dangshi yanjiushi, *Yunnan zhishi qingnian shangshan xiaxiang yundong*, 368–379.

Zhongguo renmin zhengzhi xieshang huiyi Heilongjiang sheng weiyuanhui wenshi he xuexi weiyuanhui 中国人民政治协商会议黑龙江省委员会文史和学习委员会编, ed. 2005. *Zhishi qingnian zai Heilongjiang* 知识青年在黑龙江 (Sent-Down Youth in Heilongjiang). Harbin: Heilongjiang renmin chubanshe.

Zhongguo zhiqing chanye wenhua cujing hui 中国知青产业发展促进会. 2009. "Xishuangbanna zhiqing wenhua lüyoujie jiang yu 12 yue zai Jinghong juxin" 西双版纳知青文化旅游节将于十二月在景洪举行 (The Sent-Down Youth Tourist Culture Festival of Xishuangbanna Will Be Held in December in Jinghong), November 18. http://blog.sina.com.cn/s/blog_53ce2e4d0100g7k8.html Accessed April 6, 2014.

Zhongguo zhongyang guowuyuan 中国中央国务院. 1973. "Zhonggong zhongyang zhuanfa guowuyuan guanyu quanguo zhishiqingnian shangshan xiaxiang gongzuo huiyi de baogao. 30 hao 中共中央转发国务院关于全国知

识青年上山下乡工作会议的报告。30号, in Song Yongyi, ed., *The Chinese Cultural Revolution Database CD-ROM*. Hong Kong: The Chinese University Press, 2002.

Zhou Han 周函. 2010. "Nie Weiping: Beidahuang zouchu de qisheng" 聂卫平：北大荒走出的棋圣 (The Go Master Who Came Out from the Great Northern Wilderness), October 10. www.people.com.cn/GB/198221/1988 19/204159/12909939.html. Accessed February 1, 2017.

Zhou, Xueguang and Liren Hou. 1999. "Children of the Cultural Revolution: The State and the Life Course in the People's Republic of China," *American Sociological Review* 64(1): 12–36.

Zhu Bingxing 诸炳兴. 2013. "Sishi nian hou you jian zhiqing weiwentuan" 四十年后又见知青慰问团 (Seeing the *Weiwentuan* Forty Years Later), April 17. http://blog.sina.com.cn/s/blog_8727a5b00101icez.html. Accessed December 30, 2016.

Zhu Mingyuan 朱明元, ed. 2011. *Nanwang Makuli: Heilongjiang sheng jiangchuan nonchang zhiqing huiyilu* 难忘马库力：黑龙江省江川农场知青回忆录 (Unforgettable Makuli: Memoirs of Sent-Down Youth in Jiangchuan Farm, Heilongjiang). Self-published.

Zhu Xiaohong 朱晓鸿. 2011. "Xiaxiang" 下乡 (Going to the Countryside), in Zhu Mingyuan, *Nanwang Makuli*, 185–186.

Zweig, David. 1987. "From Village to City: Reforming Urban–Rural Relations in China," *International Regional Science Review* 11(1): 43–58.

Interviews Conducted by the Authors

Chen Jiang 陈绛, Shanghai, June 29, 2013
Chen Sheng 陈盛, Los Angeles, August 18, 2013
Wang Yuan 王远, Los Angeles, August 18, 2013
Wang Pei 王培, Santa Barbara, February 12, 2014
Wei Min 魏民, Shanghai, August 4, 2013
He Xinhua 何新华, Shanghai, June 28, 2013
Xiao Qin 肖青, Shanghai, June 22, 2016
Xu Yi 徐怡, Shanghai, June 7, 2016
Zhu Kejia 朱克家, Kunming, September 23, 2012

Glossary

Aihui 瑷珲
Baoshan 宝山
Bianjiang 边疆
bihun 逼婚 (forced marriage)
bu zhengchang de nannü guanxi 不正当的男女关系 (inappropriate male–female relations)
chadui luohu 插队落户 (settle down and join a production team)
Changning 长宁
Chen Jiang 陈绛
Chen Yonggui 陈永贵
Chongming 崇明
Cui Shushan 崔树山
Dafeng 大丰
danwei 单位 (work unit）
di'er guxiang 第二故乡 (second hometown)
dingti 顶替 (children inherit their parents' jobs after they retire)
Dong Jiageng 董家耕
Donglu 东陆
Elunchun 鄂伦春 (Oroqen)
er xiancai 二咸菜 (a simpleton; a fool)
fasheng nannü guanxi 发生男女关系 (engage in sexual relations)
Fengxian 奉贤
Fuyang 阜阳
Ganchazi 干岔子
Ganlanba 橄榄坝
Ganzhou: 赣州
Guanji 官集
gao duixiang 搞对象 (dating)
Heihe 黑河
heiwulei 黑五类 (five black categories)
Hongkou 虹口
Hongqi 红旗

Hou Jun 侯隽
Hua Guofeng 华国锋
Huichun 珲春
Huaibei 淮北
Huanglong 黄龙
Huangshan 黄山
huixiang qingnian 回乡青年 (returning-to-the-village youth)
hukou 户口
Huma 呼玛
Huyue 呼悦 (happy Huma)
Huzhou 湖州
Jia Aichun 贾爱春
Jiangbei 江北
Jiang Danping 蒋旦萍
Jiang Yue 江月
Jing'an 静安
Jinshan 金山
jianwu 奸污 (sexual molestation)
Jiaozhou 胶州
Jiayin 嘉荫
jin 斤 (500 grams)
Jinghong 景洪
Jiujiang 九江
kang 炕 (large heated brick bed)
la san 癞三 (slut)
lao san jie 老三届 (the three old classes)
laobao 老保 (cadres who sided with the old government officials)
Le'an 乐安
Li Deshen 李德生
Li Jiaquan 李家全
Li Qinglin 李庆霖
Lichuan 黎川
Liu Fachun 刘发春
liumang 流氓 (hoodlum)
liumang afei 流氓阿飞 (hoodlum)
Liu Shichang 刘世常
Liu Shijie 刘世杰
luan tan lian'ai 乱谈恋爱 (casual dating; fooling around)
lunjian 轮奸 (gang rape)
Lushan bei 庐山杯
Ma Tianshui 马天水
manzi 蛮子 (barbarians)

Mengding 勐定
Menghun 勐混
Mengla 勐腊
Mengpeng 勐捧
Minhang 闵行
mu 亩 (0.16 acres)
Nancheng 南城
Nanhui 南汇
nannü guanxi 男女关系
Nenjiang 嫩江
Nie weiping 聂卫平
Putuo 普陀
qiangjian 强奸 (rape)
qiangjian weisui 强奸未遂 (attempted rape)
Sandaogou 三道沟
Sanhe 三合
Shanghai ren 上海人
Shangrao 上饶
Shanhe (Heilongjiang) 山河
Shanhe (Jiangxi) 善和
shehui qingnian 社会青年 (social youth)
Shen Longgen 沈龙根
shenghuo zuofeng wenti 生活作风问题 (lifestyle problems)
shua liumang 耍流氓 (act like a hoodlum)
Simao 思茂
sixiang gongzuo 思想工作 (ideological work)
Suiyang 绥阳
Suxian 宿县
Tan Guoxing 谈国兴
tan lian'ai 谈恋爱 (dating)
Tian feng 田峰
Tian Gendi 田根第
tiaoxi 调戏 (flirtation)
tongjian 通奸 (adulterous sex)
tongju 同居 (living together)
Tongzi 桐梓
waidi ren 外地人
Wang Chenlong 王承龙
Wang Hongwen 王洪文
Wang Qingyu 王庆余
Wang Xiuying 王秀英
Wang Xiuzhen 王秀珍

Wang Yugen 王玉根

Wei Min 魏民

weiwentuan 慰问团 (comfort teams)

weixie 猥亵 (seduction)

Wudaogou 五道沟

Wuqi tongxun 五七通讯 (*5/7 Bulletin*)

Wuyuan 婺源

Xing Yanzi 邢燕子

Xu Jingxian 徐景贤

Xu Juju 徐桔桔

Xu Shoule 徐守乐

Xu Yiming 徐逸敏

xuelihong 雪里红 (mustard greens)

xiangxia ren 乡下人 (country bumpkins)

xinfang bangongshi 信访办公室 (grievance office)

Xikang 西康

Xuhui 徐汇

Xunke 逊克

Yang Jidong 杨继东

Yangshupu fadian chang 杨树浦发电厂 (Yangshupu
    power plant)

Yang Xiaohu 杨晓沪

Yao Wenyuan 姚文元

Yaoshuilong 药水弄

Ye Jianying 叶剑英

yiban nannü guanxi 一般男女关系 (ordinary
    male-female relations)

yinfeng huanchao 引凤还巢 (calling the phoenix back to its nest)

yipianhong 一片红 (uniform redness)

Yixiken 依西肯

yiyuanhua 一元化 (unified Party leadership)

Yiziquan 椅子圈

youjian 诱奸 (luring into sex)

Yuxi 玉溪

Zhabei 闸北

Zhang Chunqiao 张春桥

Zhang Liang 张亮

Zhang Ren 张韧

Zhao Fan 赵凡

zhaoshang yinzi 招商引资 (attract investments)

Zhonggong zhongyang guowuyuan zhishi qingnian shangshan
xiaxiang bangongshi 中共中央国务院知识青年上山下乡办公
室 (State Council's All-China Office of Sent-Down Youth)
Zhongguo qingnian bao 中国青年报 (*China Youth News*)
Zhu Kejia 朱克家
Zhu Yongjia 朱永嘉
Zhuzhou 株洲
zixun chulu 自寻出路 (finding one's own road)

Index